Dolomites

and eastern South Tyrol

Dietrich Höllhuber

D1387349

SUNFLOWER BOOKS

First edition © 2010
Sunflower Books™
PO Box 36160
London SW7 3WS, UK
www.sunflowerbooks.co.uk

ISBN 978-1-85691-378-2

Important note to readers

This book is a translation from a series of *general* guides originally published in Germany (see Publisher's note on page 6). We have tried to ensure that the descriptions and maps in this book are error-free at press date. The book will be updated, where necessary, whenever future editions permit. It will be very helpful for us to receive your comments (sent in care of Sunflower Books, please) for the updating of future editions.

    We also rely on those who use this book — especially walkers — to take along a good supply of common sense when they explore. Conditions can change fairly rapidly due to storm damage. Explore *safely*, while respecting the beauty of the countryside.

Cover photograph: the church tower of St. Valentin, with the Santner peaks of Schlern in the background (Walk 3).

Translated by Pat Underwood from *Dolomiten/Südtirol Ost*, text and maps ©2006, 2009 Michael Müller Verlag, Erlangen, Germany
Photographs: the author except for pages 30-1 (Südtirol Marketing), 58 (Eggental Tourist Board), 68, 172 (Eisacktal Tourist Board), 5, 171 (Shutterstock), 15, 41, 62, 174 (istock photo)
Sunflower Books is a Registered Trademarks.
A CIP catalogue record for this book is available from the British Library.
Printed and bound in China by WKT Company Ltd

● Contents

4 Dolomites and eastern South Tyrol

Preface

In 1788 the head of the Department of Mineralogy at the Ecole des Mines in Paris, Deodat de Dolomieu, visited the southern Tyrol to explore the mountains. At that time there was no special name for these steep-sided, isolated mountains with their brightly coloured rock. In those days hardly anyone was interested in the new sciences of mineralogy and geology; most people believed that God had created the world 6000 years earlier — why worry about exactly *how* it came about?

Dolomieu found petrified tropical corals and other fossils at a height of 3000 m, which told him that these mountains were once under the sea. Above all he found a stone that, after his scientific studies were published, was named for him: dolomite. In dolomitic rock the calcium in the original limestone sediment from the sea bed or coral reefs is transformed to incorporate magnesium. Gradually the term 'Dolomites' began to appear in the scientific literature when this part of Tyrol was discussed, and it finally filtered down to common use among the inhabitants of this poor farming land.

View from Piz Boé (Walk 13)

Up to 240 million years old, these coral reefs — like the Geisler peaks and the high plateaus of Schlern and Sella — thrust up from the sea bed in an almighty upheaval, leaving deep valleys which today make a first-class holiday base — a mecca for walkers, mountain bikers, climbers, skiers and paragliders. But you don't have to be an *aficionado* of any of these sports to enjoy the fresh air in the upper valleys, the healthy mountain setting and home-made cooking, visits to working alms or taking a lift up to the high peaks.

Drei Zinnen, Langkofel, Rosengarten, Pale di San Martino, Geisler peaks, Civetta, Cristallo, Seekofel — the Dolomites present a cornucopia of landscapes, a real feast for the eyes. Wolkenstein, Cortina d'Ampezzo, Canazei, Corvara, San Martino di Castrozza, Welschnofen — all the villages have an excellent infrastructure, with plenty of action for those who seek it, yet ample breathing space for those who seek peace and quiet.

— DIETRICH HÖLLHUBER

Publisher's note

This book has been translated from the German for the Sunflower 'Complete' Series. Coverage is far wider than in our 'Landscapes' guides — full of general information, from history to restaurants (recommended hotels and restaurants are shown on the town plans, and other places with recommended **restaurants** are highlighted in the text with the symbol ✖, then listed in the Index.

The format is different, too: instead of separate car tours and walks, each chapter covers a specific area (see fold-out maps), with detailed information about the various towns and villages — from the 'sights' to lift opening times and prices. The **24 main walks** are described in the same chapters, highlighted in coloured panels. But there are also dozens of other detailed **walking and cycling** 'tips', as well as suggestions for some of the author's favourite hikes in each area — which you can follow using the relevant Tabacco 1:25,000 map (see page 22).

In addition to the eastern Dolomites (east of the A22 motorway) rising in the provinces of South Tyrol, Trento and Belluno, the book covers an area *outside* the Dolomites — the eastern part of South Tyrol. The bordering cities of Bozen/Bolzano, Brixen/Bressanone and Bruneck/Brunico are also described, with town plans. The book does *not* take in the Brenta Dolomites west of the A22 motorway.

While it is usual for guide books published in English about the Dolomites to use Italian **place names**, you won't always find these names taking precedence 'on the ground'. Italian is the main language in the Fleimstal/Val di Fiemme, Primiero, Agordino and Cadore; Ladin in the Fassatal/Val di Fassa, Buchenstein and Ampezzo. German is so widely spoken in South Tyrol that even Italians use German place names (many of the Italian names were created under Mussolini: the original, German, names were simply translated into Italian). Thus signposting is totally inconsistent. Since the maps in this book were produced in Germany, with German place names where appropriate, we generally use these names in the text. But in the Introduction, the section headings within each chapter, and the Index we give *both names* — or *all three* names, if the village is **Ladin** (see page 106).

Those of you unfamiliar with the area may be puzzled by the German word '**alm**', which can be used in several contexts. An alm is a mountain pasture above tree line, usually with one or more huts, often used for dairy farming. Many of the huts welcome visitors, selling fresh milk and cheese, or even meals.

We are fortunate to have an author, Dietrich Höllhuber, who started walking and climbing peaks in the Dolomites in his teens, then moved to northern Italy in 1985 so that he could spend most of his free (and working) time in the area he so loves. But do take into account that he is a very strong hill walker and cyclist, completely at home in this mountainous environment. It would certainly be wise to build in *plenty of additional time* for his walks, until you get the measure of his pace. And of course, we advise you *never to walk alone.*

Below is a key to the town plans and walking maps; *note that the scales vary on both the maps and the plans!*

Key to the maps and plans

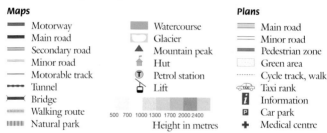

Maps
- ▬▬ Motorway
- ▬▬ Main road
- ═══ Secondary road
- ─── Minor road
- ─── Motorable track
- ••••• Tunnel
- ►────◄ Bridge
- ········ Walking route
- ▮▮▮▮ Natural park

- ▣ Watercourse
- ▭ Glacier
- ▲ Mountain peak
- 🏠 Hut
- Ⓣ Petrol station
- ⌐ Lift

500 700 1000 1300 1700 2000 2400
Height in metres

Plans
- ▭ Main road
- ═══ Minor road
- ▬▬ Pedestrian zone
- ▭ Green area
- ········ Cycle track, walk
- 🚕 Taxi rank
- 𝒊 Information
- ℗ Car park
- ✚ Medical centre

☀ Introduction

The Dolomites are located just south of the Austrian border, between the Eisack/Isarco Valley to the west and the Sexten/Sesto and Piave valleys to the east. The southern boundary lies on a line that curves roughly northeast from Trento to Belluno.

When to go

The whole Dolomites, whether it be the northern Pustertal or the southern Cadore, have a continental alpine climate. **Summers** are hot and dry, especially in the valleys. Only in areas affected by the famous 'Adriatic lows' is there significant rainfall. On the highest terrain it can freeze up and snow even in high summer! **Autumn** comes late and is mostly dry, perfect for outings. Unfortunately, most hotels in the Dolomites close by the middle or end of September; if you plan to come after this, be sure to book ahead and remember that *all the lifts will be closed*. By mid-December all the lifts are open again, and Dolomiti Superski — the largest collection of lifts and runs in the world — is in full swing. **Winter** precipitation is not very high in the Dolomites, so the pistes must be carefully (and often very artistically) prepared. Sunny days are far more frequent than they are north of the Alps, and the view from the top of many ski slopes

Climbing to the Rosengarten peaks

takes in about half the range.
Spring begins late, no earlier
than April/May in the valleys
and June higher up — that's the
time to explore the Dolomites on
foot!

Travelling to the Dolomites
By *air*
There is an airport in the
Dolomites, at Bozen/Bolzano,
but getting there currently takes
eight hours from Heathrow, with
changes at Milan *and* Rome
(daily flights by Alitalia in
cooperation with Air Alps; see
www.alitalia.com). Otherwise,
Innsbruck, Brescia and Verona
are the two airports handiest for
the Dolomites, with onward
travel by rail, bus or car taking
about two hours. Other gateways
are Milan or Bergamo (onward
travel about four hours), Venice
(onward travel under three
hours) or Munich (four hours
away). To see the latest airline
news and some flight suggestions, log on to South Tyrol's web
site: www.suedtirol. info.

By *train*
The Dolomites *can* be reached by
rail from London St. Pancras
International in under 24 hours,
but at least two changes of train
will be involved (usually with a
change of *station* as well). If your
heart is set on going by train,
details can be found at:
www.bahn.de (German railways)
or www. trenitalia.it (Italian railways). Of course there is always
the possibility of treating
yourself to the Orient Express
from London, having tea as you
cross the Brenner Pass, and
alighting at Innsbruck, Verona or

*Travelling by train is comfortable, but,
unfortunately, quite a long-drawn-out
affair from the UK*

Venice — with onward travel by
train or hired car.
The main railway stations in the
Dolomites, served by the fast EC
trains, are at Trento, Bozen/
Bolzano, and Brixen/Bressanone.
From these stations there are
direct bus services to the
northern and western holiday
areas. Only the far southeastern
side of the range, near Belluno, is
more quickly reached by train
from Padua or Venice. The
Franzensfeste/Fortezza station is
where you should change for
trains to the northern areas near
the Pustertal/Val Pusteria; these
stop at Bruneck/Brunico,
Toblach/Dobbiaco and
Innichen/San Candido.
For copious details about rail
connections — including
motorail possibilities (via Calais
and Nice or via Hook of Holland
and Düsseldorf to Verona), log
on to www.seat61.com, a
cornucopia of train information.

By *car*

Driving to the Dolomites is an option recommended for those who enjoy the flexibility and freedom of having their own transport. After crossing the English Channel by tunnel or ferry (there are also ferries from Hull and Rosyth in Scotland to Zeebrugge) it is an easy drive of about 12 hours on the Continent's excellent motorways. (For an overview of the route, motorway tolls and approximate fuel costs, log on to www.viamichelin.com.)

The best approach to the Dolomites is via the A22 motorway over the Brenner Pass. This gives quick access to the western and northern parts of the range, and there are exits at Brixen/Bressanone, Klausen/Chiusa, Bozen/Bolzano and Trento, from where you can head east and south on good roads. Other motorways which you might use if you are only visiting the southern and eastern Dolomites include the very busy A4 linking Milan and Venice. From Mestre (near Venice) the less-travelled A27 gives access to Belluno, with a good national road (SS51) continuing to Cortina.

In addition to your passports, be sure to have a valid **UK driver's licence** (preferably with **photo**), **vehicle registration document**, and **insurance** (third party compulsory); if you are involved in an accident, all three will be required. You will also need a **GB sticker**, **spare bulbs**, **warning triangle**, and a fluorescent yellow jacket for each person in the car. If you have a new or valuable car, it is worth getting special vehicle recovery insurance for the trip, offered by all automobile clubs and insurers. This covers the costs of transporting the vehicle to the nearest garage, getting you and your car back home, the cost of sending spare parts, any accommodation costs incurred, etc. Not all insurance contracts are the same, so read the small print!

Getting around the area
By *car*

Naturally the same rules apply in the Dolomites as north of the Brenner Pass, although Italians drive more on instinct than by 'rules'. But on the whole respect for motoring laws is better in the north of the country than in the south … so you can pretty much rely on traffic halting at red lights!

On **motorways** the speed limit for cars and motorbikes is 130 km/h (80 mph), for cars with trailers 80 km/h (50 mph), for caravans above 3.5 t 100 km/h (60 mph). Motorbikes under 150 ccm are not allowed. On **main roads** the speed limit for cars and motorbikes is 110 km/h (70 mph), for cars with trailers 70 km/h (45 mph), for caravans above 3.5 t 80 km/h (50 mph). On **secondary and minor roads** the speed limit for cars and motorbikes is 90 km/h, for cars with trailers 70 km/h, for caravans above 3.5 t 80 km/h.

Dipped headlights are mandatory when driving, *even in daylight*.

At **red lights**, you are allowed to turn right if no traffic is approaching from the left.

Seat belts must be worn in both front and rear seats, and an appropriate harness is obligatory for children aged 3-12.

The permitted **alcohol level** is 0.5mg/l — generally equivalent to two glasses of wine. Motorists driving over the limit will have their licenses revoked for two weeks to three months and pay high fines (258-1032 €). If you have an **accident** the car will be impounded (these rules apply to foreigners as well as Italians). There are **emergency** phone boxes at 2km intervals along the motorways. Private emergency services are not allowed. The service vans of the ACI (Italian Automobile Club) can be reached 24 hours a day on ℂ 116 but, since they will not always speak English fluently, speak slowly and carefully.

For **full information about driving to and in Italy**, see www.italiantouristboard.co.uk.

You can hire a car at all larger places; in smaller villages you can rent a bike or a scooter. There are taxis even in small tourist centres, often with a mini-bus service. Roads in the Dolomites demand the utmost concentration (as here at Arabba). When holiday traffic is heavy, you'll be crossing the more difficult passes at a snail's pace; the worst hold-ups are usually at the Grödner Joch between Gröden and the Hochabteital. Since few passes (like the Karer Pass) have any regional significance, closing them to private traffic has been considered — or making a toll payable. So far this has come to nothing.

Frequently seen traffic signs

Baccendere i fari: put on your lights;
attenzione: caution;
deviazione: detour;
divieto di accesso: entry forbidden;
lavori in corso: works in progress;
parcheggio: car parking;
rallentare: slow down;
senso unico: one way;
strada senza uscita: one-way street;
tutte direcioni: all directions;
uscita veicoli: caution: vehicle exit;
zona a traffico limitado: limited vehicle access;
zona disco: parking only with disc;
zona pedonale: pedestrian zone.

Petrol prices are about the same as in surrounding Continental countries. For lead-free ask for *senza piombo;* super = *super* and diesel = *gasolio;* octane and quality are the same as in other Continental countries.

Petrol stations are only open 24 hours on the motorways; on main roads and in towns and villages they are usually *closed* from 20.00-7.00 and from 12.00-15.00 as well as *all day Sundays*. More and more petrol pumps are fitted with credit card automats which also take Euro notes.

By *bus*

Buses in the three Dolomites provinces of South Tyrol, Trentino and Belluno are a fast, economical and reliable way of getting about — as long as you aren't trying to travel on a Sunday, when many of the smaller places are not served by bus.

On all three traffic networks (see below) you can buy tickets when boarding the bus, in the office of the bus operator, or at local shops and kiosks (usually tobacconists). Buying a ticket on boarding is significantly more expensive.

All of the companies listed below will take cycles, *if there is room* (*not* usually the case on week-ends). Depending on the line and driver, cycle carriage may be free or cost up to 4 €.

Some of the operators offer **free (or very cheap) bus travel** in winter, even serving isolated

Bus station at Bozen/Bolzano — part of an excellent network

hotels and the valley stations of the lifts. In a very few cases (like the Lake Karer/Carezza area), this is also true in summer. Ask at the operators' offices for information.

SAD (www.sad.it) is the bus operator in **South Tyrol**, with its offices in Bozen/Bolzano, from where a good number of their orange-coloured buses also depart. Other centres are in Brixen/Bressanone and Bruneck/Brunico. SAD also travels to some destinations outside South Tyrol, for instance to the Fassa Valley in Trentino (from Bozen) and Cortina d'Ampezzo in Belluno (from Toblach).

SAD offers both individual tickets and passes; the latter are good for all buses and also the trains. The ticket or pass must be validated on boarding, or you will face a hefty fine! Their '**Mobil Cards**', valid on buses and trains throughout South Tyrol, are especially useful — 3 days for 13 €. But there are also three **regional cards**, for example South Tyrol East (which covers the Dolomites) and takes in Meran, for only 15 € for a full week. These are available from the tourist board.

Trentino Transporti (www.ttspa.it) is the operator in **Trentino**, with their head office in Trient/Trento. Their blue buses penetrate the Dolomites via Auer/Ora in South Tyrol, since the very winding Fleimstal/Val di Fiemme road is little used.

Dolomitibus (www.dolomitibus.it) is the operator in **Belluno**. The buses in this province are often run by private companies centred on Belluno and Feltre. Except for the main routes, the buses are less frequent than those of SAD or Trentino Transporti, especially in summer when schools are closed and many of the services aren't operating.

By train

The Brenner railway line and the railway in the Pustertal/Val Pusteria offer good services for those based at Bozen/Bolzano, Brixen/Bressanone, Bruneck/Brunico and Toblach/Dobbiaco or Innichen/San Candido. Trains travel almost hourly every day from Innichen to Franzensfeste/Fortezza via Toblach and Bruneck. From there you change to trains for Brixen, Klausen and Bozen as well as Auer and Neumarkt. For information see www.trenitalia.com.

Since many stations are un-manned, buy tickets at automats or from *bus* drivers. Only when there is no automat can you pay on the train. But this does *not* hold good for the journey from Belluno to Calalzo di Cadore in the southern Dolomites; for this stretch you *must* buy a ticket in advance — either from the bar in the railway station or from a tobacconist. In Italy train tickets **must always be validated** before you board the train, otherwise you may be subject to a high fine! Single tickets — unless passes — are only good for a bus *or* a rail journey; they are *not* inter-changeable.

By cycle

Because of the strenuous gradients, the Dolomites are not suited for long-distance cycling. But they *are* ideal for mountain bikes. Almost all **trains** will accept mountain bikes. Carriages for bikes are at the start or end of the train. One-day tickets cost 3.50 €. All three **bus** companies will take bikes *if there is room* (see above). For information on rail transport for cycles/bikes see www.trenitalia.it.

Where to stay
Hotels

The number of rooms in hotels, *pensions,* apartments and farm-houses in the Dolomites is huge.

There are plenty of high-class hotels in Gröden/Val Gardena — like the Grödnerhof, a four-star hotel in St. Ulrich/Ortisei, built in 2001. Apart from all the other facilities, there's an internet connection in each room.

The north (South Tyrol province) has is an especially large choice. In the southwest (Trentino province) accommodation is concentrated in a few places and apartments; B&Bs and private rooms are very thin on the ground. That's even more true for the southeast (Belluno province), where beds are concentrated in even fewer locations, and most are luxury hotels or apartments. Prices are pretty much the same through-out the area — and on the high side overall. The most economical places to stay are in South Tyrol.

Accommodation standards are quite high whatever the category: all hotel rooms have bath or shower, WC and telephone. TV (usually satellite) is the rule in all 3- and 4-star establishments; the same is true for hairdryers. Mini-bars, however, are a rarity. A balcony, usually flower-filled, is standard, except in historical houses and the small houses where individuals rent out private rooms. A common feature of many 3-4 star hotels is a very luxurious 'wellness centre', with saunas, whirlpools, in- and outdoor swimming pools, gym equipment and solaria.

In many places, especially *pensions,* a week is the **minimum stay**. In high season you will also be expected to take half-board terms. Room and breakfast is generally only available in low season.

Unless you are using a travel agent or booking a package holiday, surf the web to find a place that appeals to you. Most of the sites have an English version with e-mail facility, should you have any questions. You can then **book the accommodation** on the web, or by phone, fax or letter.

Seasonal opening varies. In **South Tyrol**, for example in the Gröden/Val Gardena, places are generally open May/June to end September/mid-October, but some only open from July to mid-September and again from December to mid/end April. In **Trentino**, for example in the Fassatal/Val di Fassa, May/June to November is usual, but some places close in August. All are usually open again from December to April. In the province of **Belluno** (with Cortina d'Ampezzo and Buchenstein/Pieve di Livina-llongo) most places are open mid-June to mid-September and again (if they are winter sports centres) from mid-December to March or mid-April. **High season** in all the provinces is from the 4th week in July until the 3rd week in August, and from Christmas to 6 January; in skiing areas only, also from February to mid-March.

Family-friendly hotels

Hotels in this group are especially good at making family groups feel at home. These places (3-5 stars) take special care of the children, with playgrounds or playrooms and sometimes special programmes for kids. Log on to www.familienhotels.com (the site runs in English).

Farmhouse holidays

Agriturismo (farmhouse holidays) are possible in many areas of

South Tyrol, but are less common in Trentino and Belluno, where B&B or apartments with breakfast are more usual. For

agriturismo details log on to the relevant web sites (South Tyrol: www.roterhahn.it; Trentino: www.trentino:to; Belluno: www. venetoagriturismo.it).

Mountain huts
Mountain huts are reserved for mountain climbers and are not included in any list of accommodation *unless* they are run as guest houses for tourists. In summer, from 20 June to 20 September, virtually all mountain huts are open, and many stay open until mid-October or later. The tourist boards know all the opening dates and will supply lists on request.

Hotels for walkers
These comfortable hotels (3-4 stars) cater specially for walkers and families, with equipment hire, mini-bus for walk access, guided walks, walk 'libraries' with maps and guides. See www.wanderhotels.com; the site is available in English.

Youth hostels
Youth hostels are in short supply. The provinces in the Dolomites don't appreciate tourists who don't spend! Exceptions are the lovely youth hostel in the old Grand Hotel in Toblach/Dobbiaco (although it does not belong to the IYH), a hostel outside the area of this book in Riva Monte Agordino in the southern Dolomites, and some church centres like the Kassianeum in Brixen.

Campsites
Campsites are also very thin on the ground, and in some places (like Gröden/Val Gardena), there are none at all. For what there is, log on to www.camping.it.

Mountain azaleas at Passo Giau, in Ampezzo

Maize-based polenta is the carbohydrate of choice throughout the area — as here in Primiero.

Cuisine

Food in the Dolomites is a unique combination of Tyrolean, Imperial Viennese and Italian cooking. On top of that you have the pleasure of Tyrolean wines, from the dry white Sylvaners from the Eisack/Isarco Valley to the elegant Pinot Noir from the lower Etsch/Adige.

Broadly speaking, the Dolomites can be divided into three culinary regions where either dumplings, potato-based gnocchi or pasta predominate. In South Tyrol, even in the Ladin areas, dumplings dominate: bacon dumplings with sauerkraut and little dumplings in the soup. In Trentino's Fassa Valley the preference is for gnocchi, like the spinach-green *strangolapreti* ('priest chokers' — though no one knows how it came by this name). This is also true in the formerly Austrian Buchenstein and the Ampezzo Valley with Cortina. South of the old Austrian border, in Belluno province, pasta comes second only to polenta, the thick maize porridge.

This Italo/Tyrolean/old Austrian 'fusion' is at its most interesting in South Tyrol, where there are the most high-class restaurants, but in other provinces it also attains high standards. So traditional eating in the Dolomites is very simple: there are dumplings or the ravioli-like 'Schlutzer' or polenta, and with it maybe bacon or a soup with noodles or little dumplings. Bacon and smoked sausages are available everywhere, although 'bacon' here means something different from what you would find in Germany, Austria or Switzerland (see below).

Törggelen

'Törggelen' has almost become synonymous with the culinary way of life in South Tyrol. The meaning itself comes from the word 'Torggel', or wine press, and 'törggelen' means going to taste the new wines at the vintner's. Naturally this is best done with a little food on the side! In the autumn people walk up to the high ground, where the sun seems to linger longer, and the vintners open their premises for a short time — offering wine-tastings and home-cooked titbits. Traditionally this took place between saints' days — St. Martin (11 November) and St. Catherine (25 November) but, like all other customs today, the period has been stretched and now lasts from late October to the end of the year! The wine to be tasted is displayed in the farmer's rooms or spread out on tables in front of the house ... together with 'Schlachtschüssel' (cooked bacon, liver sausage and fresh blood sausage), roasted chestnuts, 'Speck', 'Krapfen', etc. Even if the vineyard is accessible by car, it's the walk (or cycle ride) that 'makes' the day's outing.

Dolomites specialities

Bacon (*Speck*) is made by stripping the hind legs of fat then soaking the meat in a bath of salt with cabbage. After this it is cold-smoked over juniper wood and stored for a long time. This makes the bacon extremely tender, with a mild flavour. In Tyrolean style this is cut into thick chunks and, once on the table, cut again into rashers and served on bread with a glass of red wine for the *merende* (the equivalent of a very hearty English afternoon tea). Done in the Italian way it is (like all other hams) cut paper-thin and served as an appetiser. Unfortunately it is legal to call packaged bacon 'Südtiroler Speck' — so if you are buying it in a shop, *beware*; better still, buy it direct from the farmer. (For an interesting treatise on South Tyrolean bacon, see www. recla.it/index_en.php!)

There are various **local cheeses** from the Alpine pastures. The local cheese is often grated over pasta; from Trentino, for example, there's the very good, parmesan-like *grana* cheese. In the Val di Fassa and Fleimstal/ Val di Fiemme they make the strong-smelling *puzzone,* covered with a light ochre skin. *Ziger* is a cone-shaped fresh cheese with chives; widely available in South Tyrol, it is eaten on black bread with vinegar, oil and onions.

All **desserts** in the Dolomites hark back to Austrian days: strudel, especially apple strudel, the famous 'Sachertorte', and buckwheat gateau with red berry filling. You can also expect to find 'Zelten', a fruit bread, and in Trentino a gingerbread biscuit with lots of lemon and orange zest; 'Krapfen' are a Ladin speciality — an elongated deep-fried doughnut with poppy seeds.

Practicalities A-Z

Climate and weather

The Dolomites encompass several climate zones, from the mild climate of western Lombardy in northern Italy (with an average annual temperature above 10 °C) to the hard mountain climate (average annual temperature about 0 °C). The valleys of Eisack/Isarco, Etsch/Adige and Puster/Pusteria are dry and cold in winter (sometimes with problems caused by snow) and warm and clearly wetter in summer, especially in July and August — quite like the mid-European climate. The lower Etsch/Adige, Primiero and lower Cadore enjoy mild, frost-free winters, so that not only wine but olives can be cultivated. In summer there is little rain, but it's no warmer than in the Eisacktal or Pustertal. A mountain climate characterises the areas between 900 and 1400 m, with an average annual temperature of about 14 °C and the possibility of night frosts in spring and autumn. Few settlements lie above the upper sub-alpine border (1600 m) and none at all in the alpine zone.

Weather forecasts on the web

South Tyrol: www.provinz. bz.it/meteo;
eastern Alps: www.meteoalpin. com;
Dolomites/Arabba: www.arpa. veneto. it;
Veneto: www.arpa.veneto.it/ csvdi/bolletino;
other weather forecasts at www. datameteo.com (in English).

Communications

In almost all tourist centres there are **post offices** and (card) **telephone kiosks** (buy cards

On the western side of Grödner Joch

police (112; **fire department**
(115; **breakdown/vehicle
recovery service (ACI)** (116. For
telephone information in Italy
call (12, for outside the country
(186. When making
international calls from Italy to
the UK preface the number with
0044; to North America with 001.
Calling from outside the country
to Italy, preface the number with
0039 and *include the zero* from
the area code (eg for a number in
the Bozen/Bolzano area call
0039/0471 + the number).

Festivals, customs and events

Even without the events
organised by the tourist boards,
there is always enough to see and
do in the Dolomites. One sees
people in local costume in the
farmers' markets or on Sundays
going to church. The brass bands
and 'Schützen' (see opposite),
with their attendants, gather
together at church festivals,
processions, annual fairs, the
many pilgrimages and the
autumnal transhumance with the
decorated cattle.
The following festivals and
events take place annually:
Prozesso alle Streghe, a folk
festival in remembrance of the
witches' trials (Cavalese, 1st
week in January);
Hay-sleigh and **horse-drawn
sleigh races** (Stern/La Villa,
February);
Good Friday processions in most
places that have a church;
Corpus Christi processions take
place on the Sunday after Corpus
Christi, since Corpus Christi is
not a holiday in Italy;
Oswald von Wolkenstein Ride,
with mock historical battles (on

from tobacconists). The post is
slow: try using *posta prioritaria,*
which is a bit faster. The **postage**
for letters and post cards to
Italy/the EU is about 0,43 €, *posta
prioritaria* to Italy/the EU about
0,65 €, to other countries 0,80 €.
Many towns and villages have
internet points, and more are
being added every year. A
mobile phone is worth taking, as
there is an excellent network of
masts. At present the cost is a
little over 1 €/min. **Television** is
usually confined to programmes
in Italian or German, but most 3-
and 4-star hotels and apartments
have satellite television receiving
news programmes from Sky, BBC
or CNN.

Emergency services/ telephone information

The general **emergency service**
(including helicopter ambulance)
is (118; **mountain rescue** (118;

Transhumance in Primiero

the Seis plateau, end May/early June);

Sacred Heart Festival in June, with processions in many places. In the evening eye-catching fires are lit on the surrounding mountains, showing, for instance, the heart symbol with a cross;

International Choirs Festival (in the Hochpustertal/Alta Pusteria;

Jazz Festival (in Bruneck/Brunico, July);

Estate Musicale di Fiemme, a festival of classical music, choirs, jazz and operettas (in the Fleimstal/Val di Fiemme, July/August);

Gustav Mahler Weeks (in Toblach/Dobbiaco, mid-July to mid-August) — classical music by Mahler, who lived and composed here during three summers, but also by others;

Festa delle Bande: brass-band festival (in Cortina d'Ampezzo, August);

Ascension Day (15th August), holiday processions throughout the Dolomites, with various guilds and associations (including Schützen) in traditional costume; especially noteworthy at pilgrimage churches dedicated to the Virgin Mary, like Maria Weissenstein near Deutschnofen;

Palio della Sloiza: folk festival when the hay is cut, with traditional sledges (in Primiero, end August);

Folk music and folk-dancing day: in the folk museum at Dietenheim (September);

Spectaculum, a three-day Middle Ages festival (in the streets of Bozen/Bolzano and at Runkelstein Castle, September);

Almabtrieb/Desmontegada: German/Italian words for the autumnal transhumance, when the cattle come back down from their alpine pastures. This festival is celebrated in many places, but is especially interesting when the goats are brought down in

Cavalese on the 3rd of September;
Gsieser Almhüttenfeste (festival of the huts on the Seiser Alm/ Alpi di Siusi), with tastings of specialities from the alpine pastures (mid-September);
Harvest: a procession giving thanks for the harvest (many places, on the first Sunday in October)
Kuchlkirchtag in Brixen/ Bressanone with guided culinary walks; also **Kuchlkastl** in Völs/ Fiè, a culinary folk festival on Schlern/Sciliar (both in October);
Leonhard-Ritt, a religious procession featuring riders on horseback, horse-drawn carriages, etc (in St. Leonhard/

S. Leonardo in the Abteital/Val Badia on the second Sunday in November);
Krampus Day (5 December) and the **Krampus Lauf** in Toblach/ Dobbiaco (see page 89);
Christmas markets in Bozen/ Bolzano, Brixen/Bressanone (the oldest) and other places, in the style of German and Austrian Christmas markets (in December).

Information
Tourist boards outside South Tyrol all have the abbreviation APT (Azienda Promozione Turistica) or IAT (Ufficio Informazioni Assistenza/ Accoglienza Turistica). Web sites

Schützen
'Schützen' were Tyrolean citizens charged since the early 16th century with the protection of the homeland. They played an important role in 1797, when Napoleon's troops invaded. Associations of Schützen still exist, and members see themselves in the true sense of the word as 'defenders of the homeland' and as followers of the first defenders of Tyrol.
But there are not only Schützen in South Tyrol: Mezzocorona in Trentino began in 1983 to re-establish the Schützen associations, followed by Trient, Lavis, Vezzano, Pergine and other places — in Belluno naturally in Cortina. 'Siamo italiani, di lingua italiana. Ma la nostra patria è il Tirolo' said one commander at that time in a newspaper interview. 'We are Italians, we speak Italian, but our fatherland is Tyrol'. So everywhere in the old Austrian parts of the

Dolomites, in Trentino and in Buchenstein, and Ampezzo in Belluno, you will see a growing number of Schützen at all possible festivals.
Schützen association websites are mostly in German, but if you key the word into an advanced search in English, there are some interesting references.

for the various tourist boards are shown at the top of each chapter. Naturally you can also contact the relevant **Italian Tourist Board** (see below), but they usually have less local information to offer than the bodies mentioned above.

In the UK: 1, Princes St, London W1B 2AY, (020 7408 1254, *fax* 020 7399 3567, e-mail: italy@ italiantouristboard. com, www.enit.it. There is also a 24-hr brochure request line: (090 65 508 925, but note that these calls are charged at premium rate)

In the USA: 630 Fifth Ave, Suite 1565, NY 10111 630. (212 245 5618/4822, *fax:* 212 586 9249, www. italiantourism.com.

In Canada: 175 Bloor St. East, Suite 907, South Tower, Toronto, Ontario M4W 3R8, (416 925 4882, *fax:* 416 925 4799, brochure hot-line: (416 925 3870, www. italiantourism.com.

There are excellent **internet** links on the web for South Tyrol and the Dolomites — right down to room rentals, sports opportunities, government departments and public places. *Most of the sites have English pages.*

www.hallo.com is the official site of the South Tyrol tourist PR department.

www.stol.it is a commercial site with some good facts, like traffic information and weather (but you have to pay to be connected).

www.provinz.bz.it/naturparke covers the natural parks.

www.parks.it covers *all* natural and national parks in Italy.

www.trenitalia is the official site of the Italian railways.

www.wetter-italien.de is a brilliant German site detailing the weather in the various resorts, sometimes with web

cameras. At time of writing it was not available in English but, if you can't make out the German or the icons, try the Google automatic translation facility (but don't expect too much!).

Maps

Many touring maps leave off the less-visited south of the range. An exception is **Michelin**'s 1:400,000 Regional Map 562, although it is not detailed enough for some purposes. The **General Karte Südtirol** (Mair), at a scale of 1:200,000, covers almost all the Dolomites and is sufficient for motoring and trekking by bike. Unlike Michelin, it shows almost all the villages mentioned in this book, but the typography may demand a magnifying glass! There is a 2009 edition of the popular TCI (Touring Club Italiano) 1:200,000 map **Trentino–Alto Adige**. Another, very readable map called **Trentino, Alto Adige, Südtirol** is on sale in the Dolomites (publisher Istituto Geografico/ De Agostini; scale 1:250,000). Mountain bikers, walkers, climbers and general enthusiasts should use the excellent large-scale (1:25,000) **Tabacco maps**, available at all bookshops and newspaper kiosks. The Kompass and Freytag & Berndt maps are generally less detailed but sometimes more up-to-date, as they are reprinted more frequently. The free maps from tourist offices are only useful for general orientation.

Medical care

In case of illness, the E111 card (which can be downloaded from the Internet or picked up at your post office) allows EU residents to obtain free medical treatment in Italy, so be sure to have it with you. Do *not* go to the doctor first, but to the USL (Unità Sanitaria Locale; the local medical centre), which is specially set up to deal with tourists. They will send you to a doctor or hospital. Since the opening dates and times of the USLs vary enormously, we have not given them in this book; check at the tourist office when you arrive — or look in the town halls, where opening hours are posted. If you are treated by a registered doctor with a private practice (thus not at the medical centre or a hospital), you will usually be expected to pay, then claim it back on your insurance when you return home. (It is presumed that you will take out a travel insurance policy before you travel!) **Pharmacies and doctors open or on call at night and on weekends** are posted at the town hall and on the doors of pharmacies. They are also listed in the daily newspapers like *Dolomiten, Trentino* or *Corriere delle Alpi.* The only **hospitals** in the Dolomites are at Bozen/Bolzano, Brixen/Bressanone, Bruneck/Brunico and Cavalese. People suffering serious accidents or illnesses are often flown by air rescue to Trient or Innsbruck for treatment.

Money/banks
The euro (€) is the local currency, so you will have to take euros with you or change when you are there. Almost every town and village has an automatic bill dispenser (if you hold the appropriate debit card); the relevant charge on your card will be in the region of 3,30 €. If you make withdrawals with a credit card, reckon on a surcharge of about 3%. Travellers' cheques can only be exchanged at banks, but there is (officially) no charge.

Opening times
In the Fassatal and Fleimstal/Val di Fiemme shops (including butchers and bakers) are closed Thursdays (though a very few open early Thursday mornings); in South Tyrol most shops (except in Bolzano) are closed Saturday afternoons. Banks are usually open Mon-Fri from 08.00-13.00/14.30-15.30; post offices Mon-Fri from 08.15-13.00.

Shopping and souvenirs
Shopping, usually confined to rainy days, can be quite fun on good days, if it's combined with an excursion or a walk. Products from the farms are the best souvenirs to take home (see 'Dolomite specialities' on page 16).
Woodcarvings/sculptures are a speciality of Gröden/Val Gardena, but are also found in the Fassa, the Hochabtei/Alta Badia and Ampezzo valleys. Before buying, visit the exhibition in St. Ulrich/Ortisei (see page 104). Specialised carvers produce masks (for instance, in Prettau/Predoi) and toys (especially in Gröden/Val Gardena).
Loden wear: This attractive dress never goes out of style, so it's always a good investment. It's worth shopping around: prices are cheaper in Toblach/Dobiacco, for example, than in Bozen/Bolzano! The largest manufacturers are Oberrauch-Zitt and Moessmer; there is a wide selection at the large co-op in Cortina.

Fabrics and lace: A good place to buy hand-made linen or cotton/linen tablecloths is Pederü/La Valle in the Abtei/Badia Valley, where there are three sales points in the handicraft area just by the road. There are also places in the Pustertal/Val Pusteria (for instance, shops in Bruneck/Brunico). In the upper Tauferer Ahrntal/Valle Aurina you can also get pillow lace (for instance in Prettau/Predoi).

South Tyrolean *Speck* (see page 16) is world-famous and available in all good-quality food shops. Avoid all packaged *Speck;* buy it from the farmer who has smoked it himself, to get the best, old-style quality — mild and tender.

Mushrooms: Italians go mad for the dried porcini mushrooms *(Boletus edulis),* also called ceps. Specialist purveyors (like 'Tutto Funghi' in Bruneck/Brunico) guarantee fine-quality produce.

Cheeses: Cheese from the alpine pastures is a good choice, especially the semi-hard and mature cheeses. The products of the Sexten/Sesto and Toblach/Dobbiaco dairies are especially recommended. It's a pity that the tasty (but slightly smelly) *puzzone* from the Fassa Valley is not transportable. Belluno cheeses are also good: try the dairies in Buchenstein, Colle Santa Lucia, Valbiois and any cheese from the pastures.

Sports

In both summer and winter the Dolomites are an ideal destination for sports enthusiasts. In summer the landscape is perfect for walking, long-distance hiking, climbing and mountain biking. With the first snows, the landscape changes to a paradise for skiing, snowshoe walking and snowboarding (the latest 'must-do'). It's a wonder people aren't tripping over each other, but there's such a choice of sports that this only seems to happen in a few places.

Walking and climbing

The classic Dolomite sport of mountain climbing has now threaded out into many different strands, since **walkers**, **mountain climbers**, **rock- and free-climbers** not only all have different goals but different equipment. Whatever your choice, there's an excellent network of walking routes (mostly red/white/red) and many climbing 'gardens' (like the one at Lake Dürren/Landro) and climbing walls.

In the northern Dolomites **walkers' huts** are quite close together; in the southern part of the range there are fewer huts and they are less well equipped, so that in some mountain groups (like the Lagorai or Marmarole) you'll have to rely almost entirely on bivouacs.

Obviously the **maps** from the tourist boards will *not* suffice for walking and climbing. It is best to get the excellent 1:25,000 Tabacco maps — at the very least for the area in which you are based. There are also large-scale maps from Kompass and Freytag & Berndt, but they are not as detailed.

A special feature of the Dolomites is the *via ferrata* (literally 'iron road'). There are many of these

Walkers at the Kreuzkofeljoch (Aferer Geisler and Peitlerkofel) — Walk 2

protected climbing trails: iron grips, pegs and cables enable those who are not technical experts to scale walls that would usually only be the province of Grade IV climbers or beyond. But you still have to have a helmet and other equipment — and, naturally, experience in Alpine terrain. For information contact the AVS (the South Tyrol Alpine Association; www. alpenverein. it). They also have an information desk on the ground floor of the South Tyrol Tourist Board in Bozen/Bolzano, open Mon-Fri 09.00-12.00/14.00-17.00. *Tip:* Even if you have no climbing experience, it is possible to tackle Walk 9; see page 100. You can buy the equipment in one of the sports shops or mountain guide offices.

A **mobile phone** is of little help if you're sitting in a glacial fissure! Before you go off for the day *always inform a reliable person!* The **mountain rescue** number is ☎ 118; the **alpine emergency signal** is six sound or visual signals within one minute (for instance, shout or flash your torch six times); then pause for one minute, then repeat the signal and wait for an answer. The answer is three signals within one minute.

Other sports
Fishing is allowed in the many clear watercourses in the range. Licenses for foreigners are easily obtained from tourist offices or even tobacconists. Any private fishing areas are marked in Italian with *Divieto di pesca* or *Pesca privata*.

The only people who come to the Dolomites to **swim** are those who like indoor hotel swimming pools. Actually, that's even becoming a pleasure now in the 4-star hotels, with their 'wellness' areas, saunas, whirlpools, etc. Whoever wants to swim 'naturally' can do so in Vahrn near Brixen/Bressanone or in Völs/Fiè. Or in one of the many ice-cold mountain lakes — very refreshing, if you can stand it for more than a moment or two! The lack of level terrain is a hindrance to building **golf**

courses, but there are a few — at Deutschnofen/Nova Ponente, Corvara, Campitello, Cortina d'Ampezzo and Bruneck/ Brunico.

The strong up-currents which characterise weather in the Dolomites (especially on fine mornings before noon) make the range a superb meeting place for **paragliding**. The best starting points are the mountain stations of the lifts or nearby places, like on Rodella above Campitello, Plose above Brixen/Bressanone or the Spitzbühel Hut on the Seiser Alm/Alpi di Siusi. For South Tyrol you can get up-to-date information at www.paragliding.it. Another informative site is www.parapendio-gardena.com, the site of the Gröden/Val Gardena Paragliding Club (their coverage is not limited to the Gröden Valley).

Cycling and mountain biking are one of the top sports in the Dolomites. Cyclists on racing bikes swarm along the major roads, especially around the Sella Group. Mountain bikers are competing more and more with walkers, and there are some fine cycle routes for families, for instance on the level terrain between Toblach/Dobbiaco and Lienz (see cycling tip on page 96). Since you can take your bike with you on the bus anywhere in the Dolomites (provided there is room), you can cover long distances without having a car at your disposal. **Cycle hire** is available almost everywhere. For information about cycling and mountain biking look at www.bikearena. com. Some tourist boards (especially Pustertal/Val Pusteria) also

publish free biking guides. The network of old mountain roads dating from the First World War, originally built as mule tracks, is an Eldorado for mountain bikers. These roads are generally only moderately steep, most are very well maintained, and they are closed to all motor traffic. The highest concentration of these old roads is in the supplies area for the Front — in the Fanes and Sennes groups (between the valleys of Gader/ Badia and Höhlenstein/Landro); you can really get off the beaten track here.

The Dolomites are not very suitable for **horse-riding**, which is mostly concentrated in the outlying wooded mountains and on the large plateaus like Seis/Siusi. In the valleys north of the Pustertal/Val Pusteria there are some riding stables which specialise in trekking; more information on this from the Tauferer Tal Tourist Board: www.tauferer. ahrntal.com. For South Tyrol you can get information about riding stables and farms with horses from the Tourist Board (www.suedtirol. info). If you like Haflinger horses, contact the South Tyrol Haflinger Breeders' Association, www. haflinger-suedtirol.com. In Trentino the APT Trentino can give you details or see www. trentino.to. For the province of Belluno contact www.fise.it (Federazione Italiana Sport Equestri), but the site is only in Italian at present.

Every tourist centre has **tennis courts**, and you can rely on all 4-star hotels having them.

Winter sports are becoming more and more popular in the Dolomites, and February is now

Dolomiti Superski

One ski pass, 460 lifts, 1220 km of pistes' — that's Dolomiti Superski's advertising slogan. It offers the largest selection of lifts and pistes on one pass anywhere in the world.

One of their pistes (Gran Risa in Stern/La Villa) counts among the most interesting, fastest and most popular in the world. Names like Wolkenstein/Selva, St. Ulrich/Ortisei, Stern/La Villa, Plose, Kronplatz/Plan de Corones, Cortina d'Ampezzo (1956 Olympics), Canazei, Fleimstal/Val di Fiemme (FIS World Cup/Nordic Championships 2003) make winter sports enthusiasts' hearts beat faster. The Sella Ronda, which circles the Sella Group, and the Marcialonga, the Nordic marathon in the Fleimstal, have attained mythical status. Most places have taken snowboarding and cross-country snow shoe walking to heart.

*The **Dolomiti Superski pass** encompasses almost the whole of the range (just as this book does, with the exception of the Brenta Dolomites and the Austrian Lienz Dolomites). The pass isn't exactly cheap and is only worth buying if you want to travel to more than one of the ski centres mentioned here or if you are staying in a place from where various ski resorts are easily reached — for instance in Brixen/Bressanone, with the nearby Eisack/Isarco Valley, Gröden/Val Gardena, and the Seiser Alm/Alpi di Siusi; the*

Fassatal or Fleims/Fiemme valleys; or Bozen/Bolzano, with good connections to most areas. For information on the ski pass see www.dolomitisuperski.com.

***Weather reports** from the Dolomites can be seen on satellite channel 3 from 08.00.*

***Ski pass offices** are in all towns and villages where they may be used, often at the lower lift stations.*

*The pass encompasses **12 skiing regions**, all within the area covered by this book: 1 Cortina d'Ampezzo; 2 Kronplatz/Plan de Corones; 3 Hochabteital/Alta Badia; 4 Grödental and Seiser Alm/Val Gardena and Alpi di Siusi; 5 Fassa Valley and Lake Karer/Lago di Carezza; 6 Arabba; 7 Hochpustertal/Alta Pusteria; 8 Fleimstal/Val di Fiemme and Obereggen; 9 San Martino di Castrozza and the Rolle Pass; 10 Eisack/Isarco Valley; 11 Tre Valli (Moèna, Lusia, Falcade); 12 Civetta.*

*In 2009 **prices** for various passes were: **all-in pass** for 6 days 176-220 €, 12 days 288-359 €, 15% discount for seniors over 60, children under 8 accompanied by an adult free, 30% discount for those aged 8-16. **Regional tickets**, for instance Kronplatz, 6 days 163-204 €, 12 days 267-333 €, Fleimstal Obereggen 6 days 147-241 €, 12 days 265-301 €. The **Season Pass** costing 570 € is also valid for a five-day period in the Adamello ski area in the Brenta Dolomites (west of the A22 motorway).*

considered high season; accommodation must be booked well in advance. The mountain lifts and pistes, as well as the region's ski runs are managed in cooperation with Dolomiti Superski (www.dolomitisuperski.com).

Short historical summary

From about 12,000 BC: After the Ice Age the first hunting expeditions in the area of the Dolomites.

From about 5000 BC: First Stone Age farming settlements in the wide valleys, soon followed by cattle husbandry on the mountain slopes (for example at the Seiser Alm/Puflatsch or the alm south of Croda da Lago).

About 3500 BC: Ötzi, the man from the Schnalstal, dies on a high mountain pass. When he was found in 1999, he had metal objects and goods that came from far away (flint from Monte Lessini near Verona).

From about 500 BC: Celtic invaders populate areas around the Eisack/Isarco and Etsch/Adige valleys.

16/15 BC: Roman Legions under Drusus conquer the area now known as Trentino-South Tyrol; incorporation in the province of Raetia; Romanisation of the Celtic population.

493-526: Rule from Verona under the Goth Theoderich I, otherwise known as 'Dietrich of Bern', the Ladin hero associated with the Laurin/Rosengarten legend (see page 61).

568-773: Lombards invade from the south, the alpine Romans are cut off from direct contact with other Roman groups south of the river Po. This results in a series of Raeto-Roman languages (for example Ladin in the Dolomites).

8th C: Expansion of the Bavarian influence south of the Brenner Pass; in 769 Duke Tassilo founds Innichen Monastery to promote the Germanisation of the Pustertal/Val Pusteria, which has been inhabited by Slavs since the 6th century. The Ladinised inhabitants retreat into the deeper valleys, preserving their language and culture.

773: Charlemagne conquers the area; the whole Dolomites are under Frankish control.

814: Charlemagne dies, precipitating the end of the Carolingian Empire.

843: Under the Treaty of Verdun the area of the Dolomites is split between the Italian and German kingdoms.

1004/1027: Trient/Trento and Brixen/Bressanone (bishoprics since 381/571) become Episcopal principalities, thus independent territories.

1282: The County of Tyrol also becomes sovereign territory, following which the Counts of Tyrol extend their holdings in the south and bring the principalities of Brixen and Trient under their influence. Gradually the three-language culture spreads throughout Tyrol.

1363: On the death of the last remaining member of the Tyrol family, the county falls to the House of Habsburg (up until 1918!).

1511: Kaiser Maximilian I, the Habsburg Emperor, releases the Tyroleans from war duty outside Tyrol, but obliges them to defend the land. This obligation builds the foundations for conscription in 1915, to defend the borders of the Dolomites until 1918.

1525/1526: The German Peasants' Revolt, Neustift Monastery plundered, Brixen's High Commander murdered (1532).

From about 1600: Agreements between landowners and farmers

Fresco at Rodeneck Castle dating from the Middle Ages: horseman from King Arthur's Round Table

put use of alpine pastures on a sound footing.

16th/17th C: Due to cheap exports from America, metal prices fall back sharply; mining in the Dolomites and the northern side-valleys of the Pustertal comes to a standstill.

1784: By decree of Kaiser Joseph II, German becomes the official language of the Habsburg Empire.

1788/1789: French geologist Deodat de Dolomieu discovers an unusual calcium magnesium carbonate rock in the Eisacktal/Valle Isarco; the new mineral is named after him and later is applied to the entire mountain range.

1796/1797: First war of the French/Bavarian coalition.

1803: The principalities of the German Holy Roman Empire are shattered and pull back to Brixen and Trient.

1805-1806: After the defeat by Napoleon at Austerlitz, Austria cedes Tyrol to Bavaria; other temporary boundary changes ensue.

1809/1810: Tyrolean Revolt against Bavaria and France, led by Andreas Hofer, fails.

1815: Following Napoleon's defeat, the Congress of Vienna gives all of the Dolomites to Austria, which already holds Venice and Lombardy.

1864-1867: A railroad is built over the Brenner Pass.

1866: Austria loses Venice to the Italians. The Dolomites south and southeast of Cortina (the Cadore) join the new Kingdom of Italy. Cortina and the northern and western valleys remain with Austria.

1912: The Great Dolomite Road crosses the Austrian Dolomites from Bozen to Cortina.

1914-1918: First World War. In

1915 Italy joins the Allies; bloody fighting in the mountains between Italy and Austria, with emplacements as high as 3000 m all the way across the range, from the Lagorai Group to the Sexten Dolomites. Areas at the Front (like Arabba) are evacuated and eventually destroyed by shelling (for example Toblach/Dobbiaco). In the Italian enclaves there is resistance, with many from the province of Trentino fighting on the Italian side. Heros of the Italian resistance (the 'Irriden-tisti'), such as Cesare Battisti from Trient/Trento, are executed by the Austrians and become martyrs; many Italian streets and squares are still named in their memory.

1918: Tyrol south of the Brenner Pass falls to the Italians.

1919: The Treaty of St. Germain establishes the present border between Austria and Italy. All of the Dolomites become part of Italy. New borders divide the area into three new provinces: Bolzano/Bozen, Trentino and Belluno.

1922: The Fascists take over government offices in South Tyrol by force.

1923: Edict forbidding the use of the German language in schools in South Tyrol. Illegal schools spring up throughout the area. All public offices, notices, etc must be exclusively in Italian. In the same year the Fascists forbid the name 'Tyrol' and substitute a made-up word: Alto Adige (translation from the German 'Upper Etsch Valley'). They try to break the cultural identity of the German- and Ladin-speaking people and Italianise the population.

1935: With the building of an industrial zone in south Bozen/Bolzano and the massive influx of workers from southern Italy the Italianisation is accelerated.

1938: After Austria is annexed by the German Reich, South Tyrol

expects to be annexed as well. But Hitler promises his ally Mussolini that the Brenner Pass border will be inviolate.

1939-1945: Second World War; even before the opening of hostilities, Italians and Germans unite in a settlement in the German-speaking part of South Tyrol. Up until the end of 1939 the option remains open for Italians to stay in their homeland or for people of German origin to emigrate to the German Reich: 86% of South Tyroleans opt for emigration but, because of the war, only 30% actually do so.

1946: The Paris Peace Conference reconfirms for Italy the borders that existed before the war.

1948: The provinces of Bozen/Bolzano and Trient/Trento are given administrative autonomy. This means that German can again be taught in schools. But the administration remains in Trento, where German-speaking people are in the minority. In the coming years the autonomy is constantly undermined: for instance, in 1955 a law is passed forbidding children to be christened with non-Italian names — a reminder of the Fascist era.

1956: Winter Olympics in Cortina d'Ampezzo, greatly promoting the appeal of the Dolomites as a tourist destination.

1959-1967: Austria brings the question of South Tyrolean autonomy before the full congress of the UN, which offers to help negotiations. Terrorist attacks against Italian establishments. By 1967 all parties in negotiations.

1972: Autonomy for South Tyrol grows in strength; the administration in Bozen/Bolzano receives much more authority. Equality between the Italian and German languages.

2002: Italy passes a bill allowing provincial borders to change, even when it's a matter of an autonomous province (something which was not previously allowed). The way is open for Ladin areas such as Ampezzo, Buchenstein and the Fassatal to become part of South Tyrol, with its political and cultural guarantees for German and Ladin people.

2003: The SVP (South Tyrolean People's Party) is re-elected, albeit with a marginally reduced majority.

2007: Polls in the autumn indicate that 77-85% of voters in the provinces concerned are in favour of a becoming part of South Tyrol.

View across the Seiser Alm meadows to Schlern and the Santner peaks

1 EISACKTAL/VALLE ISARCO

Brixen • Neustift Monastery • Plose • Lüsner Tal • Klausen • Lajen • Waidbruck • Villnösstal • Puez-Geisler Natural Park

Walks: 1, 2; *walking tips:* Zanser Alm and the Adolf Munkel Weg; 'Kuchlkirchtag Walk' — a guided gastronomic walk organised by the Brixen Tourist Board during the first three weeks in October; not a doddle; you'll be walking for 5-6h, with a height gain of about 650 m (gives you a great appetite!)

Web sites
www.eisacktal.com
www.brixen.org
www.luesen.com
www.klausen.it
www.lajen.info
www.villnoess.info
Opening hours: see individual attractions

From the Brenner Pass it's an easy ride to Bozen/ Bolzano, and that's all most people see of the Eisack/ Isarco Valley. They race along the motorway or on the fast EuroCity trains through the narrow valley between Brixen and Bozen without any view of the Dolomites — the wild peaks of Geisler/Odle and Schlern/Sciliar can only be glimpsed at a couple of points. Pity. It's also a pity because Brixen, Klausen and Bozen are beautiful old towns to explore — to say nothing of the many little villages with their slender church spires, culinary surprises and delicious 'Eisacktaler', the valley's dry white wine.

Brixen/Bressanone

The town lies somewhat apart from the Dolomites, but this bishop's seat is worth a stop en route, or even a longer excursion.

All **trains** between the Brenner Pass and Bozen stop here, and it's the hub for **buses** to Bozen, Bruneck/Innichen and most of the valleys in the area. The centre

The Villnöstal and Geisler peaks, with the church of St. Magdalena in the foreground (Walk 2)

is closed to cars, but there is a paid **car park** north of the old town on the Brenner Pass road. It's only around Brixen that the valley opens up enough to make room for the town. In the old town, near the cathedral (which can be seen on the approach from the motorway or train), there is a well-kept centre with shops, restaurants and good hotels. Plose, a mountain with many walking routes and ski runs, rises behind the city, surrounded by vineyards — a most attractive picture.

View from the Hofburgplatz to the Domplatz and Brixen's landmark cathedral

The façade of the **cathedral** (**Dom***) dominates the large **Domplatz**. The original building is only partially preserved. The lower parts of the towers are Romanesque and the high chancel Gothic. Today's magnificent baroque edifice was built in 1745. In the cloisters there are wonderful frescoes from the late Middle Ages. *Dom and cloisters open daily from 06.00-12.00/15.00-18.00.*

There are interesting gravestones in the arcades of the old cemetery (**Alter Friedhof**, left from the front of the cathedral). The adjacent church of St. Michael (**Michaelskirche**) is very old, but has been completely given over to the baroque. *Cemetery always open, St. Michael's about 06.00-12.00/15.00-19.00.*

The **Priesterseminar** is a late, restrained baroque building dating from between 1764 and 1771, with frescoes by Franz Anton Zeiller. The library hall, two stories high, is a real baroque jewel. *In term time limited access, no fixed opening times.* Two arcaded streets, the **Grosse and Kleine Lauben**, which meet at a right angle, were laid out in

the original 11th-century town plans. Don't miss the **Pfaundler-haus** (1581).

The old city trench (**Grosser Graben**) was filled in long ago; today it's a street. The **Säbenertor** (gate), with its high tower, breaks up the straight line of the adjacent façades.

The seat of the bishops of Brixen (**Hofburg**) is a Renaissance castle. The courtyard, with black statues on a yellow ground, is especially attractive. The **Diocesan Museum** is certainly worth a visit, with its huge collection of cribs, wood- carvings, altar triptychs, and wall paintings. *Hofburg and museum open from 15.3-31.10 daily (except Mon), 10.00-17.00; from 1.12-31.1 (except 24/25 Dec) daily, 14.00-17.00. Entry fee 7 €. www.hofburg.it.*

Neustift Monastery

This huge complex, with several courtyards, a large church, towers and well-maintained outer walls lies just 2,5 km from

Brixen, idyllically surrounded by its own vineyards. It was founded by the Augustinians in 1142, and today only monks of this order live here. The ground floor of the present building postdates a fire in 1190 and was fortified in the 15th century. In 1525 it was plundered during the German Peasants' Revolt (the

Accommodation

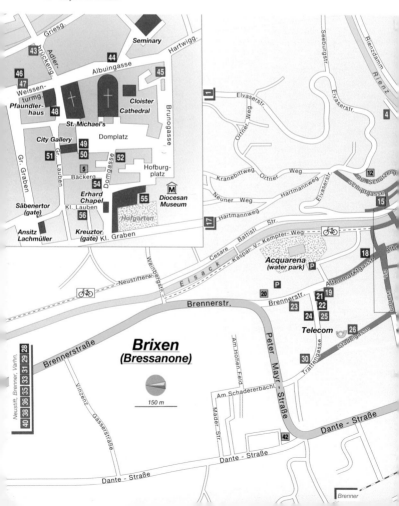

Augustinians had fled), and from 1735 all the most important buildings were restored in the baroque style. ·

You come into the grounds via an entrance dating from the Middle Ages. To your left is an interesting round building, the **Engelsburg** (Angel's Castle). It was originally a chapel dedicated

E ating and drinking

5 Senoner
7 Café/Konditorei Heiss
8 Spaghetteria-Pizzeria Valentina
10 Café-Bar Sabine
14 Schatzerhütte
18 Peters Weinbistro
21 Konditorei Pupp
22 Goldenes Lamm
24 Stampfl
27 Atrium
28 Stiftskeller Neustift
30 Elephant
44 Café am Gries
46 Adlercafé und Weinbar Vinissimo
48 Domcafé
49 Goldene Rose
50 Bar Historia
51 Art Café
52 Finsterwirt
54 Café zum Bäckergassl
55 Kutscherhof
56 Fink

N ight life

12 Theater Dekadenz
20 You 2
32 Forum Brixen
34 Kino Astra
37 Disco Max/Juke Box
39 Diesel Pub
42 Time Out
53 Belize Jazzkeller

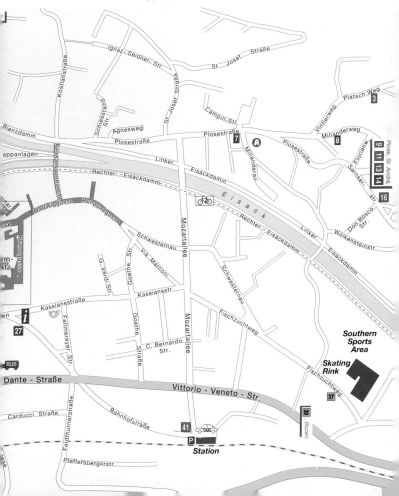

Neustift Monastery

to St. Michael and was part of the hospice for pilgrims travelling to Jerusalem — they came through Brixen en route to Venice, from where they embarked. In the 15th century the monastery was fortified with battlements and embrasures as protection against invading Turks; the **Turks' Tower** on the right dates from 1476. Next you come to the dining area and wine cellar on the left, then the first courtyard. In the building above the passageway is the two-storey **library**; a jewel of the rococo, it houses some 65,000 books, manuscripts and maps.

In the first courtyard the **Weltwunderbrunnen** immediately catches the eye. This baroque fountain, which dates from the year 1508, depicts the seven ancient Wonders of the World — and as the eighth Wonder, Neustift Monastery!

Coming into the second courtyard, the **monastery church** is to the right — a building with three naves and a high Gothic choir. Its Romanesque tower is massive. The interior of the church is one of the high points of late baroque, with magnificent ceiling paintings (by Matthäus Günther, 1736) in the form of three gigantic medallions with scenes from the life of

St. Augustine, and a marble high altar.

The **cloisters** are Gothic. The vault is still covered with some interesting frescoes, although most were ruined by gravestones being inserted at a later date. Finally, don't miss the newly-opened **historical garden**. *The monastery is usually always open; (paid) car park at the entrance. The courtyards, church and cloisters can be visited daily all year round; guided tours Mon-Sat from 10.00-16.00 every hour on the hour; from Nov to the end of Apr Sat only until 13.00. The garden is open May to mid-Oct (entry fee 5 €).*

Plose

Plose, Brixen's very own mountain, draws walkers in summer and skiers in winter. Its highest peak, Grosse Gabler at 2561 m, rises 2000 metres above the city! It's hardly surprising that the bald summits of the mountain are already powdered with snow in early autumn and that snow lies around for a long time in early spring.

A road runs via several pretty hamlets and villages to **St. Andrä**, where there is a late Gothic church with a typical high pointed tower. The chapel is an interesting octagonal central building dating from 1696. In this village you'll find the valley station for the **Plose cable car**. (Operates from Jul to the beginning of Oct from 09.00-12.00/13.00-18.00, with no mid-day break on Sat/Sun. One way 7 €, up and back 10 €, bikes 3 €.) In the hamlet of **Klerant**, a short way downhill from St. Andrä, the church of St. Nicholas is worth a

Walk 1: Circuit from Kreuztal via the Telegraph on the Plose summit and the Ochsenalm

Time: 4h
Grade: 500 m ascent/descent
Access: 🚡 or 🚐 to/from
St. Andrä (see page 36).

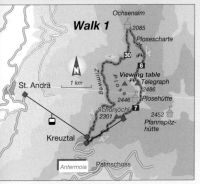

Refreshments: Plosehütte and Ochsenalm, both en route and manned
Map: Tabacco 1:25,000 N° 30, Bressanone/Brixen

Start out from **St. Andrä** by taking the cable car up to **Kreuztal**. From the top station follow **Route 7**; beyond a gate it runs up the slopes of **Schönjöchl**. In winter these slopes are very popular with skiers, as you can see! Following Route 7, you're always below a ridge up to your left — until you reach a small saddle, where another route joins from the left. Go right here, now

on the ridge itself and climbing quite steeply to a first **summit** and refuge (the **Plosehütte**, 2446 m; **1h**).
From here continue along the main ridge towards the Telegraph, the somewhat higher second summit of the massif. A motorable track takes you some way, then you pick up a track running left to the **Telegraph**, with an old Italian barracks (closed off) and a **viewing table** (2486 m; **1h20min**).
From here follow **Route 6** along the very narrow ridge, to an ideal resting spot by the **Leonharder Kreuz** (cross; 2365 m). After a break, follow the zigzags steeply down to a pass, the **Plosescharte**, from where you go left through steep meadows to the **Ochsenalm** (2085 m; **2h30min**). The return route to the top cable car station follows the **Zirmweg** (**Route 30**), undulating gently along the tree line (named for the Arolla pines which grow along here). This route is especially beautiful in the first half of July, when the rhododendrons covering the steep treeless slopes are in bloom. After about 1h30min you'll be back at the upper station at **Kreuztal** (**4h**).

visit; it has a cycle of frescoes by painters from the Brixen School (around 1475) and a famous naive depiction of an elephant. Travelling *uphill* from St. Andrä, you can get to the top end of the Plose cable car at 2050 m by car via Afers and Palmschoss. (There are also **buses** from Brixen which go via the valley cable car station as far as Palmschoss).

Driving via solitary homesteads and the hamlets of **St. Jakob** and **St. Georg** that make up **Afers/Éores** (✕), then via **Palmschoss** and the turn-off to the Villnösstal, you come to **Kreuztal** and the top of the cable car station, from where you can either take a chair lift or walk. Alpine meadows stretch up towards the Plose peaks, and in winter chair lifts run almost all the way to the top. There is a superb panorama from here, to the Zillertaler Alps in the north, Peitlerkofel and the Geisler peaks of the Dolomites in the east and south, the Sarntaler Alps and the Brixen basin in the west.

Lüsner Tal/Valle di Luson

In this narrow, deeply-etched valley there is just one village — **Lüsen/Luson**. The shady side of the valley, below the northern slopes of Plose, are quite densely wooded, but several big old farmsteads sit on the sunny side.

Here men still make a living from the land; in summer the cattle are driven up to the Lüsner Alm — a broad rolling plateau lying between 1900 and 2200 metres with breathtaking views towards Peitlerkofel and the Dolomites. **Lüsen** itself is young. In 1921 a fire destroyed the whole place, including the parish church, which has however been beautifully restored. People come here to walk, to recuperate in peace and quiet, to enjoy the intense greenery and the rustic cooking; they go to bed early. The only 'sight' is the **Pardellermühle**, a mill dating from 1646. The tourist office organises guided tours from May till October, which also include a 'Cultural Walk' through the village.

Klausen/Chiusa (✕)

This town lies in a narrow part of the Eisacktal, at the foot of a high isolated rock with several old churches and castles, and crowned by Säben Monastery, the first seat of the bishops of Bozen-Brixen. It wasn't a very amusing place for a bishop — and even

less so for the burgers of the little town below, squeezed in between river and rock. But it had the advantage of being easily defended, and remained secure until the 19th century. Moreover everyone — especially every salesman — had to use Klausen's main road to get through the Eisacktal, and had to pay a toll to do so! So it made a good base. Regional trains stop at the **railway station**; the **bus station** is in the north part of town, at the end of the market square (buses to/from Bozen, Brixen/Bruneck/Innichen, and the Villnöss and Grödner valleys). Motorists should note that the old town is a pedestrian precinct.

Take a walk along the (almost) traffic-free main street. Up until the 1960s all traffic had to funnel through here; today it's a fairly peaceful pedestrian zone. It's best to start out on the north side, by the **Säbner Tor** (gate), with the adjacent late Gothic **Church of the Apostles**. All salesmen from Germany had to pass through

Klausen's main street: up until just a generation ago, all traffic through the Eisacktal came through this narrow funnel.

From the Eisacktal you have a good view of Säben Monastery's protected site.

this gate and, after saying a little prayer in the church, pay their tolls and set out to work.

Follow the main street (called 'Oberstadt' or 'Upper Town' at this point). There's no room here for the typical South Tyrolean greenery! Instead you'll see attractively wide houses with coats of arms, bay windows and windows with stone-edged surrounds; today the ground floors are busy with shops and places to eat and drink. Just on the right (at N° 67) is a Renaissance house with beautiful frescoes; N° 57 is the beautiful old Gothic **town hall**; N° 37 (also on the right) is Säbner House, where a woodcarver works on the ground floor.

The **parish church of St. Andreas** stands a bit below the **Pfarrplatz** (Parish Square). A few late Gothic paintings, statues and galleries still remain from the date of its founding in 1498. From here the main street is called 'Unterstadt' (Lower town), but nothing changes — there are lovely houses left and right. Just before the street ends, the 'Säbner Aufgang' begins on the right, from where you can climb up to the monastery (see below).

On the other side of the Tinne stream is the somewhat isolated **Cappuchin Monastery** dating from 1701. The Cappuchins only left in 1972; today part of the complex houses the local **museum**. On display is the precious 'Loretoschatz' — a gift from the last Spanish Habsburg empress to her personal chaplain, who came from Klausen.

Museum open from the end of Mar until Aug, Tue-Sat 10.00-12.00/16.00-19.00, Sep until mid-Nov, 09.30-12.00/15.30-18.00. Entry 4 €.

The **Säbner Aufgang** is a long climb which begins in the lower town and rises to **Säben Monastery**. It has been a pilgrims' route for centuries, as can be seen from the Stations of the Cross. After a steep stretch on steps you pass **Branzoll Castle** (not open to the public) with a huge keep. Then you reach the **Liebfrauenkirche**, an octagonal baroque building. In the dome are beautiful frescoes of the Life of Mary. This is the votive church of the inhabitants of Klausen, who were saved from the Plague by the Mother of God. Via the Benedictine inner monastery one gains access to Säben Monastery's **church** dating from 1687.

Just one more set of steps and you reach the highest point, with the small **Heiligkreuzkirche** (Holy Cross). It rises above many older predecessors, since this prominent and easily-defended site was settled even in prehistoric times. Dating from around 600, it was later rebuilt in late Gothic style as the bishop's palace chapel. The magnificent crucifix on the high altar is by Leonhard von Brixen.

Liebfrauenkirche open from early Jul until 31 Oct, Thu/Fri/Sun,

*14.00-17.00; Gnaden Chapel,
Holy Cross Church and
monastery church open daily,
08.00-17.00/18.00. The monastery
itself is not open to the public.*

Lajen/Laion

This large village at the entrance
to the Ladin Grödnertal/Val Gardena basks on a sunny terrace at
1100 m. The road from Klausen
into the valley follows the traces
of the old 31.4 km-long railway,
built by the Austrian military (in
record time) from September
1915 to February 1916, to link
Brixen with the upper reaches of
the valley.

Tschöfas, **Tanürz** and **St. Peter**
with its big church (outdoor
frescoes!) are isolated villages;
St. Peter is the last German-
speaking settlement below
Raschötz, which separates the
German and Ladin parts of the
valley. This is age-old farming
country, with Tyrolean-style twin
farmhouses.

Waidbruck/Ponte Gardena

Waidbruck lies at the point where
the Eisacktal narrows into a
gorge before opening up again at
Bozen. It's been a crossroads
from Roman times: this is where
a road leaves the Eisacktal for the
Grödnertal; in Roman times the
road over Ritten to Bozen began
here.

In the Middle Ages the **Trostburg**
watched over the entrance to the
Grödnertal and still stands there
today as if it were ready to spring
into defensive action. This castle,
where Walther von der Vogelweide (the first great German
lyrical poet-knight) grew up in
the 12th century, was splendidly
rebuilt in the Renaissance —
something one can't judge from

the outside. Inside, some of the
rooms are original, and there is
also an exhibition devoted to
Oswald von Wolkenstein (14C),
the most important lyrical poet
between Walther von der Vogelweide and Goethe. *The Trostburg
can be reached on foot in 20min
from the main square in Waidbruck via the steep old access
road, now closed to traffic. Open
only on guided tours: Jul/Aug
Tue-Sun at 10, 11, 14, 15, 16.00;
Maundy Thursday until Jun and
Sep/Oct only at 11, 14, 15.00.*

Villnösstal/Val di Funes

Few pictures of the Dolomites are
as well known as the view of the
Geisler peaks with the little
church of St. Johann in Ranui in
the verdant foreground. And it's
just like that: the Villnösstal is
one of the few green, quiet and
well-farmed valleys in the South
Tyrol Dolomites.

Buses run from Brixen via
Klausen railway station as far as
St. Magdalena and, in summer,
four a day go on to the Zanzer
Alm (which in August is also
served by five mini-buses a day
from Ranui). Cars pay a toll
beyond St. Magdalena.
Travelling from the Eisacktal you
first cross a narrow, deeply-cut
and forested gorge, before
coming into the wide sunny
Villnösstal below St. Peter. This
attractive farming country once
consisted of individual farms and
hamlets; today St. Peter and
St. Magdalena, like Teis above the
Eisacktal, are more village-like.
The peaks of the Geisler Group
and the equally abrupt **Aferer
Geisler** limit the views. The
farmers live from farming, as in
the past, but today they also offer
farmhouse holidays and let

rooms. Taking a holiday here isn't necessarily a doddle: Reinhold Messner, who came from Pitzak in the middle of the valley, learned to climb on **Sass Rigais**, the highest and most eye-catching spike of the Geisler Group.

In **St. Peter** (✗) the parish church of Saints Peter and Paul lies on a sunny terrace above the valley, surrounded by the little village with its inns, post office, bank and shops. More interesting than this much-rebuilt church, however, are two chapels in nearby hamlets. **St. Valentin in Pradell** has a fine altar triptych dating from the late Middle Ages, with paintings from the life of St. Valentine, clearly influenced by Michael Pacher. The fresco of St. Christopher on the outside walls is one of the most beautiful in South Tyrol. From here it's a lovely climb up to the little chapel of **St. Jakob am Joch**. This also has an altar triptych (from 1517) to admire; like the one in St. Valentin's, it comes from the Brixen School. *Both churches are open Jun to end Oct, St. Valentin Tue/Thu 16.00-18.00, St. Jakob Thu/Sun 16.00-18.00.*

St. Magdalena (✗) lies at the point where the Villnösstal narrows again, and the view to the Geisler spires is especially beautiful (photograph page 32). The little church of **St. Johann** in **Ranui** is an unforgettable spot. It dates from 1744; its slim little tower with the onion dome and painted front, which mimics an entablature, are lovely, but what sets this tower apart is its unusual position: it's at a 45° angle to the nave. The key to the church is held in the nearby Ranuihof.

The famous '**Teiser Kugeln**' are stone spheres filled with agate, amethyst or quartz crystals. The parent rock is located by a stream near the village of **Teis** in an area of quartz porphyry. Prospecting is forbidden! To see the parent rock, you can take a guided walk organised by the Teis Tourist Office. This includes a lovely

St. Johann in Ranui

nature trail and a 'Törggelen' stop (see page 18). You meet up at the **Mineral Museum** ***(open mid-Apr to early Nov, Tue-Thu 10.00-12.00/14.00-16.00, Sat/Sun 14.00-17.00)***. The museum has a web site (www. mineralien museum-teis.it) and, although it is only in German and Italian, there are good photos.

View to the Geisler peaks from the Gampenalm: this is where Reinhold Messner learned to climb

Puez-Geisler Natural Park

A massive tectonic fault separates the gently sloping meadows of the Villnösstal from the abrupt rock of the Geisler peaks. While the meadows lie above the easily worked red sandstone, the mountain chain is made up of often blindingly-white dolomitic rock.

The Aferer Geisler/Odles Deores in the northeast and the Geisler/Odle peaks in the south (the Geisler Group), together with the high-lying plateau of the Puez Group form part of the Puez-Geisler Natural Park. Thus the park encompasses both German- and Ladin-speaking parts of South Tyrol, as well as parts of the Grödner/Gardena and Gader/Badia valleys.

The park is a truly magnificent **walking area**. One can cross the Puez Group from southwest to northeast on a straightforward trail across high alpine terrain, and the Adolf Munkel Weg (see below) has always been famous as one of the most beautiful walking trails in the Dolomites. All motorised traffic is forbidden in the park; tents and mountain bikes *are* permitted but, because of the steep trails they're not really an option. So it's much better to take plenty of time to explore on foot, and enjoy the magnificent sight of golden eagles overhead. There are other rare birds in the park, too, like black grouse and capercaillie, but visitors hardly ever see them. The Villnöss Tourist Board has an office at the Zanser Alm car park.

Walking tip: Brogles Hut and the Adolf Munkel Weg

Time: 5h
Grade: 600 m ascent; 800 m descent; *the only water en route is at the Weissbrunn (spring)*
Map: Tabacco 1:25,000 N° 30, Bressanone/Brixen

The Adolf Munkel Weg (✕) is one of the most beautiful walking trails in the Dolomites, running across Alpine pastures and through the forests at the foot of the Geisler peaks. The walk begins at the Zanser Alm car park (✕), rises to the Brogles Hut and then descends to Ranui. The middle stretch contours at 1900 m. You will see the Odle, Sass Rigais, Fermeda, and Seceda peaks from close quarters, and the walk is accessible to everyone used to mountain walking, since there are no particularly tricky sections.

Walk 2: Around the Aferer Geisler/Odles Deores

Time: 6h
Grade: 650 m ascent; 1100 m descent
Access: Bus from St. Magdalena bus stop to Zanser Alm; the walk ends back at St. Magdalena.
Alternative, shorter walk: For a really great family walk, follow the main walk from the Zanser Alm car park to the Schlüterhütte with its magnificent, far-reaching views (about 2h). Have lunch at the hut: specialities include various polenta dishes — maybe with melted cheese, maybe with goulash, and the desserts are especially tasty, too — carrot and buckwheat tart, apple strudel with vanilla sauce, and — rare for mountain huts — yoghurt with fresh fruit. Afterwards, relax with a beer while the kids explore the extensive meadows. Then return the same way (about 3.5-4h in all).
Map: Tabacco 1:25,000 N° 30, Bressanone/Brixen
The Aferer Geisler are the somewhat smaller counterpoint to the Geisler/Odle peaks. They hem the Villnösstal to the northeast. Seen from the Peitlerscharte, they merge with steeply rising Peitlerkofel/Sass de Pútia in the distance, with the next mountain range to the north being Plose (Walk 1). This walk

takes in the northern part of the Günther Messner Steig, to make a circuit around the Aferer Geisler (the southern part of this trail, which crosses the peaks, is climbers' country). The trail was named in

View west from the Peitlerscharte

memory of Reinhold Messner's brother, who died in a mountaineering accident when climbing with his brother in the Himalayas.

The **walk begins** at the **Zanser Alm car park**: follow the motorable track to the left (signposted to the Gampenalm and Schlüterhütte). When you reach an alm, cross the usually dry **Kaserill** stream to the right (well waymarked). On the far side, a good trail sees you climbing steeply (on steps). When the trail levels out a bit, there is a fine view to the Geisler peaks.

Soon you're at the **Gampenalm (1h15min)**. Pass the alm and go right, uphill, on a steep trail (**Route 35**), keeping the motorable track to the Schlüterhütte over to your right. It's a fairly tiring zigzag ascent to the **Schlüterhütte** and then up to the somewhat higher **Kreuzkofeljoch (2h**; photograph page 25), from where there is a superb view to Kreuzkofel in the Fanes Group on the far side of the Gadertal. Pilgrims on foot use this pass when coming from the Abtei and Gader valleys on their three-day Corpus Christi procession to Klausen and Säben Monastery.

From the Kreuzkofeljoch head left on the almost-level trail towards Peitlerkofel, which rises loftily ahead. At the first fork go left, at the second keep right (left is the Günther Messner Steig across the peaks of the Aferer Geisler). The normally crowded **Peitlerscharte (2h45min)** is where all those heading for Peitlerkofel stop to rest — as can be seen, sadly, both on the ground and in the nearby vegetation.

Now head left downhill on a gravelly zigzag trail. At a fork after about 20 minutes, keep left. Cross a stream (usually there's some water) and, at the next fork, go left again (even though most people will be going *right* here, to their parking place on the road from Lüsen. The mountain with the rounded top is Plose.

Now you're quite alone. Larches and Arolla pines, Alpine meadows and easily-crossed screes make up the next hour and a half (the last 15 minutes of which is a very steep descent). A massive scree descending from the Aferer Geisler is to your left. On reaching the road (**4h15min**), head left and, after 10 minutes, by a crucifix, go right on a woodland trail. You cross the asphalt road again in five minutes and now follow a forestry road (closed to vehicles) further downhill and then left into a little valley. The road rises slightly and finally descends again.

You leave the woods near a bench (**5h30min**) and see the church of St. Magdalena against the backdrop of the Geisler peaks (photograph page 32). When you reach the second farmstead, continue along the road via **St. Magdalena**, to the valley floor and the **bus stop (6h)**.

2 SEISER ALM AREA/ALPE DI SIUSI

Seis • Völs • Kastelruth • Seiser

Walks: 3, 4; *walking tips:* Laranz Woods; Tisens and Tagusens; Puflatsch

Access: cable car from Seis; up to 26 buses a day between Bolzano, Völs, Seis and Kastelruth; up to 7 a day between Völs and the Gröden via Seis and Kastelruth. Free shuttle bus with six lines between the Panider saddle, Kastelruth, the valley station, Seis and Völs via Kastelruth and Seis. In high season buses run every quarter- or half-hour from 08.00-19.00; they are free for Combicard holders, otherwise 5 € for one week, 3 € for 3 days. On the alm itself there's an 'express' bus between Compatsch (the mountain station for the Seis cable car) and Saltria.

Web sites www.schlern.info

> ### Combicard
> *You can buy a Combicard for 32 € (valid 3-7 days), allowing free travel on the Seiser Alm cable car, the 'express' bus, 1 trip on the Marinzen Hut lift in Kastelruth, all bus services from Compatsch to Saltria, all shuttle buses and 3 days of 'Mobilcard' travel on SAD buses (see page 12). There are also Combicards for 7 and 14 days, and — of course — a 'gold' Combicard …*

www.seis.it
www.voels.it
www.kastelruth.com
www.seiseralm.it
www.bolzano-bozen.it
Opening hours: see individual attractions

Völs/Fiè, Seis/Siusi and Kastelruth/Castelrotto lie on a plateau high above the Eisacktal/Valle Isarco. Rising 1000 m above them are the broad meadows and pastures of the Seiser Alm/Alpe di Siusi, one of the most extensive pasturelands in the Alps. Even higher — another 600 m up — is the high limestone plateau of Schlern/Sciliar. It is not often that one sees such a breathtakingly beautiful landscape, so don't be surprised if you're not alone. During the autumn harvest festival in Kastelruth, you can't get a room in the area for love nor money; it's a weekend to avoid. Instead, why not visit in early spring, with mild days and so many wild flowers in bloom. Or in summer, when sports possibilities are endless and there's a chance to swim in an ice-cold lake. Or late autumn, when the larches stand out bright yellow in front of the limestone flanks of Schlern.

Seis/Siusi (✕)

Even for a province with as many spectacular backdrops as South Tyrol, few villages are as blessed as Seis. It lies in a green basin below the wild, bare Santner peaks, an offshoot of the adjacent Schlern. Once a small farmers'

hamlet, it is now a first-class holiday centre. There is a large **car park** by the **bus station**, at the corner of Schlern and Valier. There are good hotels and *pensions,* the cuisine is excellent, and walking possibilities are first class.

miss the short walk from Seis via waymarked Route 8 and then Route 3, which first goes to the castle and then **Bad Ratzes**. It begins at the end of Hauenstein-strasse opposite the tourist office. There's little left of this Middle Ages castle, which was built in the 12th century by the Hauensteins. Later it passed to the Wolkensteins, who enlarged it and made it habitable. One of the family members was the poet Oswald von Wolkenstein (commemorated by a marble plaque). After the German Peasants' Revolt in 1525 the castle was abandoned and fell into ruin.

Walking tip: Laranz Woods (see Tabacco 1:25,000 map N° 5). There's a little walk in the Laranz Woods west of Seis, which would be nothing special except for the giant mushrooms of all varieties to be seen scattered around. None are poisonous; they are all painted sculptures — done by a talented wood carver who has come to an arrangement with the park authorities to display them there.

Völs/Fiè (✕)

The setting of this old village on one of the hills overlooking the plateau is most attractive, and the church square is particularly harmonious. There are two **car parks**, both on the main village road — one near Boznerstrasse, the second on the other side of the village, near the start of the trail to Hauenstein Castle. Inside the old parish Church of the Ascension (**Maria Himmel-fahrt**), with its slender clock tower and eye-catching onion dome, is a Romanesque 13th-

Seis has an old tradition as a summer resort: people have been coming to the Ratzes baths since 1715, and in the 19th century the Norwegian playwright Henrik Ibsen bought himself a house here. In the forest above the village (near Walk 8) are the remains of **Hauenstein Castle**, where Oswald von Wolkenstein (see page 40) once lived. There's little of note in Seis itself, even the baroque parish church is nothing special. But the church of **St. Valentin** (see cover photograph and Walk 3) above the town, definitely *is* worth a visit. From here you'll have the best possible view of Schlern (take binoculars too!). The little church with its slender tower and golden onion dome has lovely frescoes inside and out, dating from the end of the 14th century. *Only open Thu 14.00-15.00.* **Hauenstein Castle ruins:** Don't

century crucifix and an altar triptych (1489) by the master craftsman Narziss of Bozen. The vicarage near the **cemetery chapel of St. Michael** houses the small but interesting **parish museum**. This has a most attractive collection, especially of late Gothic sculptures taken from various chapels in the parish for safe-keeping. *Parish museum open only in summer, Tue/Fri from 11.00; guided tours.*

Schloss Prösels: The forerunner of the little castle you see today was given by the Kaiser to the Bishop of Brixen in 1027. The bishop then turned it over to a ministerial family who named it after the castle of the Lords of Völs. The columns on the Völs coat of arms came about when Leonhard von Völs, governor of the province under Kaiser Maximilian, took the new name of 'Colonna' (column), since his family originally came from old Roman Colonna. This energetic owner had the castle rebuilt in modern Renaissance style, turning it into a prestigious castle complex which spread the fame of the Völs-Colonna name.

Some rooms are magnificent — like the large sitting room with fireplace and wooden beamed ceiling, the riders' room with Renaissance panelling and wonderful woodcarvings on the balustrade of the large staircase. The walls were painted with frescoes, and in the castle chapel Hans Leonhard Schaufelein — a master from the Dürer School, showed what modern art was north of the Alps. The contrast between the late Gothic building technique and the Renaissance paintings, frescoes and woodcarvings are often especially

striking — as in the loggia of the inner courtyard, where portraits in the Renaissance style are displayed between the late Gothic arches. *Castle open from May-Oct daily (ex Sat). Guided*

Hay baths — a Völs speciality

For many people a summer holiday in Völs will be their first opportunity to take a 'hay bath' — as generations of local farmers did to keep themselves fit and fresh. The Hotel Heubad is a reminder of the time, in the early 20th century, when a doctor, Josef Clara, first sent tourists here for the hay. And they loved it.

So what is a 'hay bath'? The 'bath scrubber' buries the guests in a hay-pit and fills it with hay up to their necks, then covers them with towels and leaves them to their fate: they sweat. After 10 to 25 minutes (depending on age, gender and general state of health), if their pulse has risen substantially, the guest has sweated enough and then moves on to a rest room to recuperate, wrapped in warm blankets.

As with the sauna, this is the time for the client to take a lot of liquid on board — not alcoholic, of course — but who's to say if the guest's hand reaches for the wine bottle rather than the water? After that one must eat heartily, and South Tyrolean cooking fits the bill perfectly.

The effect of the hay bath is de-toxification through sweating and a good feeling in one's body; the joints especially are lubricated, and arthritic pains are lessened or even disappear entirely. When the pains come back, just take another hay bath...
www.badkultur.com.

View from Kastelruth's Calvary Hill (Kastelruther Kofel or Kalvarienberg) down onto Tisens

tours at 11.00, 14.00, 15.00 (Apr, May, Oct); at 11.00, 14.00, 15.00, 16.00 (Jun/ Sep); at, 10.00, 11.00, 15.00, 16.00, 17.00 (Jul/Aug). Entry 4 €.

South Tyrol has few good swimming lakes, and as a result the little lake in Völs (**Völser Weiher** in German — or Völs *pond;* **Lagetto di Fié** in Italian; ✗) has become popular for swimming. It was originally created as a carp fishing lake for the lords of Schloss Prösels, since fish was needed for the many annual fasting days. The shore is boggy in places, and sometimes the pond dries up, but there is a small bathing complex and a little wood-built restaurant nearby serving regional dishes. There are also rowing boats for hire, and on Sundays in August the pond is full of rowers. You can reach the lake by car on roads from Völs or on foot via waymarked Route 2 from the Vigilerhof on the road to Seis.

Kastelruth/Castelrotto (✗)

Kastelruth is an extremely pleasant place for a holiday — green and beautifully sited, with the Seiser Alm and Schlern in the background and with a mostly intact historical old centre at the foot of its castle hill (which today lacks a castle). It has top-class infrastructure: excellent hotels and a wide variety of pastimes for both summer and winter. There is a large **car park** near the village centre. Kastelruth is often full up, so book early. But be aware that there are many older visitors, so you may find the atmosphere a little too low-key…

The old part of Kastelruth has some houses with outside frescoes, like Felseck House, the Gasthof zum Wolf and the Mendelhaus. But the village landmark is the massive detached **clock tower** of the baroque parish church of Saints Peter and Paul (1756-58) with its onion dome. The church itself, which is also very large, is more recent (19C).

A steep lane rises from the village centre (by the solid Gasthof Turmwirt on the right). You can either follow this lane or take the track to the right, just where the lane starts. Either way you will reach the **Kalvarienberg** (Calvary Hill, also called the **Kastelruther Kofel**). The well-waymarked circuit takes about 30 minutes. There was once a castle atop this hill, but it was destroyed in 1202. The rump of the keep was converted into two baroque Calvary chapels; next to them is another chapel dating from the 17th century.

Walk 3: From Kastelruth to Seis via St. Valentin

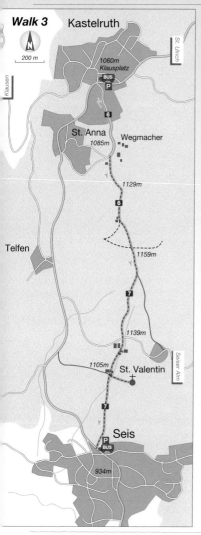

Walk 3

Kastelruth

200 m

1060m
Klausplatz
BUS
P

6

St. Anna
1085m   Wegmacher

1129m

6

Telfen

1159m

7

1139m

1105m   St. Valentin

7

Seis
P
BUS

934m

St. Ulrich

Klausen

Seiser Alm

Cover photograph
Time: 1h
Grade: 100 m ascent, 180 m descent
Access: several buses daily between Kastelruth and Seis
Map: Tabacco 1:25,000 N° 5
For almost the whole of this short, easy walk you have Schlern and the wild spikes of adjacent Santner in front of you.

Begin in **Kastelruth**: after looking round **Klausplatz**, return to the main trunk road, cross over, and walk south up the lane signposted to 'Guns/Marinzenweg/Farmacia'. You soon see the **Route 6** way-marking as you climb gently away from the village. The lane becomes a cinder track and reaches its highest point by a signposted crossroads; from here just continue in the same direction, still on Route 6. The views are fantastic!

After about 300 m turn off right on **Route 7**, a gently descending grassy path. This runs straight across meadows, crosses the Seiser Alm road and comes to a group of houses. On the left, a little off the route, is the church of **St. Valentin**; you'll have seen its tower on the approach. Keep straight downhill to nearby **Seis**, which you reach near the **bus station/car park** (150 m to the left; **1h**).

Walking tip: Tisens and Tagusens
(✕). See Tabacco 1:25,000 map N° 5: by following waymarked Route 1 from Kastelruth you can reach the nearby village of **Tisens** on foot in half an hour. The starting point is the central Klausplatz: follow Plattenstrasse, then turn right after 150 m onto Sabine Jäger Strasse, a very lightly-trafficked road that goes all the way to Tisens. Like so many other churches in South Tyrol, **St. Nicolas** at Tisens has a huge St. Christopher on the outside wall.

From Tisens you could carry on to **Tagusens**. To walk there (allow 1h), follow waymarked Route 2, which forks right where the

Seiser Alm: meadows with walkers, Schlern and the Santner peaks in the background

motor road makes a left-hand curve in the valley, about 750 m *before* Tisens. The trail crosses the wooded Moosbüchl and takes about 50 minutes from the turn-off. Tagusens is a solitary outpost set above the exit from the Grödnertal (the village opposite is Lajen). Below the hamlet is the chapel of **St. Magdalena**. Its tower dates from the 14th century, the nave (later rebuilt in baroque style) from about 1500. The baroque altar, with a painting by Franz Xaver Unterberger is especially lovely. Don't miss the school museum in Tagusens, which cleverly depicts what classrooms were like about 50 years ago (the building was used as a school up until 1993). *Museum open from Easter to 31 Oct, Mon/Wed/Fri from 10.00-16.00; no entry fee, donations welcome.*

Seiser Alm/Alpi di Siusi (✕)

The Seiser Alm is well known as one of the most beautiful holiday destinations in all Europe, and with good reason. Hardly any other mountain area can offer so much throughout the seasons and yet remain so little changed by tourism. Dominated by Schlern and the Rosszähne — and with Langkofel in the east, the Seiser Alm is pure heaven for those who want an active holiday.

It is strictly forbidden to drive on the Alm, and the road from Seis/Kastelruth to **Compatsch** (where all the infrastructure is concentrated; ✕) is closed in summer from 09.00-17.00; you can only reach the alm via the cable car from Seis. (The only exception is that overnight guests can obtain special licences from their hotels or the tourist board, but even they must use the roads before 11.00 and after 15.00.) The cable car runs from Seis daily from 08.00-19.00 (in case of rest break or maintenance stoppage there is a shuttle bus); one way 9 €, up and back 13 €, families 28 €; www. seiseralmbahn.it. From near Compatsch a second (chair) lift rises another 150 m to the Panorama Guest House (May-Oct, from 08.30-13.00, then 14.00-17.00; one way 4.50 €, up and back 6.50 €.

The rolling high plateau of the Seiser Alm, lying between 1700-1800 m and 2100-2300 m, is bedded with soft stone, which collects surface water. So there are many little ponds and wet places with interesting vegetation and, between them, large areas of meadows and pastures which have been grazed by cattle from time immemorial. Before machines and chemical fertilisers became common, the meadows were managed by hand and brought in moderate but high-quality returns. To judge how good the hay was, you only have to taste the local milk, butter and cheese. The locals have known for centuries how good the oil from this hay was for treating arthritis and bone diseases; the '**hay baths**' (see page 47) now offered to tourists date back to a traditional treatment for the local people.

If you cross the plateau with its alms and sprinklings of huts where dry hay is stored for the winter (and then taken by sledge into the valley), you come into the mountainous region — as spectacular as the Alm itself. From the plateau it is easy to climb mighty **Schlern** which rises so majestically over Völs and Seis; the same is true for the well-named **Rosszähne/Denti di Terrarossa** (Ross 'teeth'). Schlern is a fantastic mountain for its panoramas and much loved by climbers — especially the Santner and Euringer crags that rise up from the plateau. These were named for the first climbers to

tackle them, Johann Santner and Gustav Euringer. The Rosszähne also attract rock climbers: from the Tierser Alpl with its homely shelter, the Maximilianweg traverses the ridge all the way to Schlern. In terms of rock-climbing *ferratas*, it is not a difficult route.

Walking tip: excursion to Puflatsch/Bulacia.

This is a lovely route up to a panoramic mountain north of Compatsch (allow about 4h, ascent/descent about 330 m; see Tabacco map 1:25,000 N° 5). Take waymarked **Route A** up to the **Puflatsch Hut** (or go by chair lift, end May to Oct from 09.00-17.00, one way 4.50 €, up and back 6 €). From the hut turn right on **Route PU**. This takes you up to the **Fillner Kreuz**, a fine viewpoint over the Grödnertal. Turn left here on **Route 24** to the **Puflatsch summit** and the so-called **Hexenbänke** (Witches' Seats), where porphyry rock columns, angled down towards the valley, take on the shape of an easy chair. The local people have always referred to this natural phenomenon as a seat, and numerous legends tell of its supernatural genesis — and how the 'Witches of Schlern' sat here to take in the beautiful views. (Take care; there is some exposure!) Route 24 continues down to the Arnika Hut, from where you take **Route A** back down to **Compatsch**.

Bozen/Bolzano

Bozen, the capital of South Tyrol, lies outside the area of this guide. But many visitors to the Dolomites travel via Bozen or take a day trip to the town, which is

Walk 4: From Seiser Alm to Schlern and the Tierser Alpl Hut

Time: 7h
Grade: 800 m ascent and descent; you must be sure-footed and have a head for heights
Access: cable car or bus to Compatsch
Refreshments: Saltner Schwaige (snack bar), with rustic food and fresh alm milk; Schlernhäuser (CAI, only open in summer); Tierser Alpl Hütte, below the Rosszähne, with a friendly atmosphere and good food.
Map: Tabacco 1:25,000 N° 5.
Start out in Compatsch (1850 m): walk south on the little road signposted to 'Panorama' (the top station of the chair lift), but turn right on **Route 10** just after the first left bend. You rise gently over alm meadows, walk under the lift to the Laurin Hut, and rise to a ridge (1957 m). From here

walk 100 m downhill, to a little road.

Follow the road (**Route 5**) to the left, to the pleasant **Saltner Schwaige** (1820 m, **1h45Min**), just at the start of the climb to Schlern. Cross the stream and go right on the 'Touristensteig', a rapid ascent in deep zigzags, huffing and puffing up through mountain pines. When you come to the meadows of the **Schlern plateau** (2318 m), stride out across almost level ground to a fork (**3h15min**). The **Schlernhäuser** are to the right (2450 m) and are worth a visit, but the main walk goes left here.

You are now following **Routes 3/4** over the Schlern plateau, with a beautiful view to the Rosengarten. Beyond a saddle there is another ascent — to the end of

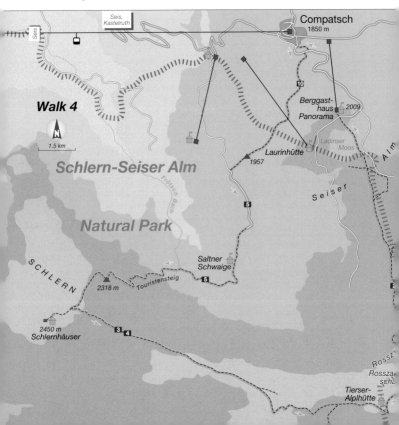

the plateau under the Rosszähne (2520 m, **4h**), where the trail heads right, into a wild gorge. For the next half hour you must be sure-footed and have a head for heights; the path is good, but narrow and, if you slip, it's a long way down...

Beyond a traverse at the foot of the **Rosszähne** (2375 m) and the path forking through the Bärenloch to Tiers you rise again, to the **Tierser Alpl Hut** (2440 m, **4h45Min**), which has been in view for quite some time. It sits on a saddle between the Rosszähne and Rosengarten. After taking a break, carry on to the left on **Route 2** to the **Rosszahnscharte**. Again you need to be sure-footed on the steep descent over loose rubble in a corrie above the Seiser Alm.

The pleasant Tierser Alpl Hut at the foot of the Rosszähne

Then the route heads right and is less steep. Keep left at a fork, crossing meadows and a damp little valley (the **Ladinger Moos**). When you reach the **Panorama Guest House** (2009 m, **6h**), you can either take the chair lift down, or walk down the road to **Compatsch** in an hour (**7h**).

situated in a sunny south-facing basin, surrounded by vineyards in the north. Of the 100,000 inhabitants, about 75% are Italian-speaking; even English speakers are more used to the name Bolzano. But the old town still exudes a Middle Ages/baroque German character.

All trains running between Munich and Verona/Milan/Rome and Venice stop at Bolzano's **railway station**. It is also the **hub of the SAD bus company**, which has a very large network covering the whole of South Tyrol. Travelling by car, note that there is a **covered car park** on the south side of the railway station.

The meeting place of the town is **Waltherplatz**, with cafés, shops and a large memorial dedicated to Walther von der Vogelweide (see page 40).

The **Dompfarrkirche** (parish cathedral church) is Gothic; its 62 m-high tower finely-carved late Gothic. Once inside, don't miss the Gothic chancel and baroque high altar. There is also a museum. *Church open Mon-Fri from 09.45-12.00 and 14.00-17.00; Sat 09.30-12.00; museum open Tue-Sat 10.00-12.00.*

The **Dominikanerkloster** is a Dominican monastery and late Gothic hall church with three naves; the choir has beautiful baroque ornamentation. There are frescoes from the Giotto School in the Johanneskapelle and more frescoes dating from around 1490 by Friedrich Pacher in the cloister (which is only accessible from the adjacent conservatory of music). *Open Mon-Sat from 09.30-18.30, Sun from 12.30-18.00.*

The **Franziskanerkirche** is late

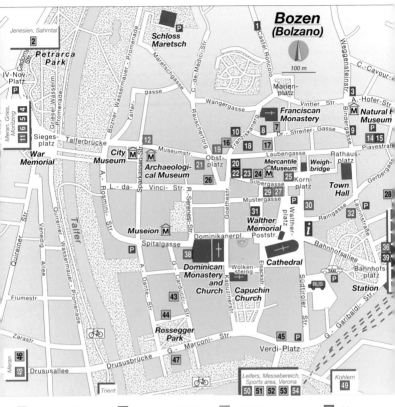

Accommodation

6   Post Gries
11   Camping Moosbauer
14   Luna Mondschein
25   Figl
29   Stadthotel Città
30   Greif
32   Parkhotel Laurin
33   Rentschnerhof
34   Magdalenerhof
35   Jugendherberge
36   Regina A.
38   Kolpinghaus
49   Kohlern
50   Camping Steiner
54   Sheraton Four Points

Eating and drinking

1   Gummer
3   Batzenhäusl
4   Weingartenhof
5   Pizzeria Geier
8   Fischbänke
9   Pizzeria Nussbaumer
10   Nadamas
13   Löwengrube
15   Mondschein
18   Anita
20   Vögele (Roter Adler)
22   Hopfen & Co
23   Hostaria Argentieri
31   Kaiserkron
32   Laurin
37   Sonnleithenhof
39   Arma
40   Ebnicherhof
41   Signaterhof
49   Kohlern

Night life

2   Kinoki
7   Sonderbar
10   Nadamas
16   Theater Cortile
17   Capitolkino/Filmclub
24   Theater Carambolage
26   Pogue Mahone's
28   Haus der Kultur/
       Waltherhaus
32   Laurin Bar
42   Primo Piano
43   Konzerthaus 'Haydn'
44   Disco Okay
45   Neues Stadttheater
46   Internetbar Fantasy
47   Pub Caffè Latino
51   Pub Alumix
52   Pub Restaurant Soul
       Kitchen
53   Ku.Bo.

Cafés

12   Subito Tutto Co
19   Café-Konditore
       Hofer
21   Café-Konditore
       Streitberger
27   Stadtcafé
48   Café-Konditore
       Zingerle

Gothic inside and out (badly restored), with a Nativity by Hans Klocker (1500) on the reredos.

On the west side of the river is the **Piazza della Vittoria**, a square and war memorial dedicated to the Italian Fascists of Bolzano.

Schloss Maretsch is a Renaissance castle surrounded by vineyards, with interesting frescoes in the reception room on the first floor. Today it is a conference centre. *Ask the tourist office for information about visiting.*

The fruit and vegetable market (**Obstplatz**) has been serving the town for centuries; it's always busy and very photogenic.

The **Lauben** is the main shopping street, with old-established shops and modern boutiques under the arcades of impressive town houses.

The large **Muri Benedictine Abbey** is in the Gries district; only the lovely late Gothic monastery church is open to the public. In the late Gothic **Gries parish church** there is a magnificent carved altar by Michael Pacher dating from 1475, depicting the coronation of Mary. *The anteroom of the monastery church is open all day, and you can get a good view of the church; Gries parish church is open from Apr to Oct, Mon-Fri, 10.30-12.00, 14.30-16.00.*

Runkelstein Castle is on the north side of town, an easy stroll from the centre. Dating from the Middle Ages, it has some very unusual frescoes depicting country life — for example men and women playing ball, lance-throwing competitions and round dancing under the trees. *Open daily (except Mon) from 10.00-18.00 (entrance fee 8 €).*

Naturally Bolzano has a wealth of **museums**, too interesting to be saved for rainy days!

Chief among them is the **South Tyrol Archaeological Museum**, Museumstrasse 43 — also called the 'Ötzi-Museum' in honour of its most famous exhibit. Ötzi, the 'man in the ice', is displayed on the first floor, in a darkened room behind armoured glass in a cold-storage chamber at -6°C. There's information about his discovery by hikers in 1991; radiocarbon dating revealed the body to be more than 5000 years old. *Open daily (ex. Mon) from 10.00-18.00 (Thu 20.00); entry 8 €; concessions 5.50 €; families 16 €.*

The three-story **Stadtmuseum** (City Museum), Sparkassenstrasse 14, exhibits the art, culture and customs of Bolzano and South Tyrol. *Open daily (ex. Mon) from 10.00-18.00; entry 5 €; concessions 3.50 €.*

The **Naturmuseum Südtirol**, Bindergasse 1, is a modern museum focussing on the natural history of South Tyrol, with eye-catching dioramic displays. *Open daily (ex. Mon) from 10.00-18.00; entrance fee 5 €; concessions 3 €; families 10 €.*

The **Museion**, Serenesistrasse 1, is a museum for modern art, with continually-changing displays. *Open daily (ex. Mon/holidays) from 10.00-20.00 (Thu until 22.00); entrance fee 6 €; concessions 3.50 €.*

The **Merkantilmuseum**, Silbergasse 6, is an impressive baroque town house, once the commercial court. *Open daily (ex. Sun) from 10.00-12.30.*

3 THE ROSENGARTEN AREA/CATINACCIO

**Tiers and the Tierser Tal • Steinegg • Eggental • Welschnofen •
Rosengarten • Karersee • Latemar • Deutschnofen**

Walks: 5, 18; *walking tips:* the
'Elizabeth Promenade' and
circuit round Lake Karer
Web sites
www.rosengarten-latemar.com
www.tiers.it
www.welschnofen.com
www.eggental. com
www.obereggen.com

Tip: **Bonus Card:** This free card is
a gift to all visitors to the
Rosengarten-Latemar area and
offers discounts on things like
entry to museums, travel tickets
(including the lifts) and special
events (like guided walks).
Opening hours: see individual
attractions

The rose garden … why would anyone give this rugged, untamed mountain range such a romantic name? There's a secret behind it: when seen from the Tierser Tal, Eggental or Regglberg, the mountain walls glow red after sunset — as if by magic.

Before it was transformed into a massif, the mountain was a rose garden, and King Laurin was its master. It doesn't matter if you find this hard to believe, because the legend is so pretty anyway (see page 61). And you won't escape the legend — it's everywhere around you when you're in Tiers, Welschnofen, Deutschnofen and at Lake Karer. There are Laurin inns, Laurin chair lifts, Rose Garden hotels and endless Laurin souvenirs.

The proper name of this tourist region is Rosengarten-Latemar, taking in not only Rosengarten but the adjacent, equally rugged (but less legendary) Latemar range. The area is also home to South Tyrol's most important place of pilgrimage — the church of Maria Weissenstein, near the friendly holiday village of Deutschnofen on Regglberg, a mountain characterised by meadows, round wooded hills and sprinklings of solitary farms and hamlets.

Tiers and the Tierser Tal/
Tires and Val di Tires

One can hardly imagine a wilder ravine than the far reaches of the Tiers Valley. Up until the 1970s, when a small road was built, there was no motor access from the Eisacktal to Tiers, the only real village in the valley.

Only the young people take the road to Völs and Seis for granted. But the long isolation of Tiers is still noticeable today, at least in the village itself. With the new road came tourism — a whole range of friendly hotels, guest houses, holiday homes and private rooms for rent. The skiing and walking areas of the Rosengarten, Lake Karer and the Latemar are all nearby, affording good business opportunities. But what attracts visitors above all is the magnificent natural setting, with the massive walls of the Dolomites in the background and the age-old farming traditions — including harvesting the hay by hand in the mountain meadows and cheese-making on the alms. Transport is easy too; the road is good, and there are frequent **buses** to and from Bozen: up to five times daily on weekdays and twice a day on Sundays. Two or three buses a day go all the way to the Karer Pass. There is also a free walkers' bus from the beginning of May till about June 20, when the school holidays start and the summer timetables for the local SAD bus company provide good scheduling for walkers.

Tiers is made up of three separate sections: the village itself with the parish church, the hamlet of St. Cyprian, and the spa area at Weisslahnbad. The **parish church** of St. George has a Romanesque tower; the late baroque porch (1766) was built onto the late Gothic choir. A signposted walking route leaves from the upper part of the village to the isolated **plague chapel of St. Sebastian** in a clearing in the woods. This was built in 1635, the year of the Plague, after 124 people had died — almost the entire population. From the chapel there's a motorable track to **Weisslahnbad**, where people have long sought relief from rheumatic pain. The hot water is slightly acidic, with low-level radioactivity. The baths, in the hotels, are now regulated by the local government. From Weisslahnbad you can walk back to **St. Cyprian** on the upper road (starting from the church), with a fine view over the Tierser Tal and to the Rosengarten Group. West of Tiers, in the narrow valley between Tiers and Blumau, is the hamlet of **Breien/**

Brie. There's nothing special to see here except for a little church on the sunny slopes 200 m above the hamlet, dedicated to **St. Catharine of Alexandria**. The Gothic wall paintings on the southern outside wall depict her martyrdom. To get there, walk 40 minutes along the track from the bus stop, keeping left at a fork. The upper frescoes may be shaded by the overhanging roof; noon is the best time for photography.

Tschamintal and Schlern Natural Park

If you walk from Weisslahnbad up into the **Tschamintal/Valle di Camin** *which divides Schlern and Rosengarten, you will come face to face with wild primeval nature. Just how wild can be judged by the fact that a neighbouring valley is called Bärenfalle (Bears' Trap) and that the climb to Schlern is called the Bärenloch (Bears' Hole). This valley is part of the* **Schlern Natural Park**. *Not far beyond Weisslahnbad you pass the Park Information House, in a restored sawmill dating from 1598. There is a large* **car park** *(driving beyond this point is forbidden) and an inn.* **Naturparkhaus open Jun-Sep, Tue/Wed/Fri/Sun 09.00-12.00/15.00-18.00; Sat 15.00-18.00.**

The road from Tiers to Lake Karer runs via the **Niger/Nigra Pass** and below the walls of the Rosengarten. It is one of the most beautiful high-level roads in the whole Alps. There are several places to park and walk, and lifts to the Rosengarten Hut; for details see Welschnofen overleaf.

Steinegg/Collepietra

Steinegg, part of Karneid, lies on a sunny terrace at the lower end of the Tierser Tal. It can be reached from Blumau or from the Eggental below Birchabruck. This road only dates back a couple of decades; before, there were only trails and a bad haulage track. Since the road was built the village grows a little every year: visitors who appreciate the freshness of summer and the beauty of autumn here have spread the word — how beautiful it is up here when the sun shines, while the Etsch and Eisack valleys are lost in mist. The local museum below the church is interesting, and at the edge of the village there are some earthen pyramids composed of a most attractive moraine rock.

Museum open from Palm Sunday to 31 Oct; guided tours until 30 June Tue-Fri at 11.00, Sat 15.00, Sun/holidays at 15.00, 16.00.

Eggental/Valle d'Ega

Welschnofen is the largest village in the Eggental. The valley itself begins as a narrow gorge by Kardaun on the eastern edge of Bolzano and splits into two at Birchabruck — the Eggental and Welschnofen branches. Both the new and old roads over the Karer Pass into the Fassa Valley run via Welschnofen; today these are the most travelled stretches on the Great Dolomite Road.

But you don't have to be a fan of high-mountain roads (and none is greater than the Dolomite Road) to come here, since the landscape alone is reason enough — Rosengarten and Latemar, widespread woodlands, and many walking trails with well-placed huts. And then there's Lake Karer as a focal point, its waters reflecting the image of Latemar.

Welschnofen/Nova Levante (✖)

The village can be reached via the Great Dolomite Road from the Eisacktal (Bolzano or Karneid); take the Bozen Nord exit from the motorway. Coming from the east take the Fassatal road via Vigo and the Karer Pass. **Parking**

Alm below the Rosengarten

On the Great Dolomite Road

The first part of what is today the famous Great Dolomite Road between the Eisacktal at Bozen and Cortina d'Ampezzo was the road through the Eggental to Welschnofen. The wild gorge of the Karneid stream between the Eisacktal and Birchabruck below Welschnofen was an insurmountable obstacle for road-builders up until the middle of the 19th century. The gorge walls are only a few metres apart at their narrowest points, and when the water was high the gorge was impassable. But some clever engineers found the solution: they built the road as a succession of suspension bridges below the rock overhangs and so high above the stream that even high water did not reach them; the rock itself was breached with tunnels. By 1860 Welschnofen was finally accessible on the Eggental through road. That gave the local people an idea: up until then Welschnofen had been part of Kardaun; by 1870 they were proud to announce their own municipality.

At this point a Viennese, Dr. Theodor Cristomannos, came along with his idea of a Dolomite Road to run all across the Austrian Dolomites from Bozen to Cortina. A huge hotel for tourists near lovely Lake Karer above Welschnofen (the Grand Hotel Carezza, see 'Walking tip' opposite) soon attracted many tourists to the area, and the local businessmen smugly thought that the road would stop there. But in the same year (1896) the Karer Pass was breached and by 1909 the road had been extended to its current length of 110 km.

Whether you travel the Great Dolomite Road by car, motorcycle or even bicycle, today you'll be on a very well engineered asphalt road. It's not steep at any point (the maximum gradient is 12%), but it's full of curves (caravans can't use it east of the Fassa Valley). From the Karer Pass the road runs through the Fassa Valley (Vigo, Pozza and Canazei in the province of Trento) to the Pordoi Pass, then down to Arabba in Buchenstein (Belluno Province) and from there over the Falzàrego Pass to Cortina d'Ampezzo.

places in the village are limited; petrol is available further up the valley on the road to Lake Karer. There are eight **buses** daily between Welschnofen and Bozen, up to five a day to Lake Karer (three of which go further — to the Karer Pass and Vigo in the Fassatal as well as Moèna and Predazzo with connections to the San Pellegrino Pass and San Martino di Castrozza.) There are bus stops at the tourist office and the supermarket. For walkers there is also the free Eggental service every Tuesday and Thursday in summer, linking the

Karer Pass, Welschnofen, Birchabruck, Eggen and Obereggen, Deutschnofen, Petersberg (and Weissenstein).

You can drive through the old part of Welschnofen in the wink of an eye — from the Mondschein Inn to the church takes only five minutes. The modern part of the village, with its hotels, pensions and the like is bigger, but you can easily miss it out. To get to the ski area you follow the road to Lake Karer or down to Birchabruck and then up to Obereggen. Summer visitors to Obereggen are really spoiled:

Welschnofen: the Frommerbachtal (top) and old house in the centre

meadows above it and views to the Rosengarten. The **museum**, housed in the community centre next to the church, portrays farming life (changeable opening houses, ask at the tourist office).

Walking tip: Elizabeth Promenade. In 1897 Empress Elizabeth ('Sissi') of Austria spent a holiday at the Grand Hotel Carezza. One of the paths she used to walk has been upgraded and named the 'Elizabeth Promenade'. There's a monument in memory of this glamorous but unlucky woman, who was murdered in Geneva a year later. It's best to begin the walk at the Hotel Rosengarten in the Frommerbachtal just northeast of Welschnofen (see Tabacco 1:25,000 map N° 6): follow **Route 3** straight up to the monument (by Hof Zenai). From there you can pick up the Promenade itself (**Routes 6/9**) and stroll along to the Grand Hotel Carezza; the second part of the route is a track closed to motor traffic. Along the way you pass the Schönblick Inn (refreshments). Reckon on 1h to reach the highest point of the walk, above the monument (ascent of 300 m), and 1h30min from there (mostly contouring) to the Grand Hotel Carezza, where there is a bus stop for your return.

Rosengarten/Catinaccio

Rosengarten looks so steep that one would never dream of its walking possibilities. But there are several routes across the range which are suitable for the average hill walker, and even inexperienced walkers can stroll from the top lift stations or places where they can be dropped off

walk out the front door of the hotel and you're on lovely walking Route 7. Just follow it to the 'Schwarzen Adler' — for a meal or a coffee, then take the next bus back.

People come to Welschnofen for the exhilarating surroundings and activity holidays, not to see the village itself. Its 'sights' are quickly listed. There's the **parish church**, slightly above the centre and the road, with green

King Laurin and the Rosengarten

The Germanic tribes who migrated from the Etschtal must have been astonished when they saw the red glow of sunset in the Dolomites — especially over the massif that is today known as Rosen-garten/Catinaccio. They'd never seen anything like it. Clearly, they must have thought, this was not a natural phenomenon. It appeared to them that, in contrast to the tall blue-eyed Goths, the small dark alpine Romans (today's Ladins) must know some secret. It's all the stuff of legend — like the bit about the magical belt and hat. Dietrich von Bern, who would eventually become associated with the Rosen-garten legend, was in fact the Goth King Theoderich, whose seat was in nearby Bern (Verona). And so (to make a long story short) here's the Rosengarten legend — or at least one version of it! Where today there is only bare rock there was once the castle of the dwarf King Laurin. His pride and joy was his rose garden, in which red roses bloomed all year round.

Laurin had a belt which gave him the strength of 12 men, and a magical hat which made him invisible. He was in love with the blond (naturally) Princess Simhilde; he kidnapped her and took her away to his castle, to live happily ever after. But her brother Dietleib turned to Dietrich von Bern, and the two of them rode off into the mountains with a large party to rescue Simhilde and punish Laurin. By trickery they managed to snatch the hat and destroy the belt. Laurin could not fight any longer, but he could at least make his kingdom inaccessible, so that his conquerors went away with empty pockets (but with Simhilde, one supposes). He cast a magic spell: the castle disappeared and the rose garden faded away. But Laurin had made a mistake: he forgot about twilight. And that's why today we see the Rosengarten glow between day and night, full of glowing red roses, as it was back then, when it was the pride and joy of the unlucky dwarf king.

by the hut taxis — enjoying the high Alpine experience with little effort.

The most famous peaks of the Rosengarten Group are not necessarily the highest (Catinaccio d'Antermoia/ Kesselkogel, 3004 m, with two protected climbing paths), but the group called the Vajolet Towers in the north of the range. In the evening, when seen from the west, they are exceptionally beautiful in the red light — the Ladins call this the 'Enrosadüra'. These three towers were first climbed under precarious conditions, as can be imagined, and still attract experienced climbers. The first tower to be climbed was the Winklerturm (1887; named for the Munich mountain climber Georg Winkler, who did it in three hours, climbing on his own). The Stabeler and Delago towers are also named for the first climbers to master them.

Various lifts, funiculars and taxis serve the huts on the mountain: — the **Paolina Hut** is reached by the Paolina chair lift from Lake Karer (open end May to mid Oct, midday break from 12.30-13.30, one way 3 €, up and back 7 €); — the **Rosengarten Hut** by the

Laurin lift II from Welschnofen;
— the **Rifugio Ciampedié** via the Ciampedié funicular from Vigo di Fassa (mid-Jun to mid-Oct, mid-day break from 13.00-14.10, one way 7 €, up and back 12 €);
— the **Gardeccia Hut** and **Rifugio Stella Alpina** by taxi from the Fassatal;
— **Rifugio Micheluzzi** (Baita Duron) by taxi from Campitello di Fassa.

Karersee/Lago di Carezza

Emerald-green Lake Karer, mirroring the wild rock towers of Latemar and surrounded by thick green forest, are one of the best-known images of the Alps. The downside is that the lake is also one of the easiest in the Alps to reach, since when the road was built over 100 years ago the intention was to skirt the lake. But because of the terrain it was only possible to build the road somewhat higher up.

Sir Winston Churchill called for his paints when he spotted the lake en route to the Grand Hotel Carezza in the summer of 1949, and dashed off a very large canvas in 20 minutes!

Today the lake is surrounded by a fence, but there are many viewpoints and benches. Often in late summer and autumn there is so little water that its western part is cut off and the lake looks like a little pond. It seems that the water level is decreasing every year, so we shall have to see how long there will even *be* a Lake Karer.

Walking tip: Lake Karer. There's a really pretty little **walk round the lake**, easily reached by

Time: 4h30min

Grade: 800 m ascent/descent; you must be sure-footed and have a head for heights, as well as some *climbing experience*. The climb to the Santner Pass is protected, but should only be attempted by sure-footed hikers with no fear of heights: *a few places are Grade 1.*

Access: 🚌 or 🚗 to the lower lift station at Welschnofen (in summer there is a walkers' bus from Tiers and Lake Karer); then chair lift to the Rosengarten Hut

Refreshments Rosengarten Hut (Rifugio A. Fronza), run by the CAI Verona, at the top of the Laurin II lift at 2339 m, where the walk begins; Santner Pass Hut, private, 2741 m; Rifugio Re Alberto (Gartl Hut); Rifugio Vajolet (Vajolet Hut), run by the CAI Trento, 2243 m; Preuss Hut

Map: Tabacco 1:25,000 N° 6, Val di Fassa

Start out from the **Rosengarten Hut** (2339 m): take **Route 542s** (signposted to the Santner Pass Hut). This rises quite gently in a

traverse below the western walls of Rosengarten. But the going gets tricky below the Santner Pass: horizontal ledges and steps on this rocky upthrust are overcome with the help of iron ladders and hand-holds; there are also wire ropes at some awkward places. After a small saddle the route descends a bit in a steep ravine, usually at least partially filled with ice: take great care on these steps! Then you have to get over another upthrust, helped by pegs and cables, before emerging at the Santner Pass and the **Santner Pass Hut** (2741 m, **2h**). Big sigh of relief and pause for refreshments…

From here go down through a corrie to the nearby **Gartl Hut** and carry on — steeply again, but with less difficulty — to the two huts below. The larger one, on the left, is the **Vajolet Hut**; the one on the right, closer to the edge of the cliff, is the **Preuss Hut**. The route descends just below the **Vajolet Towers**, which you can really appreciate when you get to the huts (2245 m, **2h30min**).

From here take the wide motorable track down the valley — but not for long: on the third curve turn right on **Route 541**. This heads south, rising steadily below the rock walls of Rosengarten. When you approach the foot of the rock walls (2416 m, **3h**) fork right on **Route 550** to the Tschagerjoch — a steep climb, with scree and rocks on both sides. From the narrow **Tschagerjoch** (2630 m) you dive back down to your starting point; two wire ropes are in place to help for the final, very steep descent to the **Rosengarten Hut** (**4h30min**).

descending to the water from either of the car parks. The circuit itself is only 25-30 minutes, but with climbs up to the individual viewpoints you should allow a good hour.

Latemar

The jagged limestone peaks of Latemar, so beautifully mirrored in Lake Karer, crumble so easily that the rock even breaks up in your hand. This means that the greatest level of care is needed for mountain- and rock-climbing here! And in fact there is only one walking route over Latemar — Route 18, which runs to the Bivacco M. Rigatti on the **Latemarspitze** (2800 m). This isn't the highest peak on the mountain, but the most easterly tower (2848 m). On the other hand there are very beautiful walks at the foot of the mountain, between the Karer Pass, Latemar meadows, and in the 'Geplänk', the massive scree *cirque* at the northern foot of the walls. Another fine route runs from the Karer Pass over to Obereggen in 1h30min (Route 21, then 21a).

Deutschnofen/Nova Ponente

Reached by road from the Eisack-tal via Birchabruck/Ponte Nova, Deutschnofen has up to 10 **buses** a day to/from Bolzano and two a day with Obereggen in summer. For walkers there is also the free Eggental service mentioned on page 59.
From the village there is a brilliant view to Latemar, Rosengarten and Schlern; looking west one sees Mendel and Adamello and in the northwest the Sarntaler and Texel groups. The village, surrounded by fairly gentle terrain, is an ideal base for easy walks. And mountain bikers don't have to overcome any of the more difficult Dolomite routes; they can come here with their families and explore the Regglberg, the wooded hills to the south of Deutschnofen. On the other hand, mountain climbers and hill walkers have more challenging routes on their doorstep — easily reached by car or bus.

The late Gothic **parish church of St. Ulrich** has a Gothic altar triptych (with neo-Gothic framing) by Hans von Judenburg (1421-24). It was once in the parish church at Bolzano — until they decided to have some fun with baroque and gave some of their 'old-fashioned' things to the people of Deutschnofen. Today this altar is the pride and joy of the village and surroundings; the five wooden reliefs work wonderfully in the high altar (and a side-altar), which are complemented by the beautiful net vault of the ceiling.

In the middle of the open fields in the east part of the village is the **chapel of St. Helena** (key nearby in the Kreuzhof). Both the chapel and massive tower date from the 12th century. Inside is a wealth of frescoes from the Bolzano School (from 1410), showing scenes from the Old and New Testaments. It only takes about half an hour there and back on foot: follow the good lane closed to motor vehicles from the Gasthaus Pfösl on the road to Birchabruck or Obereggen.

The famous **pilgrimage church of Maria Weissenstein** (✗) stands in an isolated position on a flat slope south of Deutschnofen, but it belongs to the village of Petersberg. Its

Obereggen, backed by Latemar

founding dates back to a vow. According to legend, one Leonhard, a farmer on the Weissenstein lands and probably an epileptic, was rescued by the St. Mary after falling into a gorge and built the chapel in thanks. People seeking cures began to make pilgrimages to the place. Soon the little chapel was too small, so it was replaced by a church (1561), which was turned over to the Servite Order in 1718. They had the church enlarged, added the baroque touches in 1752 and built the two small towers and dome. The frescoes, by the 18th-century Viennese painter Adam Mölk, are the most interesting artistic features inside the church. The cloisters were built between 1787 and 1836, and both the cloisters and church have had some of their ornamentation stolen. On the left side of the church the old chapel still stands, with a collection of votive gifts dating over the centuries. The church is the goal of tens of thousands of pilgrims on the saint's day, August 15. Even the Pope visited in 1988.

The undulating hilly landscape south of Deutschnofen is called **Regglberg**. A wealth of forestry roads and walking trails crisscross this sparsely-settled terrain. The only real 'mountain' rising up from the green woods in the area is **Weisshorn** (easily climbed from the Jochgrimm in the east). Regglberg is also ideal terrain for mountain bikers, as long as they avoid the **Bletterbach Gorge**, which cuts across the southwestern part. This steep valley is walkers' country — but keep away from the valley floor in wet weather. **European Long**

Distance Route E5 from Deutschnofen crosses the gorge; it's a well-waymarked, magnificent trail.

Although the little village of **Obereggen/San Floriano** belongs to Deutschnofen, it lies quite far out in the valley, below the rock needles of Latemar. It's best known for the Fiemme/Obereggen Skicircus. But while Obereggen is a very comfortable ski village, you can have a good summer holiday here too: walks up Latemar begin right in the centre — like the magnificent route to the Latemar Hut (Rifugio Torre di Pisa). Or you can take the chair lift up the mountain and start at 2150 m.

From **Rauth/Novale** a road runs up to a little lake at the **Lavazè Pass** (provincial border) and then down to **Cavalese**, the main village in the Fleimstal/Val di Fiemme. The lifts up here — and all those on the Reiterjoch and in Pampeago (reached from Obereggen via the road to Tèsero) — are included in the Fiemme/Obereggen Ski Pass. From the Lavazè Pass there is a road to the Jochgrimm under Weisshorn, from where Radein and Kaltenbrunn can be reached by mountain bike.

4 PUSTERTAL/VAL PUSTERIA: THE LOWER VALLEY

Mühlbach and the Valser Tal • Meransen • Vintl and the Pfunderer Tal • Terenten and Pfalzen • Bruneck • Sonnenburg Nunnery

Walks: none; *walking tips:* Lindenweg from Mühlbach; Mills Nature Trail at Terenten
Web sites
www.gitschberg-jochtal.com
www.vintl.it
www.bruneck.com
www.st.lorenzen.com

www.provinz._bz.it/volkskunde museen
www.kiens.info
www.dolomitisuperski.com (for Kronplatz)
Opening hours: see individual attractions

From Franzensfeste/Fortezza almost all the way to Bruneck the valley of the Rienz River is narrow and shady. So most people stick to the sunny side-valleys or make straight for Bruneck.

The lower Pustertal is not really suitable for settlement and is sparsely populated apart from market and administrative centres like Mühlbach and Vintl. Two sunny neighbouring valleys, the Valser Tal and Pfunderer Tal, run in from the north; both of them have pretty farming villages and many solid Tyrolean twin farm buildings. From here one can climb the ice-capped peaks of the Zillertaler Alps — like Hochfeiler on the Austrian border, but also explore the lovely high alpine landscape around Lake Eisbrugg.

The sunny terrace between Terenten and Pfalzen is quite heavily populated — more grows here, the days with sunshine are more frequent than in the deep valley below or in the side-valleys. The landscape is also very suitable for strolls and short walks. Bruneck, the most important town in the whole Pustertal, lies in a wide basin; it has a well-preserved old centre, worth seeing.

Mühlbach and the Valser Tal

The Eisacktal narrows some 2km above Mühlbach by the Mühlbacher Klause, the remains of a Middle Ages defensive wall and toll-house. A prehistoric stone-slab track, the Lindenweg, runs up to Meransen on a sunny terrace, which can also be reached by cabin lift or road. Up here the old farms have been converted into apartments and hotels. In contrast, the **Valser Tal/Val di Valles**, despite having a small ski area, has remained

essentially unchanged — especially when you walk up into the end of the valley, where you can take a break on the Fane Alm, one of the few alm villages in the region.

The **Mühlbacher Klause**, dating from 1269, marked the border between the lands of Brixen and the Pustertal (which belonged to the Counts of Görz-Tirol) up until 1500. Mühlbach was the administrative seat at the time; the Kandelburg in the centre of Mühlbach still recalls these days.

The building has been restored. *Open Jun-Sep; guided visits can be booked ahead at the tourist office: Thu at 10.00, 14.00, 15.00; entry 4 €.*

Mühlbach/Rio di Pusteria was an important place in the old days, as can be seen in several important old buildings — like the **Ansitz Strasshof**, where once the guardian of the bishopric was housed (the most important government official, in charge of the tolls). Others are **Ansitz Freienthurn**, today cloisters and a school, and **Ansitz Kandlburg**, where the court was once held (today a château-hotel).

The **parish church** is Gothic, with beautiful frescoes dating from the Middle Ages, really worth seeing. Many Roman remains have been uncovered in the late Gothic **Floriani Chapel**, which is open to the public. *Parish museum, with (among other displays) remains from the Floriani Chapel, open Wed/Sat from 10.00-12.00.*

Walking tip: the Lindenweg

From Mühlbach the **Lindenweg**, an ancient, probably prehistoric stone-slab track climbs up to Meransen. Allow about 1h30min for this ascent of 600 m (way-marked **Route 12**, Tabacco 1:25,000 map N° 37). About halfway up, on a flat stretch, you walk below a roof protecting a simple altar and memorial stone with three female figures called the **Jungfernrast**. It depicts the three holy maidens Aubet, Cubet and Cuere (the king's daughters according to legend), who fled the Huns and collapsed half crazy with thirst in the mountains. As they fell to their knees and prayed to God for help, a spring emerged from the rock and a cherry tree sprouted, laden with fruit.

Most visitors ignore the village of **Rodeneck/Rodengo** itself and make straight for the castle, **Burg Rodeneck**. Like all good castles, this one stands on a rock on a steep slope above the Rienz Valley. The setting is charming, the long building with its pre-castle in front most eye-catching. In the 13th century a knight who owned the castle had the '12 Adventures of Iwein' (from the courtly romance better known as 'Yvain, the Knight with the Lion', dating from about 1200) depicted as frescoes. There is also a fresco of one of the knights of King Arthur's Round Table (photograph page 29). These frescoes are one of the earliest examples of non-religious painting in the Alps and were only discovered by chance in 1972. *Castle open daily except Mon from mid-May to Oct; guided tours at 11.00, 15.00 (mid-Jul to mid-Aug also at 16.00); entry fee 4 €.*

The **Fane Alm**, with its huts, barns and chapel lies on a sunny meadow in the highest reaches of the Valser Tal at 1740 m. The huts are closely packed together; the alm looks like a village, although it's only inhabited in summer. In the past the whole village lived up here, taking care of the cattle and making butter and cheese. There are still cattle, but now you can reach the alm by road. The alm caters for walkers, with hearty snack food at the Gatterer Hut. I heartily recommend **two walks** from the alm up into high alpine terrain (Tabacco 1:25,000 map N° 37): one goes to Lake Grossen and the Wieser Hut,

Pustertal, with the Bruneck basin and Tauferer Tal

from where you can get back to Vals via the Altfasstal; the other goes way up the Valser Tal to the Brixner Hut, with possibilities of going even further — to Wilde Kreuzspitze (3134 m) with its fantastic view, or completing a magnificent but very strenuous circuit via Lake Wilden back to the Fane Alm.

Meransen/Meranza (✖)

Until a generation ago Meransen was the preserve of local farmers, but tourists are warming to the place. The farms still exist, and on Sunday mornings, when the churchgoers are out in force, you will see Meransen for the the old farming community it still is — despite the lively winter season at the Gitschberg ski area. You can get there by road or lift from Mühlbach (all year round from about 07.00-18.40).

Meransen's **church** is beautifully situated on the sunny village plateau. The walled-in cemetery is quiet and affords far-off views into the Pustertal and to the Dolomites. A fresco in front of the entrance under the massive tower depicts St. Christopher. Nothing outside gives a clue to what lies within: one of the most beautiful rococo interiors in Tyrol —magnificent and bright, with decoration, frescoes, altar paintings and ivory-white wooden sculpture. On the right-hand side altar are late Gothic statues of the three holy maidens mentioned on page 68, to their right a box containing interesting votive offerings.

Vintl and the Pfunderer Tal

The Pfunderer Tal runs from Vintl far into the mountains; only a short ridge separates Weisszint (3264 m) from the high peaks of the main Alpine ridge. Since there are no lifts in the valley itself, winter is quieter than summer, despite the proximity of the Gitschberg-Jochtal skicircus. But the valley is an eldorado for walkers and climbers, as well as really fit mountain bikers.

'Marble' has been quarried in the

valley for centuries; it's not real marble, but a green to bright grey serpentine.

Vintl/Vandóies (✖): Two churches stand on the hill in Untervintl, the old parish church and the new one. But the **new parish church** isn't really so new, it's a true baroque building. The painting is by Josef Anton Zoller (1763), who has a street in the village named after him. On the other hand, the **old parish church** is *really* old; it's referred to as far back as the 14th century when it was already old, having been started in Romanesque style. Inside, frescoes by Leonhard von Brixen have come to light: in comparison with the church, they are relatively new, since they are only about 500 years old.

Pfunders/Fundres (✖) lies high up in the valley. There is a beautiful view from the church with its late Middle Ages fresco of St. Christopher. Pfunders is made up of little hamlets and solitary farms that are attractively dispersed above the valley floor. The farms at **Kammerschien/ Camporsino** comprise the highest settlement in Pfunders, at 1520 m! Now it is served by a road, but until quite recently it could only be reached on foot (a two-hour ascent). This trail was called the **Kirchweg** (Church Walk), since naturally all the farming families from Kammerschien went to mass on Sundays — half a day's undertaking. If you go further up the valley from Pfunders, the road ends at a car park beyond the 'Duner Heuschupfe' (✖). From here a private road continues to the outermost farms of **Dun**, the highest in the valley, at 1480 m. There are

several signposted **walks** from Dun — to the Edelraute Hut and through the Duner Klamm to Engberg and the Weitenberg alm (5h return; easy to moderate).

Terenten and Pfalzen (✖)

The hoteliers up in these villages have been heavy-handed with their hackneyed slogans: 'sunny terrace', 'great view to the Dolomites', etc. But it is an accurate description of the south-facing terraces between Terenten and Pfalzen. Apart from these two villages there are only hamlets and isolated farms. The farms and the large families needed a lot of space and thus settled quite a distance from each other. So there is a large network of tracks joining these old hamlets, groups of houses and single farms. A few have been improved to roads which await your discovery — perhaps by mountain bike, which is the ideal transport up here. But don't be fooled by the road map; between Terenten and Pfalzen it's *not* all flat terrain, although even casual cyclists manage most of the climbs.

Thanks to tourism the centre of **Terenten/Terento** (stress the first syllable) is heavily built-up today. A bypass road called the 'Pustertaler Sonnenstrasse' avoids the centre, and one can wander round the pedestrian zone undisturbed. The scattered settlements, including those on the hill where the grouped farm buildings stand, date back thousands of years.

The **parish church** has a Gothic choir and tower, but the rest dates from the 19th century. The church cemetery is typical of the Tyrol.

Walking tip: Mills Nature Trail

Above Terenten attractive **earthen pyramids** are constantly appearing, due to water erosion. This area lies in the Ternertal and can be reached in about half an hour by following the **Mills Nature Trail**. Some of these old water mills, once used for grinding corn, are still in good condition, and one of them is used for show purposes. *Show mill open Jun-Sep, Mon only, from 10.00-13.00.*

Between Terenten and Pfalzen, in the hamlet of **Issing**, you can visit the Bergila distillery, which has been distilling herbal oils for more than 90 years. Some of the herbs come from gardens around Issinger itself. *Open for visits May-Nov, Mon-Fri; in Jul/Aug also open Sat/Sun from 08.00-12.00 and 13.00-18.00.*

The houses and extravagant façades in **Pfalzen/Fálzes** are testament to the fact that people once earned a good living here, when court was held in nearby Schloss Schöneck above Issing (private; not open for visits). The baroque **parish church** is very pretty, but of far more interest to art historians is the inside of the little Gothic **Valentinskirche** in the open meadows east of Pfalzen. To get there take the road to the right above the Gasthof and after about 800 m turn right to the church. A complete cycle of frescoes painted by Friedrich Pacher in 1487 was discovered on its north wall in 1979/80.

Bruneck/Brunico

Bruneck is certainly worth a visit. But take the lift up **Kronplatz** before you explore the town.

From up there you have the best view of its position at the confluence of two important valleys.

There is ample **parking**; the old town is a pedestrianised zone. You can also come by train, with good connections from Brixen, Bozen and the Hochpustertal, or by bus: the **bus station** is near the **railway station**, and there are connections to all the valleys in eastern South Tyrol.

Old Bruneck is a small town dating from the Middle Ages, which really must be seen. Gates, old village houses, a castle, museum, churches (from Gothic to baroque), a fascinating folk museum in nearby Dietenheim, good places to eat and drink, the best shopping between Brixen and Lienz, theatre — all this brings a lot of visitors. In the evenings the 'Spaziermeile' (Strolling Mile) outside the old town gates is a long open-air café. The tourist office organises walks for all abilities, and can also tell you about special events — like the classical concerts in July and August, the day-long jazz festival in July, street theatre during the first week in September, and various winter events including the Christmas Eve market in the old town, with displays of local crafts.

You enter the walled old town via the **Ursuline Gate** beside the Gothic **Ursuline Church**. The row of townhouses on **Längsachse**, the main thoroughfare, is most attractive. Some of the buildings still have old signs hanging outside; in times past, not only inns, but all business premises had these signs. Walk through the **Ragenertor**, decorated with frescoes, and into

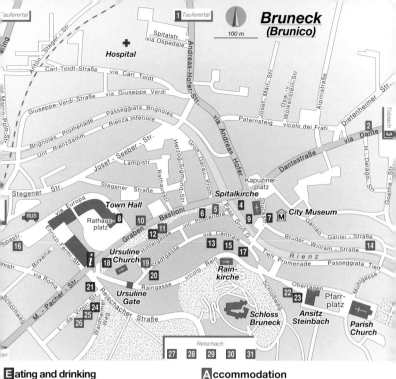

Eating and drinking

4 Testa Rossa Café
6 Café Roth
7 Künstlerstübele
8 Eisdiele/Konditorei Ice Marlu
9 Enoteca Bernardi
12 Forst Bierstuben
13 Pizzeria Café Arc
15 Stadtcafé

17 Wörz Bäck
18 Bar Café Lolita
20 Café Pub Caipi
21 Café GiBo
23 Bistrokücherle
24 Enoteca Bologna

Accommodation

1 Andreas Hofer
3 Camping Schießstand
5 Goldene Rose
10 Post
11 Corso
14 Haus Ragen
16 Blitzburg
22 Krone
25 Bologna
27 Majestic

28 Royal Hinterhuber
29 Messnerwirt
30 Olympia
31 Edelweiß

Special

2 City Theatre
19 City Library
26 Odeon Cinema

Platz Oberragen. This is where the craftsmen and civil servants had their premises outside the Middle Ages town. There's a baroque column dedicated to St. Mary and, at the end of the square, the **Ansitz Sternbach**, a massive townhouse with bay windows and tower dating from 1664. The neo-Romanesque **parish church** (1855) is one of the first churches built in this style. In Paul von Sternbach Street the Renaissance **Ragenhaus** is worth seeing (today it is a music school).

The **Rainkirche**, dedicated to St. Catherine, has a good tower with a two-storey baroque onion dome and a baroque nave. In the little adjacent park there's an open-air bar in summer. Founded in 1250, at the same time as the town, **Schloss Bruneck** has been heavily restored. But it is still an attractive castle, with the coats-of-arms of the Brixen archbishops in the courtyard, and a round tower with a spiral staircase. The rooms are in both the Renaissance and baroque styles; those fitted out in

1500 for Kaiser Maximilian are especially splendid. In summer a small café in the front courtyard sells drinks and snacks. At time of writing part of the castle was being made into a branch of the Messner Museum (see page 176), with the theme 'Mountain People'. *Castle open Tue-Fri from 15.00-18.00, Sat/Sun 10.00-12.00; in Jul/Aug Tue-Sat from 10.00-12.00 and 16.00-19.00. Combi-ticket available, giving entrance to the Stadtmuseum (see prices below).*

The baroque **Spitalkirche** (1761) has an attractive façade and interior. Part of the altar still has the original marble ornamentation so popular at that time. When you leave the church, take Dantestrasse to leave Kapuzinerplatz and head towards the outside of town. At the first crossing you come to an old shrine-like pillar with crumbled frescoes protected by a roof. These were painted by Hans von Bruneck at the beginning of the 15th century.

Old and new combine to make the **Stadtmuseum für Graphik** a really original attraction. Exhibitions include works by Michael and Friedrich Pacher, Albrecht Dürer, Simon and Veit von Taisten (altar triptych) and modern classics from the likes of Oskar Kokoschka, Alfred Kubin, Paul Klee, Paul Flora, Alfred Hrdlicka and Kurt Moldovan. *Museum open Tue-Fri from 15.00-18.00, Sat/Sun from 10.00-12.00; in Jul/Aug Tue-Sat from 10.00-12.00 and 16.00-19.00, Sun 10.00-12.00. Entry fee 2.50 €, concessions 2 €. Combi-ticket with Schloss Bruneck 6/4 €.*

On the other side of the valley, at the foot of Kronplatz, **Reischach/**

Riscone sits on a sunny terrace with fine views. Today the village forms part of Bruneck. Up here you'll find most of the hotels, *pensions* and rooms to rent. There's also a Gothic church and the huge **Ansitz Angerburg**, dating from the 17th century.

Dietenheim/San Theodone

The **South Tyrol Folk Museum** is located in the village of Dietenheim on the northern edge of the Bruneck basin. It is laid out in the Mair am Hof residence (1690-1700) and three hectares of

Votive offerings in the folk museum testify to St. Mary's help.

surrounding land. Just the house itself, with its outbuildings, would have been sufficient for a wide-ranging museum, but the old farmhouses, stables and mills on the open land make the visit even more enjoyable. The buildings have been brought here from all over South Tyrol, balcony by balcony and stone by stone, then carefully reconstructed. The three-story Höfelerhof from Mühlwald is especially impressive. *Museum open from Easter to end Oct, Tue-Sat 09.30-17.30, Sun/holidays 14.00-18.00. Entry fee 3.60 €, families 7.25 €.*

St. Georgen and Giessbach

The old village of **St. Georgen/San Giorgio** (✕) lies some way up the Tauferer Tal/Val di Tures in a loop of the Ahrn. Its presence is thanks to an old ford, where today a bridge crosses the stream over to Giessbach. Romanesque and pre-Romanesque remains have been found beneath the floor of the Gothic **parish church**. The Crucifixion group on the outside wall is probably the work of Hans von Bruneck. The buildings of Giessbach are very impressive: there are two old gabled houses with artistic doors and coats-of-arms (one of which is Schloss Gremsen, now offering rooms with kitchens), as well as many other beautiful old houses.

St. Lorenzen (✕) and Sonnenburg Nunnery (✕)

St. Lorenzen/San Lorenzo is the oldest settlement in the whole Bruneck basin, as evidenced by the many engravings and the remains of pilgrimage castles in the vicinity. Even the name harks back to ages past, since St. Laurentius is a typical saint of late antiquity. The place must also have been founded before the Bavarian land acquisition. It's also known that **Sebatum**, the most important Roman site in the whole Pustertal was located here, and there is a Roman milestone on the road to Sonnenburg. If you walk along that road today it's difficult to take in its original meaning. In the Middle Ages St. Lorenzen was the outpost of the Tyrolean prince who held court at the nearby **Michelsburg**, while the Archbishop of Brixen had his seat at Schloss Bruneck. Whoever travelled from Bruneck to St. Lorenzen had to pay a toll. The Madonna on the high altar of the **parish church** is the work of Michael Pacher.

The Sonnenburg château-hotel, on a hill, was originally **Sonnenburg Nunnery**. It was an autonomous order with pretty relaxed rules, and the nuns were a law unto themselves. Under the Brixen Archbishop Nikolaus von Kues, who wanted to carry out long-overdue reforms, a conflict arose between Sonnenburg and the bishopric which only ended with the intervention of Prince Sigismund von Tirol, after excommunication and some bloodshed — and even then it was a draw, with the departure of the abbess and the resignation of the bishop. The cloister was half in ruins until 1975, when part of it was rebuilt as an hotel; today of course it is an impressive and well-kept building. The contrast between the refurbished parts and the still-intact ruins is especially delightful. During construction the crypt of the earlier collegiate church was uncovered. *Crypt open daily from 10.00-12.00.*

Kiens/Chienes

The parish of Kiens comprises three villages: Kiens, Ehrenburg and St. Sigmund, all lying a little above the Pustertal. **Ehrenburg** (✕) is known for its eponymous castle, which is a must. There's peaceful walking all around, and canoeing on the Rienz.

The **parish church** of St. Sigmund has a triptych dating from 1480 and the little **pilgrimage chapel** on the road to Vintl some frescoes by Josef Anton Zoller.

Schloss Ehrenburg was the Archbishop of Brixen's castle. It acquired its Renaissance polish in around 1500 when a new section was built with a marvellous three-storey arcaded courtyard. The old Romanesque castle with its original keep was left untouched. But none of this was good enough for the later baroque princes from Brixen, the bishops. Archbishop Caspar Ignaz Künigl and his brother had the building re-created in the baroque style. A magnificent castle is the result: much of the luxurious interior decoration is well preserved, as in the Bishop's Room and the aristocratic 'Blue Room' with its cobalt-blue tiled ceiling. Although the family of the Counts Künigl still live in the castle today, it can be visited. *Castle open for guided tours in Apr, May, Oct on Wed only at 15.00; in Jun and Sep from Mon-Sat at 11.00 and 15.00; Jul/Aug Mon-Sat at 11.00, 12.00, 15.00, 16.00. Entry fee 4 €, concessionary tickets 2 €.*

Kronplatz/**Plan de Corones**

All the winds around Bruneck have their advantage: clouds carrying snow from the north are happy to deposit their white load at the first obstacle south of the main Alpine ridge — like **Plose** (see page 37) and **Kronplatz**. This flat-topped mountain always can be sure of snow, making it the skiing mountain *par excellence,* more developed than any other in the Dolomites. And all that so easily within reach — five minutes by car from Bruneck or by town bus to Reischach and then by lift to the peak. It's even worth driving up in summer; despite the lifts, roads, huts and other features that mar the summer landscape, there are beautiful walking routes and even more beautiful mountain bike tours (you can take bikes on the cabin lifts).

Olang/**Valdaora** (✖)

Olang comprises four villages on the east side of Kronplatz, with two direct lift connections. The green basin in which these scattered villages lie is bordered in the west by the wooded slopes of Kronplatz and overlooked in the south by the sharp ridges of the Dolomites — like Piz da Peres (2507 m) and Maurerkogel (2567 m). Staying in Olang is a good idea if you want to walk in summer (there are over a dozen manned alms in the mountains above) but don't want to be far from the action (Bruneck is just around the corner). It's also fairly quiet in winter, despite its proximity to Kronplatz. Olang rises to the occasion with 28 hotels.

At Mitterolang there's a memorial in the square to Peter Sigmayr; the house where he was born is now a hotel. Sigmayr was a much-loved Tyrolean freedom fighter who, with Andreas Hofer, rebelled against the Bavarian/French rule. After the fighting of 1809 he went into hiding but, when the French arrested his father and threatened to kill him, Sigmayr gave himself up. He was shot in 1810, his body strung up at a crossroads for 48 hours (*'pour encourager les autres'*).

5 TAUFERER TAL AND AHRNTAL/VAL DI TURES AND VALLE AURINA

Sand in Taufers • Mühlen • Reintal • Rieserferner-Ahrn Natural Park • Arhntal • Luttach • St. Johann • Steinhaus • Prettau • Kasern

Walks: 6; *walking tips:* Kofler zwischen den Wänden; St Francis meditation path; Lake Klaus; Kehreralm; Krimmler Tauern; *cycling tip:* from Bruneck to Sand
Web sites
www.tauferer.ahrntal.com
www.taufers.com

www.kofler-zd-waenden.com
www.muehlwald.com
www.ahrntal.it
www.ahrntal.org
www.mineralienmuseum.com
www.prettau.it
Opening hours: see individual attractions

The long axis of the Tauferer and Ahrn valleys runs from Bruneck in the Pustertal to the high Alpine ridge and the northernmost part of Italy. Here, and in the two neighbouring valleys (Reintal and Mühlwalder Tal) walking and mountain climbing are the main draws for tourists.

Bruneck lies at a height of 835 m; Grosser Möseler in the Zillertaler Alps reaches up to 3478 m, and Hochgall on the border with East Tyrol attains 3495 m. In between these landmarks nature is at its finest, with green meadows, alms, woods and high alpine pastures, glaciers and a couple of pretty old places like Sand in Taufers.

Bring your mountain bike — or rent one! Every alm and every farm has its own lane (while in contrast the trails between the isolated high farms and alms are often so steep and exposed that they are only accessible to experienced mountain climbers). But you will also find castles, old stately homes, a mining museum with old tunnels, and rustic cooking in even more rustic local inns. And it's also possible to experience the age-old way of life on farmhouse holidays.

Sand in Taufers/ Campo Tures (✕)

Sand in Taufers lies just where the almost-flat Tauferer Tal suddenly forks and, after a steep gorge section in the Ahrn and Rein valleys gets much narrower and far from flat!

In the past, whoever wanted to cross the mountains to the Salzburg area had to go through Sand. For merchants it was a necessity. Wine from Bolzano was taken over the Krimmler Tauren

Pass to the north, where it was needed for Communion wine. Salt from Hallein and other salt-producing places was taken south (where it was in equally heavy demand) on the same route. Sand profited from all this trade and, just where the Ahrntal begins, an early castle rose to protect the route — spectacular **Schloss Taufers**. The view is impressive, unforgettable: from the meadows by Sand you look out to the Neumelans estate with its mighty hipped roof and delicate bay windows, Schloss Taufers above it, surrounded by woods, and all that crowned by the snow- and ice-capped peaks of the high Alpine ridge.

There is a large **car park** in the southern part of Sand. Parking on the road in the Ahrntal is not allowed. There are up to 25 **buses** a day to/from Bruneck and either Kasern or Prettau.

Cycling tip: tour from Bruneck to Sand in Taufers: The cycle route between Bruneck and Sand (Tabacco 1:25,000 map N° 36) is well marked and family-friendly, thanks to the very limited ascents. For most of the way this is a wide asphalted cycle path built over an old railway line. There are benches en route where you can take a break. The only time you might get lost is when you leave Bruneck, and for that you have two choices. You *can* take the main road into the Tauferer Tal, but as soon as you reach the beginning of St. Georgen, take the first road to the right — *watch for the sign!* But it is prettier to start out along the road to Dietenheim and from

Pseudo-Tyrolean architecture in Sand, with Schloss Taufers in the background

there take the road to Aufhofen and St. Georgen. As you reach St. Georgen via this route, the cycle path crosses your way and you can join it. Allow 2-3 hours return.

While Sand is small, it has an excellent infrastructure, in fact it's the shopping centre for several valleys. Most of the shops are on Ahrntaler Street, on the western edge of town. The old town is partly pedestrianised, its centre lying around Josef Jungmann Street; here's where you'll find the town hall, post office, bank, tourist office, bookshops and the new '**Naturparkhaus Rieserferner-Ahrn**'. It has a very good multi-media presentation about the natural park (see page 78). You may never get past the entrance hall with its film taken from a helicopter! *Park House open from May to end Oct and from Christmas Eve to mid-Mar Tue-Sat 09.30-12.30 and 16.00-19.00; open also on Sun in Jul/Aug (same hours). Entry free.*

The **parish museum** displays sacred art from the churches and chapels around Sand. Many of their treasures had to be brought here for protection in the 1960s and 70s, when there were a great number of thefts. *Museum open from mid-Jun to end Oct, Mon-Sat from 17.00-18.30; from mid-Jul to end Sep also Sun (same hours). No entry fee; please leave a donation.*

South of Sand (towards Bruneck) is the impressive **Ansitz Neume-lans**, already mentioned, in its own park. The building was com-missioned by the lord of the manor, Hans Fieger, in 1582 and finished in just 12 months. It must have been more comfortable down here than up in the drafty castle.

The difference in height between the Ahrntal and the Tauferer Tal in the gorge above Sand is almost 100 m, and the Almbach breaches the drop in cascades. The gorge is so narrow that only in modern times were the road builders able to blast a way through the rock. Before that the route through the gorge went just past the perched castle, **Schloss Taufers**. The castle's mighty grey granite walls and high keep make a deep impression even today. The Taufers, a noble family, had it built in the 13th century as their base, so it is an early Middle Ages building. The Taufers were a very important family, for quite a long time able to measure up to the Counts of Tyrol and the House of Andechs (forerunners of the well-known German brewery).

During your visit you will see the Romanesque chapel; its frescoes were uncovered during restoration. They are among Michael Pacher's masterpieces; the Byzantine Christ is majestic. The dining room, with the large tiled oven, the courtroom, the war chamber with Middle Ages and Early Modern arms and armour, the knights' room with portraits of noblemen, and the lovely library can all be visited — as can the private quarters of Margarete von Taufers, a beautifully panelled Renaissance room. It is said that her husband was killed on their wedding day, and so she shut herself away in this room (just fiction, but a pretty story). *Castle open daily from mid-May to 31 Oct; guided tours 10.00, 11.00, 14.00, 15.15, 16.30; also daily from 31 Oct to early Dec,*

Tue/Fri/Sun at 15.00. Entry fee 7 €, concessions 4/3 €. www. burgeninstitut.com.

Sand's **late Gothic parish church** is not in the village, but somewhat south of **Taufers**, a hamlet comprising just a few houses. It was completed in 1527. The ensemble makes a very impressive picture: the church, the cemetery chapel (also late Gothic) and the sexton's house on the other side of the square, with its beautiful entrance gate and bay window.

Walking tip: visit to Kofler zwischen den Wänden. The area of scattered isolated farms on the sunny slopes above Sand is called **Ahornach**. Today the farms are all joined by roads, but just a generation ago they were only accessible by tracks and trails. East of Ahornach, on cliffs high in the Reintal, is one of the most isolated alms in South Tyrol, **Kofler zwischen den Wänden** ('between the walls'). The steep trail that rises from just below (today no longer an official route), involves ladders. But a flatter access track (in the past extremely narrow and dangerous) has been widened and protected. You can reach the alm by one of three routes (see Tabacco 1:25,000 map N° 35): Route 6c from Ahornach is a straightforward walk of about 1h (road as far as the Stockner Hof); Route 6c from Tobl in the Reintal, at the junction with the road to Ahornach, is a steep ascent of 1h30min; Route 10 from Rein follows a motorable track, then Route 6c — all well-waymarked and taking about 2h. But though access is now easier (there is even a drive to the alm *for overnight* *guests only*), the setting — on a small flat meadow between steep cliffs (the 'walls') — will still astonish you, as you enjoy some fantastic local cooking.

Mühlen/Molini di Tures

Mühlen, south of Sand, is named for the many mills in the area, driven by its stream. There's a lovely drive from here up the **Mühlwalder Tal**, a valley which attracts both walkers and climbers. You go via **Mühlwald/ Selva dei Molini** with its impressively-sited parish church to **Lappach/Lappago**, the highest village in the valley at 1436 m. From here a motorable track, closed to private cars, runs to the **Neves Reservoir**. This beautifully located lake is the starting point for two interesting **mountain walks**. To the west you can reach Pfunders (see page 69) via the Eisbruggjoch; to the east you can climb to the Chemnitzer Hut on the Nevesjoch and then go down to Weissenbach, where you'd meet the Ahrntal road. From Mühlwald itself two hours of steep climbing would take you to idyllic Wenger Lake, in a corrie surrounded by larches and Arolla pines (but no hut/refreshments).

Reintal/Valle di Riva

A minor road leads from Sand along the **Reintal**.

Walking tip: Franziscusweg. Park at the Toblhof (inn), to see one of South Tyrol's most spectacular waterfalls, the three-tiered **Reinbachfälle**. You reach it on a meditation path dedicated to St. Francis (the '**Franziskusweg**'; ascent of 160 m; allow 1h return).

Higher up, the Reintal widens out a bit and, after some fine new views to the surrounding 3000 m-high peaks, you come to **Rein in Taufers/Riva di Tures** (1595 m; ✕), the main village in the valley. Rein is far from the highest settlement in the valley, since mountain farms like Hirber (1674 m) and Eppacher (1687 m) lie even higher up. Meadows, old tracks and trails, unspoilt farmhouses, alms and the isolated mountain world are the strong points of this area. The **Rieserferner-Ahrn Natural Park** completely encloses the settled and farmed parts of the village. This natural park is probably the most isolated and untouched in all South Tyrol. A straightforward but magnificent ascent (Route 3, the 'Erlanger Weg') leads from south of Rein to the Rieserferner Hut on the main ridge of the range; it's an ascent of some 1280 m, for which you should allow *at least* 8h return.

Rieserferner-Ahrn Natural Park

The Rieserferner Group almost met the same fate as so many other mountain ranges with a lot of water and steep declivities. Plans were in place for reservoirs, power stations, tracks and roads, with plenty of ski lifts for good measure. But all this was vetoed by the South Tyrol provincial government, so that today we have a natural park of national interest — and of international significance, because it is virtually untouched.

The terrain in the park is composed of impermeable prehistoric rock and slate, and a lot of rain falls here. So there is plenty of water in the streams. Ice-Age glaciers scoured the whole area, carving steep valleys topped by

A cemetery like a garden — in the Ahrntal nature is never far away.

the flat terraces that are today dotted with alms. From these terraces with their little lakes the streams bounce down into the valley as noisy waterfalls. It's true that the glaciers here are contracting at a great rate, but if you look up to Dreiherrenspitze (3499 m) or Hochgall (3436 m), you'll find that they still look quite impressive.

Ahrntal/Valle Aurina

People staying at the bottom of the Ahrntal are often disappointed to learn that the holiday area lies further uphill. But it doesn't take long to drive the 30 km of good road between Sand in Taufers at 870 m and Kasern at 1600 m. There are also **bus** connections: up to 15 buses a day ply the route from Bruneck via Sand to Kasern in the upper valley, although some end at Prettau.

From a car, the bottom of the valley is a rushed haze of unsightly buildings. But doing the road by bike you notice the little wayside chapels, the barns, old farm buildings and farm gardens with pear trees on the south-facing walls. Only walkers and mountain bikers experience the upper reaches: beyond the zone of the mountain farms there is an almost unbroken forest belt. It's not old forest, however, since it took a lot of wood to build all the hotels down in the valley! And what wasn't used for the hotels went to the furnaces: there is still a half-ruined chimney stack visible on the road above Prettau. Going up even higher you come to the alms, where the farmers took their cattle to graze

in summer and cut hay to provide for both the animals and themselves during the long winter. Even further up sheep and goats graze around the lakes in the mountain corries — lakes Griessbach, Waldner, and Klaus (the latter can be reached by the Klausberg lift, but is thankfully not too busy). Above all this shine the ice-capped peaks — territory only accessible to experienced, properly equipped climbers.

Luttach/Lutago

This old village has been completely transformed, thanks to the Speikboden ski area on the doorstep and the typical Italian industrial and trading settlement parallel to the road. The new wooden buildings can't make much impact on that. The lovely two-storey **Maranatha Museum** is worth a visit (cribs and folk art). *Museum open May-Oct, Mon-Sat from 09.00-12.00 and 14.00-18.00 (Sat 17.00), Sun from 14.00-17.00; entry fee 4 €, families 8 €.*

A lift runs from Luttach up to **Speikboden/Monte Spico**. In summer the peak (2523 m) is a goal for walkers; it can be reached from the top station (1974 m) via meadows full of rhododendrons in about 1h30min (2h45min return). The onward route via the Kellerbauerweg to the Chemnitzer Hut (Nevesjoch Hut) is only recommended for experts and only in fine weather.

St. Johann in Ahrn/ S. Giovanni

The old main village street still has a couple of lovely façades, due to the fact that there is a bypass road. The **parish church of St. Johann**, which towers above all the other buildings, has beautiful and well-preserved baroque frescoes; the whole impression is colourful and cheerful. The church dates from 1783-1785; it was built on high ground, as the whole valley was subject to flooding. St. Johann's **Kirchler Mineral Museum** houses the beautiful collection of a private donor; the displays are from the Ahrntal mines. This is really worth seeing, as it gives a good grounding in the colourful mineral world of the valley. There is also a sales room with local, regional and international objects. *Museum open May-Oct daily from 10.00-12.00 and 15.00-18.00, otherwise by request; entry fee 3 €, concessions 2 €.*

Steinhaus/Cadipietra

Steinhaus is the only really self-contained village in the valley. The administration and stores of the mining area was once located here in the **Ansitz Gassegg**. The houses are imposing, but lack out-buildings, since they were not built as farms. The **Bergbaumuseum** (Mining Museum) is located in the 'Kornstadel', the former mining stores. It is

extremely interesting — one of five establishments which together make up the South Tyrolean Mining Museum (others are the show mine in Prettau and museums in Sterzing, St. Leonhard im Passeier and Ridnaun). The collections are housed in their original setting, which has been beautifully restored. There are multi-media displays (PCs with good reference programs on the top floor). What comes over most forcefully is the everyday life and the harsh working conditions of these miners. There are special exhibitions on the ground floor. *Museum open Apr-end Oct daily (except Mon) from 09.30-16.30 (Thu 22.00); entry fee 6 €, children 3 €; combination ticket giving also entry to the show mine at Prettau 10/5 €.*

Walking tip: Lake Klaus. The fact that the cabin lift from Steinhaus up **Klausberg** (✗) only goes up to 1600 m keeps the number of people visiting the wild mountain corrie holding the **Lake Klaus** at 2162 m to a minimum, so if you go there, you won't be overwhelmed by tourists. The lift operates daily from mid-May to the end of Oct, 08.30-11.45 and 13.00-16.45 (18.00 from Jul-Sep and in winter). There is a large **car park** at the bottom station. The Berggasthof Klausberg, up by the top station, is open all year and offers hot food, snacks and cakes.
A good trail (Route 33; Tabacco 1:25,000 map N° 35) climbs 120 m from here via the Moareggalm to the Speckalm. A lot of people manage this. But then the route hairpins up another 450 m to the lake, and this is a very effective

filter … as is the fact that there's nowhere at the lake for refreshments! So despite the lift, the peak itself, like Durreck (3135 m) rightly belongs to the unspoilt Rieserferner-Ahrn Natural Park. Allow 2h30min-3h return.

Prettau/Predoi

Up at the old farming village of Prettau it's noticeably cooler than down in the lower valley; larch and birch are among the trees lining the road. The **show mine of the South Tyrolean Mining Museum** is a must; it's reached by taking a short minor road off the main valley road (**car park**). Since the temperature will be only about 7-8 °C, dress warmly (no sandals)! Copper mining here dates back 4000 years, until the mining industry proper was established in the 20th century. Prettau copper was much sought after and expensive. You board a pit train and travel through one of the many tunnels (protective clothing is provided), then follow a circuit on the floor, 6 m below

the level of the gallery. Down here you'll see working techniques depicted by models and machines. *Museum open Mar to end Oct daily (except Mon) from 09.30-16.30; in high — and even shoulder — season be sure to book ahead. Entry fee 8 €, children 3 €; combination ticket also*

giving access to the Steinhaus Mining Museum 10/5 €.
A mining **'teaching' trail** that runs up into the high mountains is a good continuation of the trip into the galleries, but only recommended for strong walkers. There are information panels along the way.

As mining fell into crisis at the end of the 19th century, the situation was dire for many families. One of the parish priests had the idea of starting a **lace-making** business to help the economy. The village women learned fast. In summer you'll see women working on the lace pillows. Another source of income is the carving of wooden masks, usually carried out by the men; it's an older trade than lace-making, but cannot compete with the mask carving of the Gröden Valley.

Kasern/Cassere (✖)

The hamlet of Kasern is just a handful of houses, an information kiosk for the **Rieserferner-Ahrn Natural Park**, a snack-bar, three hotels and a large car park.

Walking tips

Kehreralm: From Kasern a road (closed to traffic) runs 5 km to the **Kehreralm** (1842 m; see map overleaf), where it ends. This is a popular walking route for the less energetic who won't want to tackle Walk 6, with an ascent of little more than 200 m. En route you can visit the late Gothic **pilgrimage church of the Holy Ghost** (always open), just 1 km from the Prastmann Snack Bar at Kasern; it's on the other side of the stream and was once a votive chapel for the mountain people of Prettau.

Krimmler Tauern: The straight-forward but quite strenuous route from Kasern to the Krimmler Tauern (**Route 14**; see map) is the old Tauernweg, which was used for trade back in the Middle Ages. You can still see the slabs of the old cobbled route. There is no hut on Tauern, so for this 5h round trip you will need to take plenty of sustenance! The route is still used twice a year by the cattle of the Ahrntal farmers who own alms high up in the Austrian Krimmler Tauerntal. In spring this usually means that they must cross large *névés*, since the pass lies at 2633 m!

Walk 6: From Kasern to the Birnlücken Hut

Time: 5h
Grade: ascent/descent of 900 m
Access: bus or car to Kasern
Refreshments: Birnlücken Hut (2441 m), open early Jul until early Oct; food, beds and bunks.
Map: Tabacco 1:25,000 N° 35

View down into the upper Ahrntal from the Birnlücken Hut

From the car park in **Kasern** (1580 m) follow the good road (closed to traffic) further into the valley. When it ends at the **Kehreralm** (1742 m; **1h30min**), go right, over the stream on **Route 13**, winding up to the **Lahneralm** (1986 m; **2h**; refreshments). The floor of this alm is flat as a pancake; it's an old dried-up lake. From the end of the lake floor the route hairpins up to a higher flat area in glacier terrain, where you come to the **Birnlücken Hut** with panoramic views (2441 m; **3h**). Not far above is the **Birnlücke**, a pass usually covered by a snow field. From here the view to the glaciers on Dreiherrenspitze (3498 m) is magnificent. Retrace your route back to **Kasern** (**5h**).

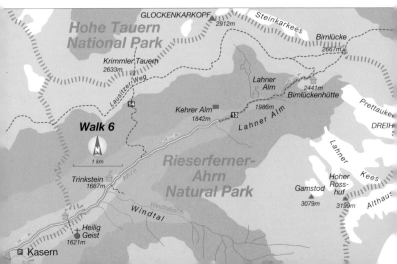

6 ANTHOLZER TAL AND GSIESER TAL/
VAL DI ANTERSELVA AND VALLE DI CASIES

Rasen • Mittertal • Lake Antholz • Welsberg • Gsieser Tal • Taisten

Walks: none; *walking tips:* Grente-alm and Kumpfleralm; Lake Antholz

Web site: www.antholzertal.com
Opening hours: see individual attractions

These are two of the least-developed valleys in eastern South Tyrol, ideal for anyone who wants a peaceful holiday — to relax, do a little sport (nothing too ambitious), get to learn about the farming culture of the area and perhaps have a farmhouse holiday.

The Antholzer Tal strikes off from the road in the Pustertal at Niederrasen and climbs 1050 m over 23 km to the Stallersattel on the boundary with Austria. That sounds steeper than it really is. The last 450 m, from Lake Antholz to the saddle are covered in under 3 km as the bird flies (but with corresponding hairpins, 10% gradient, one-way traffic with waits of up to 45 minutes and closed to caravans). It's an ideal area for short walks and long-distance skiing in winter.

The Antholzer Tal (✖) is the best valley in the Dolomites for long-distance and biathlon runners and the goal of the Pustertal Cross-Country Ski Marathon which starts in Innichen. To quench the thirst and stave off the hunger pangs of the brave walkers who are making long sweaty treks in the Rieserferner Natural Park or the mountains around Rote Wand in the south, there's a whole array of alms and mountain huts taking guests. Some of these have every modern convenience and are as comfortable as can be. It's worth while, too, taking your bicycle. There's little traffic on the road and you can pedal up and whiz down; there's also a plethora of forestry roads and drives leading from the valley floor up to alms on the slopes.

There are up to 12 **buses** a day *(not Sundays!)* between Bruneck, Olang and Antholz-Mitteltal; about 5-6 a day run up to

Obertal. At the top end of the valley is the Stallersattel. Bear in mind that if you plan to cross the border with Austria here, the pass should be open *during daylight hours* from mid-May to the beginning of November. Take documents for the border crossing. Despite the one-way traffic (uphill every 30 to 45 minutes on the hour, down every 1 to 15 minutes), this pass draws both motorists and cyclists. Because of the hairpin bends the buses can't handle it, but once at the pass, there is an Austrian bus (summer only) which you could take to Lienz.

Rasen/Rasun

Rasen is the first settlement in the Antholzer Tal. An eye-catching row of really stately farm houses runs from the chapel in **Niederrasen** at the valley exit to the church at Oberrasen. **Oberrasen** is the more important village, where the upper-crust lived — in

83

what is today the **Neurasen castle ruins** on a wooded rocky spur above the road.

Heading up to Oberrasen you'll see on the right a most impressive castle-like building with towers and bay windows, the **Ansitz Heufler**. The Heuflers of Rasen (they had already been here for several generations) had this built in 1580 in what was then the modern Renaissance style. The property is not the only one of its kind in South Tyrol, but certainly one of the most beautiful; today it's a château-hotel. The three-storey building is square and completely symmetrical, with diagonally placed corner towers. The first floor contains some represen-tative decoration and beams, especially in the 'Herrnstube', which is one of the most magni-ficent rooms in Tyrol.

Antholz Mittertal/Anterselva di Mezzo (✕)

Just a generation ago Mittertal was a strung-out settlement with a church, but today it's a compact village with guest houses, mini-markets, bakery and butcher. Above the village are two alms in panoramic settings: Grentealm and Kumpfleralm.

Walking tip: Grentealm (and Kumpfleralm). You can get to the Grentealm and its two manned huts from Niedertal or Mittertal on a delightful walk: take **Route 6** from Hof Huber (signposted from the main road; Tabacco 1:25,000 map N° 32). This hairpins up through woods to 2002 m. The Messnerwirt is manned from 20 Jun to 5 Oct, the Pfaffing from end Jun to end Sep; both offer typical rustic alm cooking — try the *graukäs* (grey cheese)! From the Grentealm other routes run to the **Kumpfleralm** and Mittertal. Allow 3h30min-4h up to the panoramic Grentealm and back down the same way; if you come down via the Kumpfleralm, allow 4h-4h30min. Both routes involve an ascent of 750 m.

Antholz Mittertal, with the Rieserferner Group rising above the village

Walking tip: Lake Antholz/Lago di Anterselva (✕). Lake Antholz is often referred to as the Lower Lake, since there is another lake by the Stallersattel called the Upper Lake (Obersee), although today that lies in Austria. Although the southern stretch of Lake Antholz is a bit spoiled by the nearby road with its hotels and restaurants, the northern part lies in the natural park and is still pristine, so it's worth doing the circuit (1h-1h30min). Leave your car at the large **car park** at the **Huberalm** (or take the bus to the next, **smaller car park** by the lake) and walk in a counter-clockwise direction around the lake, leaving the best part till last. The road which you have to follow at first sees little traffic, since most people stop at the car park. Marvellous views await you: first you see mighty Hochgall (3436 m) and Wildgall (3273 m), and later the Rote Wand (2818 m).

Welsberg/Monguelfo (✕)

The road between Olang and Welsberg has to make a long climb, since the electricity works have used the wide part of the valley for a reservoir. **Welsberg** (photograph overleaf) is a lovely well-knit place, almost looking like a town. Beautifully kept Welsberg Castle stands above the mouth of the Pieding stream which opens out from the Gsiesertal.

The narrow road through the village, which used to be subject to kilometre-long hold-ups, has been bypassed. There is a good **bus** service: Welsberg is on the Bruneck/Innichen route, with many buses. There is also a **railway** station.

A stroll around Welsberg should first take in the **parish church of St. Magdalena**, with its high- and side-altar paintings by the baroque artist Paul Troger (1698-1762), who was born in the village. The church was newly built in the baroque style. A large shrine-like pillar, with frescoes by the great Michael Pacher, stands on the square near the main road; unfortunately the frescoes were almost completely destroyed by high water in 1882. Beautiful properties attest to Welsberg's past, when court was held here — like **Ansitz Zellheim** on the main through road, with its gables, double-arched window and splendid wrought-iron gates. On a hill somewhat outside the village towards Toblach is the **Rainkirche** — today the cemetery church. A beautiful net vault in the choir and Gothic frescoes adorn the otherwise baroque embellishments of the church.

A road runs from the village to **Schloss Welsperg**, the oldest castle in the upper Pustertal between Bruneck and Lienz. It retains its old, very high keep. At that time (1126-1140) the castle was the seat of the House of Welsberg (later Counts and Princes of the Realm), who ran their extensive holdings from here. The castle was rebuilt and extended at a later date, but partly burned in 1764; it has only been restored in recent years. *Castle open Jul to early Sep, Mon-Fri from 10.00-13.00 and 16.00-18.30; Sun 16.00-19.00; closed Sat. Open from mid to end Sep Mon and Fri from 15.00-17.00. Entry fee 2 €, concessions 1 €. Also open for occasional concerts.*

Welsberg and the lower Gsiesertal from the walking path to Olang

Gsieser Tal/Valle di Casies

If you follow this still-pastoral valley, mainly frequented by walkers and a few tourists, you'll be on an old smugglers' route; they used it to take their goods over the Gsieser Törl (2205 m) to Austria.

The valley begins with a small climb via Taisten, a mecca for art lovers. Further up are Durnwald, Unterplanken (✕), Pichl, Oberplanken, Preindl, St. Martin and St. Magdalena; only these last two have any 'character'. There are about 12 **buses** a day from Welsberg to St. Magdalena (no Sundays service).

Although most **alm huts** open at the end of June at the earliest, those in the Gsieser Tal open from mid-May — a boon for walkers and enthusiasts of alm cooking! Ask the tourist office to tell you which will be open.

St. Martin/S. Martino is the setting for an annual 'Alm Hut Festival' in the middle of September (exact dates from the tourist office), with brass bands and a two-hour procession from alm to alm, with each serving up its culinary speciality.

Another plus point: quite a few **winter walking** routes are open, so if you enjoy winter holidays but don't like skiing, you can still commune with nature. These routes link the valley floor with various alms — which are also

open in winter (addresses from the tourist board).

Taisten/Tésido (✕)

Two churches, a chapel and a shrine-like pillar attract art lovers to Taisten: the original Romanesque church of St. George, the baroque parish church, the cemetery chapel and the Gothic pillar at the entrance to the village. Simon von Taisten (about 1460-1530), an important painter of the late Middle Ages, came from Taisten and painted the frescoes in the **Jakobskapelle** at the cemetery. The baroque **parish church** was decorated by Franz Anton Zeiller, whose frescoes also adorn the parish church in Toblach. Even Michael Pacher is represented, with his Madonna in the arch of the gothic **Welsbergkapelle** adjacent to the parish church. The second church is the **Georgskirche**, with a large fresco of St. Christopher and other frescoes by Simon von Taisten and Leonhard von Brixen.

Border traffic in the Gsieser Tal
Except for a handful of farmers, valley people were poor and most had to take lowly jobs like stable-boy, maid or shepherd — badly paid, or not paid at all, but given food and 'lodgings' in a covered haystack. Food was at best ham, noodle and milk soup. No wonder smuggling flourished once the crossing into the Defreggental suddenly became the Austrian border in 1919. Today you can still see the Italian toll watch hut at the Gsieser Jöchl (somewhat hidden, so that it can't be seen from the Austrian side).

Toblach • Niederdorf • Pragser Tal • Lake Prags • Plätzwiese • Innichen • Sexten • Fischleintal • Sexten Dolomites Natural Park • Helm

Walks: 7, 8, 9, 10; *cycling tips:* from Toblach through the Höhlensteintal; Pustertal cycle path between Mühlbach and Lienz

Web sites
www.hochpustertal.info
www.festivalpusteria.org

www.toblach.it
www.niederdorf.it
www.pragsertal.info
www.innichen.it
www.sexten.it

Opening hours: see individual attractions

This area, near the junction of the Rienz and Drau valleys between the Austrian border and Niederdorf, is the setting for some of the most famous pictures of the Dolomites: the Drei Zinnen, Zwölferkofel, Lake Prags, Innichen's baroque church, and the view from the Sennesalpe to Monte Cristallo.

Sexten, Innichen, Toblach, Niederdorf and Prags offer plenty of beds for the visitor returning from a long walk, a strenuous day on the mountain bike or a car tour along the endless hairpin curves. You may even be glad to sink into bed after a hard day lazing about — like swimming in one of the icy mountain lakes (Prags, Dürren or Toblach). Or there's always Aquafun in Innichen for the odd rainy day.

Three valleys stretch south from the Hochpustertal. From Niederdorf the Pragser Tal reaches far into the Dolomites. (This, and the Sextental, are the only German-speaking valleys in the Dolomites; in all others the language is Ladin or Italian.) From Toblach the narrow Höhlensteintal, hemmed in by high walls, runs to romantic Lake Dürren. In Innichen — historically the most important of all these villages — yet another valley branches off: the Sextental. On its south side are the Sexten Dolomites and the Drei Zinnen; to the north the Karnische Alps delineate the Austrian border.

The road through the Pustertal bypasses Niederdorf, Toblach and Innichen, all of which have plenty of **car parks**. There's a relatively good **bus service** in the valley ('Corriera'), which also serves Cortina d'Ampezzo. By **train** there are connections to Franzensfeste, Innsbruck and Bolzano as well as to Lienz in Austria.

Some events are organised by the whole Hochpustertal area, among them the **International Choir Festival** (www.festival pusteria.org). This involves performances in all five parishes, including open-air concerts near the Haunold Hut or the restaurant on Helm, etc. Programmes include church music, folk music, spirituals, jazz.

Also common to the whole valley is the **'Drei Zinnen Card'**, a pass

The Höhlensteintal from Monte Piana, with the 'Alemagna' below in the valley

for walkers (42 €). This gives you seven days' travel on all the buses in the Hochpustertal as well as the lifts up Haunold, Rotwand and Helm. You can also use the pass to gain free entry to the museums, sports centres (like Acquafun in Innichen or the tennis courts and climbing facilities in Sexten).

The '**Hochpustertaler Wander-pass**', available free in tourist offices, is *not* a pass, but a booklet giving 71 walking suggestions, with an overview map and very sketchy descriptions.

Toblach/Dobbiaco (✕)

Toblach lies at the point where the 'Alemagna' — the old trading route from Venice to southern Germany — meets the Pustertal. There is a large **car park** on Mittelweg, the **bus station** is at the top end of Dolomitenstrasse, and the railway station is located in Neutoblach (the station is not manned, so there is an automatic ticket dispenser).

The little village centre, with its magnificent late baroque church, is now surrounded by a host of new buildings — hotels, *pensions* and apartments. Toblach is one of the most important holiday bases in South Tyrol.

And has been for a long time: even in the 19th century there were hotels like the Grand in **Neutoblach/Dobbiaco Nuovo**, at that time a 'new' settlement, as the name implies. During the First World War Toblach lay in the firing line of the Italian emplacements on Mt Cristallino, and Neutoblach — except for the Grand Hotel, which was in a well-sheltered area — went up in flames; even the parish church was hit. The one-time enemy is now the most important visitor in August, at Christmas/New Year and in February — and of course during these times the people of Dobbiaco (as the place was christened in 1919) naturally speak Italian.

But it is for Toblach's setting that

people come. Top of the list of course are the Drei Zinnen in the background (they can be seen from the higher village of Wahlen), but there is also the Höhlensteintal with Lake Toblach and Lake Dürren. The 'Alemagna' runs the whole length of the Höhlensteintal towards Cortina, which is under an hour's drive away. Toblach is well situated not only for Cortina; Innichen, Bruneck and Lienz in Austria are easily reached by bus or train. At Toblach there are hikes and strolls on your doorstep.

Among the most popular events are the **Gustav Mahler Weeks** — four weeks in July/August (www. gustav-mahler.it), with concerts by regional and international orchestras and ensembles, conferences and seminars.

For winter visitors, St. Nicholas Day (6 Dec) or the day before ('Krampustag', 5 Dec,), sees St. Nic's black companion, the '**Krampus**', making his rounds in Toblach and many other towns in South Tyrol. The Krampus impersonators, wearing masks and dressed as the Devil, gather for the large 'Krampus Run', which takes place throughout the entire 'Krampuszone' of the German-speaking areas. Participants come from all over South Tyrol, North Tyrol, Carinthia, Salzburg, southern Bavaria and German-speaking Switzerland. If you're frightened by the Krampuses, who carry huge brooms (… and frequently use them on young ladies), then find a safe spot in one of the roped-off areas and enjoy your *glühwein* in peace.

Restored after the damage caused during the First World War,

Toblach's **parish church** is a splendid example of late baroque. The ceiling paintings (the Life of St. John the Baptist) and those on the altar are the work of Franz Anton Zeiller. Everything is decorated with plaster and gilded, but not excessively so. The Calvary alongside the church is the oldest in Tyrol.

The **Calvary** along Maximilian-strasse (which runs to the church and cemetery) ist the oldest in Tyrol, dating from 1519; five Stations are still in good condition. Together with the old Gorizian chapel in the parish church and the round hilltop chapel at the eastern exit from the village they make a complete 'sacred mountain', as was the vogue in northern Italy at that time.

The **Naturparkhaus** is located in the Cultural Centre of the old Grand Hotel in Neutoblach. This is a visitors' centre for the two parks bordering Toblach, which make up a large part of the Dolomites — the **Sexten Dolomites Natural Park** and the **Fanes-Sennes-Prags Natural Park.** Nature and culture, geology and fauna, plants and Alpine farming are presented in a modern setting. *Park House open Tue-Sat from 09.30-12.30, 16.00-19.00 (22.00 Thu); in high season also open Sun. Closed Nov and Apr. Entry free.*

The farming village of **Wahlen/Valle San Silvestro** lies on sunny slopes where the Silvestertal comes into Toblach. There are a few *pensions* and large farm houses. From the village a wide level track (closed to motor traffic) runs out of the valley: in five minutes one comes to a **chapel** with a breathtaking view to the Sexten Dolomites including the Drei Zinnen. The village church, dedicated to **St. Nicholas**, is worth seeing for its beautiful late Gothic net vault and the interesting fresco near the door depicting the Poor Souls in Purgatory.

Aufkirchen/Santa Maria lies in a

sunny spot high up between Toblach and Niederdorf. The village is dominated by the pilgrimage church of St. Mary (**Marienwallfahrtskirche**), built in late Gothic style (1475) on the site of an older church which had become too small for the congregation. One can't miss the outsized fresco on the south wall, attributed to Simon von Taisten. It's a beautiful view for St. Christopher and the Christ Child — and for us as well. From St. Mary's you can follow the 'Meditation Path' (Besinnungsweg) with its seven Stations of the Cross to the little church of **St. Peter im Kofl**. At a height of 1450 m, this is reputed to be the oldest church in the Pustertal.

The Mahler festival in Toblach is a reminder of the three summer visits the composer made to the village. As the very busy Director of the Vienna State Opera, he escaped to the Trenkerhof in **Altschluderbach**, where he worked simultaneously on his Ninth and unfinished Tenth symphonies, as well as the 'Lied von der Erde'. In the adjacent '**Wildpark**' (game park) there's a small wooden house that Mahler had built, so he could work undisturbed. *Access is via Rienz (from the road into the Höhlensteintal turn right on a small road just past the railway overpass). Park open mid-Jun to early Oct, daily from 09.00-17.00; his rooms in the Trenkerhof can be visited during the same period, but only Tue and Sat from 11.00-12.00. His so-called 'Summer*

Top: Rienz River at Niederdorf; below: the baroque parish church at Toblach is a gem.

Residence' in the park is only open one day a week for a guided tour (ask at the tourist office).

Niederdorf/Villabassa (✕)

The Pustertal road towards Toblach is referred to in the Niederdorf region as 'Frau Emma Strasse'. Frau Emma was Emerentia Hausbacher (1817-1904) and widely known throughout Tyrol: together with her husband, who came from Niederdorf, she built up an early hotel empire. The 'Schwarze Adler' in the Rathausplatz was the first step; next was a hotel at Lake Prags, then hotels in Meran, Innsbruck and the Vinschgau. Her cooking was as famous as her hospitality. One anecdote tells of an American who sent her a letter addressed simply to 'Frau Emma in Europe, Austria'— it was delivered, no problem! The **Hochpustertal Tourist Board Museum** between Niederdorf and Sexten, with its displays about early tourism in the area, was probably set up here because of her. It's housed in the late Middle Ages **Haus Wassermann**, with its beautiful coffered ceilings, old panelling and tiled fireplaces. *Museum open Jul-Sep, Tue-Sun from 16.00-19.00, Dec-Feb and May/Jun, Fri-Sun from 16.00-19.00, Sat also 09.00-12.00; entry fee 3 €, concessionary tickets 1.50 €.*

Apart from the attractive houses in the town hall square (Von-Kurz- Platz) with the courthouse and church (Spitalkirche), it's worth crossing to the other side of the Rienz, to visit the **parish church** with its chapel dedicated to St. Anna as well as the somewhat higher church of **St. Magdalena im Moos** (open May to end Sep, Sun 14.00-18.00), where there are occasional concerts. This church was founded in 1491 and holds frescoes dating back to the period of Simon von Taisten.

Dolomiti Superbike

One of the classic mountain bike races, the Dolomiti Superbike, begins in Niederdorf. It's been run on the first weekend in July since 1995. Experts and trained amateurs compete on the routes: 111 km with 3000 m height gain or 59 km/1500 m height gain. Since 2002 even beginners can enter the short race (25 km/800 m height gain). The race mostly uses forestry roads and tracks, via Toblach, Innichen, Sexten and Prags.

Pragser Tal/Val di Braies (✕)

The Pragser Tal has a really flat area lower down (called **Ausserprags**), then the valley forks at **Schmieden/Ferrara**: the branch to the left leads towards Plätzwiese, the one to the right to Lake Prags.

First taking the branch to the right, you come to **Innerprags/Braies**, where farmhouses lie on the sunny slopes — some grouped together, others singly. Early tourism to the area (to Frau Emma's hotel at Lake Prags!) meant that hotels and guest houses sprang up in the valley, especially alongside the road to the lake.

Lake Prags

The Pragser Wildsee/Lago di Braies is one of the jewels of the Dolomites: it's 36 m deep and lies at an altitude of 1489 m, below the massive north wall of

Seekofel (2810 m), the most northerly of the Fanes peaks. The water changes colour constantly — sometimes emerald, then blue and somewhat milky, sometimes black — and so clear that you can see the bottom. And cold, cold, *cold*. Just right for trout and the delicious char. You can hire boats at the Hotel Pragser Wildsee boat house and row to the south end of the lake, where there's a lovely pebble beach. Or you can circle the lake on foot — see the short version of Walk 7 opposite.

Plätzwiese/Prato Piazza

At the top end of the other fork in Schmieden is **Plätzwiese**, huge undulating alm meadows between the Prags and Höhlenstein valleys. Buses come up here from Prags from 10 Jul-20 Sep, and during this period private cars can only use the road before 10.00 and after 16.00 (toll 4.50 €). The Plätzwiese Hut offers refreshments all year round. With its wind-tousled Arolla pines, the place is a panoramic balcony. The **Fanes Group** is to the right, with Hohe Gaisl; the **Cristallo Group** is straight ahead (so close that you can see every little glacier and *névé*); to the left, alms rise up to **Dürrenstein**. The cattle up here graze on common alms, in contrast to other places in South Tyrol and the Dolomites. Farmers don't go to the alm, but entrust their animals to paid shepherds. From Plätzwiese there's an old military road down to the main Toblach/Cortina road, popular with mountain bikers.

Cycling tip: from Toblach through the Höhlensteintal/Valle di Landro
Time/length: 3h with ease; 32 km
Grade: 300 m ascent between

Toblach and the Gemärk Pass, then descent of 300 m to Cortina. The cycle path is in very good condition. *An excellent day out for the whole family;* take a bus back from Cortina.

The deeply-etched Höhlensteintal south of Toblach was scraped out by glacial action. The route runs over a small pass called **Im Gemärk/Passo di Cimabanche** to the Ladin area and Cortina (described on page 168). The mountain giants on both sides — Dürrenstein, Drei Zinnen, Cristallo — are too steep for normal walkers. Up until the 1960s a branch railway ran through the valley to Cortina and on to the Cadore. Now the old line is a pleasant and easy **cycle path** through one of the most beautiful landscapes in the Dolomites.

Starting just south of the railway line at **Neutoblach**, almost at once you pass **Lake Toblach**, covering an area of 14.3 ha (but only 3.5 m deep). It's a protected area; its southern, silted-up banks are an important habitat for amphibians and birds. The route runs almost flat to a signposted **Austrian military cemetery** on a slope to the right (**car park**).
Lake Dürren announces itself with the Drei Zinnen Hotel and the **car park** for the viewpoint. The Italian name for the lake is Lago di Landro, and that was the name of the hotel that preceded the current one; it was shot to pieces in the First World War. The lake is very shallow and in autumn often only half as large as in spring when it's full of melt-water. Just to the south is mighty **Monte Cristallo** (3216 m); the canons of the Italian emplacements on Monte Cristallino

Walk 7: From Lake Prags to the Seekofel Hut

Time: 5h30min
Grade: ascent/descent of 900 m; quite a steep mountain hike; some protected places higher up, but they are not difficult.
Access: bus or car to the Hotel Pragser Wildsee
Refreshments: Seekofel Hut/Rifugio Biella, open from end Jun to Sep
Special interest: You may well spot ibex in the Seekofel area!
Short walk: You can **circle the lake** on foot in under 1h30min: on the west side you'll be on a wide track closed to motor traffic, then you follow another good track below Seekofel and finally, on the east side, you take a 'balcony' path beside almost vertical edges dropping 30 m to

the lake (protected with fencing at all exposed points).
Map: Tabacco 1:25.000 N° 31
Start the walk at the **Hotel Pragser Wildsee** (1494 m; large car park). Take the wide track to the right and walk past the lake, to where it ends below the walls of Seekofel. You will be following **Route 1 (= Dolomites high-level Route 1)**, which branches off from this lakeside circuit.
Follow Route 1 uphill over loose scree, through woods and mountain pines. As the valley that you're following gets narrower, the way bears right and climbs in zigzags to a rocky spine (benches before and after). Go right here, slightly downhill, back to the original stream bed and cross it (1970 m; **2h**). From here the way climbs the steep slope to flatter alm terrain and heads left below a steep rock wall.
Beyond here you're in the upper valley, from where tight zigzags (protected as necessary, but take *care* in any case) take you up to the **Seekofelscharte** (2388 m). The **Seekofel Hut** (run by the Pächter family from Cortina) lies below and to the left (2327 m; **3h30min**).
Return the same way, and complete the circuit of **Lake Prags** (5h30min).

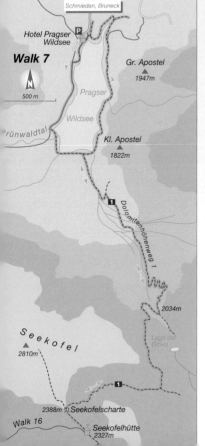

(2786 m) to its left were those that left Neutoblach in debris and ashes. The wild mountain flanks on the east side of the lake belong to **Monte Piana**, most of which lies in Belluno. Piana also saw heavy fighting in 1915-17, and there are still many emplacements which are being made into an open-air museum. A farmer called Ploner from Alt-Schluderbach near Toblach once built a guest house in **Schluderbach**; today the site is the Hotel Ploner, with apartments and a restaurant. An old military road (closed to motor traffic) runs from Schluderbach up to **Plätzwiese** — great for mountain bikers (see page 92).

The top of the route is **Im Gemärk**. The mountain half-right above this pass is **Hohe Gaisl** (3146 m), called 'Croda Rossa' by the Italians on account of its red-coloured rock. Descending, one passes the **Ospitale**, an old hospice on the 'Alemagna', of which only the small Gothic chapel on the other side of the road remains. From the hairpin bend 3 km down from the pass there is a panoramic view to the **Fanes Group**.

Excursion to the Drei Zinnen via Lake Misurina

A good but steep road (11%) runs from **Schluderbach** over a low pass to famous **Lake Misurina** in the Cadore. The view from the car park on the north shore across the lake to the Sorapis Group (3205 m) is one of the finest not only in the Dolomites, but all the Alps. The fashionable Grand Hotel on the south bank is one of the oldest in the whole region.

A road runs from the north shore towards the **Drei Zinnen** and ends at a large car park below the Auronzo Hut. Anyone can walk from here to the Drei Zinnen Hut along the motorable track, but if you want to make the most of the excursion, see Walk 24, page 173.

Innichen/San Candido (✕)

For the whole length of the Pustertal, Innichen is rivalled only by Bruneck and Lienz; in the Hochpustertal there's no competition. Only Innichen has a town-like atmosphere and can live without tourism — although it's quite happy to profit from it all the same.

There are free **car parking** places by the side of the road at the south end of Freisingerstrasse, a **railway station**, and **bus station** on Mantingerstrasse at the west end of P. P. Rainerstrasse, above the bridge over the Drau (but some buses set off from the area in front of the station). Good direct connections with Bruneck, Brixen, Sexten.

History books record that the coming of Christianity to the Pustertal began with the building of Innichen's collegiate church. In the dark interior of this Romanesque church the past comes alive, and you can almost feel yourself back in the times when the little settlement was surrounded by thick woods full of bears, wolves and lynx. The building of this church, in a total wilderness, must have been an epoch-making event for the few Slav settlers in the valley, all of them heathens.

The huge water park, Acquafun, is today's most impressive bit of infrastructure, together with the two mountain railways, the chair lifts to Haunold (the town's local mountain), and the lifts from Vierschach to Helm on the main ridge of the Karnische Dolomites.

The collegiate church (**Stiftskirche**) is on the busy Pflegplatz, but separated from it by the cemetery. In 769 Duke Tassilo III of Bavaria gave Abbot Atto von Scharnitz a large area around what is today Innichen, to found a monastery. The present church is the third building on this spot. The first church was replaced in 1000 by a larger building, of which the crypt is still preserved under what is today the choir. Both the village and the church burned down in 1200, making way for a third church. This was built in Romanesque style and dedicated in 1284 — today's collegiate church. The south door, entered from the Pflegplatz, is deeply recessed, with a magnificent relief in the tympanum. Above the doorway is a still fresh-looking fresco by Michael Pacher. The interior of the church has three naves in a most attractive Romanesque style. The middle nave is wide; a wooden Crucifixion group dating from

Collegiate church at Innichen

1240 draws the attention. The choir is raised, with the crypt below, accessible from both sides.

The church museum (**Stiftsmuseum**) is reached from Attostrasse; the collection comprises the cathedral treasures, sacred art and manuscripts. The rooms are as spectacular as the exhibits: in the 'Kapitelsaal', where the cathedral treasures are exhibited, frescoes depict the coats of arms of the canons, and the choirboys' schoolroom (Schulstube), with panelling and a huge green-tiled fireplace (dating from about 1550) is a real eye-opener. *Museum open Jun-mid Oct, Thu-Sat from 17.00-19.00, Sun from 10.00-11.00; in high season also Tue-Sat 10.00-11.00 and Tue 20.00-22.00. Entry 3 €.*

Squeezed between the road and the railway line, and deep below today's street level, is a curious, unique complex. Three little towers signal the three adjacent churches within. Inside, the complex consists of an octagonal building with tower (the **Altöttinger Chapel**), the adjacent nave with a little tower (the **Passionskapelle**), and a round building with a little tower and the Holy Sepulchre Chapel (the **Heiliggrabkapelle**). The complex dates from between 1633 and 1653. The donor was a religious man of Innichen, who made many pilgrimages. From the shrine of Altötting (near Munich) he brought a copy of the statue of St. Mary and a plan of the church housing it, which he had copied here in miniature. From Jerusalem he brought the plan of the Church of the Holy Sepulchre, which was also copied. In niches and on pillars there are statues and even whole scenes — like the Life of Mary in the Altöttinger Chapel and a wooden statue of the dead Christ in the Holy Sepulchre Chapel. Truly striking! *Museum open: Tue/Thu/Sat/Sun from 10.00-12.00 and from 16.00-18.00; donations welcome.*

The yellow-painted **Franciscan church** takes up a large flat area in the western part of the old town. The church is plain, but the altar is baroque, with a very good painting by Christoph Unterberger dating from 1764, depicting the Holy Mother and Child with St. Francis and St. Leopold of Austria kneeling before her. The cloister was also decorated in the baroque style by a naive painter, with more than 70 scenes from the life of St. Francis. It is interesting to see how he depicts the reality of his own era (around 1700) — the contemporary dress the women are wearing and the décor. *Church open daily 08.30-16.30; cloister Tue-Sun 08.30-12.00, also Tue-Sat 14.30-16.30.*

Mt Haunold: Wooded Mt Haunold at Innichen is fairly unimpressive. But in winter you can ski down the north side all the way to Innichen, and for summer there are many pleasant, easy walks. There are two huts at the top, the Haunold and the Jora. The 4-seater chair lift to the upper station (1500 m) runs from Jun to Sep and Dec to Mar, basic summer hours 09.00-12.30 and 13.30-17.15; one way 5 €, up and back 8 €. www.baranci.it.

Cycling tip: Pustertal cycle path between Mühlbach and Lienz
The cycle path beside the river

Drau from Toblach to Lienz, is very popular in summer. You can pedal along the river, then let the Austrian Railways (which have cycle wagons just for this purpose) take you back to Toblach or Innichen in the evening. This section (45.5 km) is just the eastern part of a long cycle route through the whole valley from Mühlbach in the west to the main European watershed at Toblach (where the Rienz flows west to the Etsch and Adriatic and the Drau flows east to the Donau and Black Sea and across the border to Lienz, where the Pustertal ends). Except for a small stretch near Brixen, the path is all built, mostly asphalted and very well signposted. Since the Pustertal is served by bus and train, you can break off at any point. Better still, you can rent bikes in many centres and, for a small additional cost, leave them somewhere else.

Sexten/Sesto (✖)

Sexten, home to mountain guides and climbers, lies in a wide green valley between the gentle slopes of the Karnische Alps and the rough walls of the Sexten Dolomites.

From Sexten and Moos/San Giuseppe, a bit higher up the valley, the Fischleintal runs right into the Dolomites, at the foot of Zwölferkogel and the Drei Zinnen. Sexten's mountain guide dynasty, the Innerkoflers, used to take climbers from England, Germany and Austria up to these peaks. Sexten was destroyed in the First World War — the Italian artillery was encamped at the nearby Kreuzberg Pass. Today's pseudo-Tyrolean houses are often less than 20 years old. But

Sexten Dolomites Natural Park

people don't come for the architecture!

There is a large **car park** by Congress House at the valley station of the Helm lift; good **bus connections** to Innichen and Toblach and to the Kreuzberg Pass (but no buses from there into the Cadore).

Fischleintal/Val Fiscalina

From Sexten and Moos the best way to visit the deeply-cut Fischleintal is by going up the left-hand side of the valley, past meadows loosely scattered with old larches. From the Hotel Dolomitenhof there is a lovely view to the wreath of peaks called the **Sextener Sonnenuhr** (Sexten Sundial). People in Sexten have always been able to read the time by looking to see where the sun is on the Elfer, Zwölfer, and Einserkofel (the 11th, 12th and 1st summits). Only dirt roads run to the hut at the end of this valley, from where there are various walking routes.

A 6-seater cabin lift runs from **Bad Moos/Bagni di San Giuseppe** (✖) at the entrance to the Fischleintal up to the meadows of **Rotwand** (✖) at 1921 m. It operates from 08.30-12.30 and from 13.30-17.30; closed from the end of the first week in Apr to early Jun and from Oct to 21 Dec; one way 6 €, up and back 8 €. At the top there are fantastic views, several walking routes (shown on large plans at both the bottom and top lift stations), ski-runs — and two huts with good cooking: the Rotwandwiesen Hut and the Rudi Hut. In most cases those who want to go higher will have problems, unless they are experienced and well-equipped climbers. But there is one relatively straightforward protected ascent (see Walk 9).

Sexten Dolomites Natural Park

This park encompasses one of the most important areas in the whole Dolomites: the **Sonnenuhr** around Sexten, between **Rotwand, Elferkofel, Zwölfer-kofel** (3094 m) and **Einserkofel**, the isolated **Dreischusterspitze** (3145 m), the world-famous **Drei**

The Drei Zinnen Hut backed by the famous peaks

Zinnen (up to 2999 m) and the **Haunold Massif** (2966 m).

From the Kreuzberg Pass to Lake Dürren the park boundary follows the boundary with the province of Belluno. Wild rock walls like the 'Zwölfers' and the Drei Zinnen, and jagged rock towers like those on Rotwand are just one side of this mountain landscape. The other is the alm landscape between the Drei Zinnen and the Toblingerknoten and between the Toblingerknoten and the Büllelejoch: little lakes, green meadows, and rhododendrons.

Around the Fischleintal and Drei Zinnen the park is well served with tracks and huts; in contrast the northwestern stretch between Bullköpfe and Neunerkofel is quite empty. During the First World War, the Front ran right through this area, via Monte Piana, the Toblingerknoten north of the Drei Zinnen, the Büllele-joch Hut, upper Fischleintal and Rotwand. The emplacements are still there today, just by the trails.

98

Many rare flora can be seen in the park, like the alpine Rhaetian poppy, with its bright yellow- to orange-coloured blooms, which proliferate for instance on the scree slopes between Büllelejoch and the Drei Zinnen Hut.

For information about the park visit the Park House (see page 89).

Kreuzbergpass/Passo Montecroce Comelico

It's just a few minutes from Bad Moos to the **Kreuzbergpass** (1696 m), which links to the Cadore. There's a good hotel at the pass and **walking routes** on both sides. One of the most attractive walks is to the **Rifugio al Popera A. Berti** at 1950 m — Route 124, which begins at the hotel car park (2h30min up, 1h30min back). From the hut there's a very unusual (but equally appealing) view to the Sextner Rotwand and 'Elfer' (the eleventh summit, see page 97) — from its southeast side.

From the north side of the pass

Time: 7h

Grade: straightforward mountain walk on mostly good paths, but you must be fit for the climb and descent of 1100 m. *Note:* For an easier walk round the Drei Zinnen, see Walk 24 on page 173.

Access: bus or car to the end of the motorable road in the Fischleintal, at the Hotel Dolomitenhof (1456 m; large car park, bus stop). From here you can either continue into the valley on foot or take one of the horse-drawn carriages to the Talschluss Hut at the end of the valley (shuttle service from the Hotel Dolomitenhof).

Refreshments: Büllelejoch Hut, Zsigmondy Hut/Rifugio Comici, Drei Zinnen Hut/Rifugio Locatelli. The tiny Büllelejoch Hut (just 11 bunks) is served by helicopter and mini-tractor. It's a magnificent place to spend a night in the mountains, with Tyrolean cooking and the chance to watch the sun set on the Drei Zinnen.

Map: Tabacco 1:25,000 N° 10

Start the walk at the **Talschluss Hut** at the end of the **Fischleintal**, where the north wall of Einserkofel dominates the view. Follow **Route 102/103 (Dolomite High-Level Route 5)** diagonally to the right uphill, until you come to a fork just short of a stream: go uphill to the right here (the way to the left is your return route).

At first you rise alongside the stream, then you curve to the right and the terrain is steeper. When the route flattens out again you reach the **Bödenalm** with its little lake; a little higher up is the **Drei Zinnen Hut** on **Toblinger Riedl** (2438 m, **2h**). It's all happening here, with lots of people coming from the nearby Auronzo Hut, where the road from Misurina in the south ends (see Walk 24). There is a fantastic view to the Drei Zinnen and Paternkofel, which was so doggedly contested during the First World War (an old tunnel is still passable).

From the hut go back to the Bödenalm, but this time take **Route 101** to the right, above the lakes (**Bödenseen**). After crossing several scree gullies you reach the **Büllelejoch** (2522 m). Contour left from this pass to the nearby **Büllelejoch Hut** (2428 m, **4h 15min**) and on to the **Obernbacher Joch** (2519 m). From here you look down to the end of the valley below Zwölferkofel (right) and Hochbrunnerschneid (ahead). Now descend in zigzags. Take a break at the **Zsigmondy Hut** (2224 m, **5h**), then continue on **Route 103**, a high-level route out of the valley. After crossing the Altenstein stream you reach your outgoing route and quickly regain the **Talschluss Hut** (**6h30min**) and the **Hotel Dolomitenhof** in the valley floor (**7h**).

Walk 9: Rotwand/Croda Rossa di Sesto

Time: 6h
Grade: relatively easy, protected climb, but you must be sure-footed and have a head for heights as well as some climbing experience and the right equipment (helmet, etc). The protected climbing path is even accessible to beginner climbers, provided they have the right equipment. From the top station of the Rotwand lift to the peak takes about 3h30min; the return is about 2h30min. But since the total ascent/descent is 1100 m and you'll be reaching an altitude of almost 3000 m, this 'easy' ascent is still *very strenuous.*
Access: car or on foot to Bad Moos, then cabin lift to Rotwand (operates from 08.30-12.30 and from 13.30-17.30; closed from the end of the first week in Apr to early Jun and from Oct to 21 Dec)
Refreshments: Rotwandwiesen Hut and Rudi Hut at the start and end; none en route *(and no water!)*
Map: Tabacco 1:25,000 N° 10
Alternative walk: Rotwand circuit. Shorter than the main walk (by 30min to 1h), *but the same grade and requiring the same equipment.* Follow the main walk to the second crossroads, then keep straight ahead on Route 15a/15b — to the Burgstall, from where steep steps take you up to the main walk route. Turn right and follow the main walk in reverse, down the Rotwandsteig and Route 100, back to the start.

Start the main walk from the **top station of the Rotwand lift**. Go down past the **Rudi Hut** (on your right). Just past it, at a crossroads, you'll see Route 100 — a circuit trail — heading off to the right. *Ignore it* and walk straight ahead across the lovely Rotwand meadows to a second crossroads signposted left to the Kreuzberg Pass and straight ahead to the Burgstall (Alternative walk). Turn *right* here, now following **Route 100** round the northern and western flanks of **Rotwandköpfe**.

At a junction, *leave* Route 100 by turning left up the **Rotwandsteig** (red triangle, signposts), climbing steeply to the ridge. Ladders and cables protect the first steep steps. After a descent into a small cleft, you come to another fork, where you keep right. You pass ruined military emplacements, another ridge area and, after more protected steps, reach the top of the **Sextener Rotwand** (2965 m, **3h30min**).
From here the continuation of the climbing route through the south wall of the mountain is much more difficult and only accessible to really experienced climbers. So retrace your route to the **Rotwand lift** (**6h**).

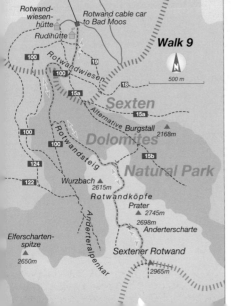

the **Malga Coltrondo** makes a good outing. Take Route 149 about 1.2 km past the pass towards Auronzo (ascent about 300 m; up 2h, back down 1h30min). Or you can drive there: the access road turns off left after about 5 km. This alm has real mountain cooking — with noodles, polenta, alm cheese, apple strudel and honey from their own hives. The area near the *malga* saw fierce trench warfare between Italians and Austrians from 1915 to 1917.

Helm/Monte Elmo

The Karnische Alps stretch from Sexten to Tarvis, forming the border between Austria and Italy. Only the far western stretch of the massif, with **Helm**, lies within the area of this book. Two lifts run up to the alms beneath this peak with its far-reaching views (and ruined hut). The 6-seater cabin lift from Vierschach/Innichen rises to 1500 m; one way 9 €, up and back 12.50 €. Operates Jul to mid-Sep and in winter, from 08.30-12.30 and from 14.00-17.15. The cabin lift direct from Sexten (82 places) rises to 2050 m; prices and operating dates/times as for Vierschach lift.

Time: 3h15min
Grade: easy mountain walk on good paths/tracks; ascent/descent 450 m
Access: car or bus to the large car parks at the valley stations for the Helm lifts at Sexten or Vierschach
Refreshments: Helm restaurant, 2050 m; Sillianer Hut, 2447 m
Map: Tabacco 1:25,000 N° 10

Start out from the **top station of either Helm lift** (fantastic panorama of the Sexten Dolomites): take **Route 20** (between the two stations and signposted '**Hüttersteig**'). After a short climb the way levels out in high alm terrain.

After 20 minutes, *leave* Route 20: go right on an unmarked but well-trodden path, coming to the main ridge of the **Karnische Alps**. Heading steeply up to the left, you meet **Route 20** again, pass ruined barracks and rise to the summit of **Helm** (2434 m), with its closed, ruined hut and a wonderful panorama.

Continue along the crest, sometimes crossing the border into Austria (keep left at a fork) and coming onto a motorable track. From a **saddle** (2381 m) continue up to the **Sillianer Hut** (2447 m, **2h**), where east Tyrolean (Austrian) food awaits you — not very different from South Tyrol's. Return along the wide main route on the Italian side of the ridge. Pass the turn-off to Helm and the Hanspiel Hut and walk back to the **top lift stations** (3h15min).

101

8 GRÖDNER TAL/VAL GARDENA

St. Ulrich • St. Christina • Wolkenstein

Walks: 11, 12, 22; *walking tips:* Luis Trenker Promenade and old railway line to Wolkenstein; Col Raiser to the Regensburger Hut/Rifugio Firenze; Pra da Rì in the Langental; *cycling tip:* from the Seiser Alm down into Gröden by mountain bike

Web sites
www.valgardena.it (for all three above villages)
www.gardena-starbike.com (mountain bike event)
Opening hours: see individual attractions

The Grödner Tal (in Ladin Gherdëina, but usually referred to simply as 'Gröden') may appear to be peaceful farming country, but today the fast-growing villages of St. Ulrich, St. Christina and Wolkenstein virtually merge into each other, and the area is 100% touristic. So naturally the sports possibilities are unbelievable, there are pleasant rooms in all price categories, and even the night life is passable.

It's always 'the season' in this valley — and that doesn't just refer to the hotel and restaurant prices. Perhaps with the single exception of November, you *must* reserve a room in advance. Christmas, February, Easter and from the middle of July to the end of August are simply packed out. Every year Wolkenstein alone has one million overnight guests, and that says it all. Germans and Italians are the principal visitors, then Austrians, Dutch and other nationalities — most recently the Poles. What remains of 'tradition' is limited to Ascension Day, when the young girls wear traditional dress and little 'crowns'.

Sports possibilities are unbeatable: there are 81 lifts (a record for South Tyrol and the Italian Alps), hundreds of kilometres of walking paths, countless hiking trails of all grades, some of the most famous protected climbing routes in the world, and mountain bike routes that leave from the front door of your hotel and follow good little roads and tracks up to well over 2000 m. The mountain huts cater for everything from snacks to overnight stays.

There are good **bus connections** into the valley (SAD bus company) all year round, linking it with Bolzano (via Kastelruth) and Brixen (via Lajen); departures are frequent. In summer there are also buses to the Grödner Joch and Sellajoch, with onward connections via Sella Ronda buses to Canazei, Arabba and Corvara running round the Sella Group in both directions.

As in the Hochpustertal, many events are organised by the whole valley in both summer and winter: concert weeks like the Gardena Winter Festival open-air concerts in March, the Val Gardena Music Festival with

At the Sellajoch Hut under the Langkofel Group

classical music in the summer, walking weeks, evening shopping in high season (until 22.30), the 'Gardena Starbike Mountainbike Event' in mid-July, and the 'Fest Gröden' in typical costume in early August.

The **Valgardena Card** (60 € for one week) gives you free use of 12 lift areas and free travel with the buses in the whole valley between St. Ulrich and the Grödner Joch and Sellajoch, as well as the Sella Ronda buses round the Sella Group. This card is available from the tourist offices. For winter there's the ski bus **Gherdëina Ski-Express** (2 € for one week) allowing you to travel to all the lift areas including Plan de Gralba.

St. Ulrich/Ortisei

St. Ulrich (Urtijëi in Ladin) is the largest village in the Grödner Tal, very touristic, with good hotels — and not cheap! In winter all age groups come here for the skiing, in summer there is a mixture of active sports enthusiasts, walkers and those just looking for some fresh air. Although there is a bypass round the village, traffic jams are common. There are large **car parks** by the valley station for the Seiser Alm and Seceda lifts; otherwise park further out, on Streda Rezia, Streda Trebinger or on the road to the railway station. The most central **bus stop** is on the Plaza S. Antone (Antoni-boden) at the lower end of the pedestrian precinct.

Today you will be hard-pressed in St. Ulrich to find the 'welcome intimacy of a mountain village', which was trumpeted in a Ladin book in 1985. If you stroll around the little town from the main road by the church (Streda Rezia) down to the Antoniboden, you'll pass a couple of beautiful old houses, but that's it. Nothing is left of a 'village', there are no more old farmhouses in the surrounds. Only in the (well worth seeing) museum in the Cësa di Ladins will you see the old dress of the area, the way the

103

farmhouses were once equipped, and the old farm tools. So: leave town as soon as possible and get out on the tracks, paths and trails! Walking is the classic sport in this valley; almost everywhere you can walk out the door of your hotel, step onto a lift and start out. That's the only reason to stay here. Even from town the slim form of Langkofel stands out as a landmark; the massif catches all the last rays of the sun. What if you were up there at sundown? Well, why not? Don't forget — apart from the Grödner Heimatmuseum (a must; see below) there's not a lot to see in St. Ulrich. The shopping area stretches along **Streda Rezia** from below the church square down to the so-called 'Antoniboden' with its little church. This bit of road is full of boutiques, cafés and inns with terraces. Somewhat above the west end of the street is the **parish church of St. Ulrich**, dating from 1797 (built over older foundations). The pews, dating from the 18th century, are especially attractive.

Between the church and the street is an ugly concrete monstrosity dating from the 1970s: the '**Kongresshaus**', where you'll find the tourist office. The building also houses a permanent exhibition of **Gröden wood-carving**.

At the **Antoniboden** the simple church separates the pedestrian zone from the wide square with the bus stop and taxi rank.

St. Anton in Boder (Plaza S. Antone), with its pointed roof and ridge turret, dates from 1673 and is dedicated to the desert hermit Antonius.

The **Museum de Gherdëina** in the **Cësa di Ladins** is a folk museum located in the Ladin Cultural Centre on Streda Rezia, with a number of very interesting objects on display, above all exhibitions of **Gröden lace-**

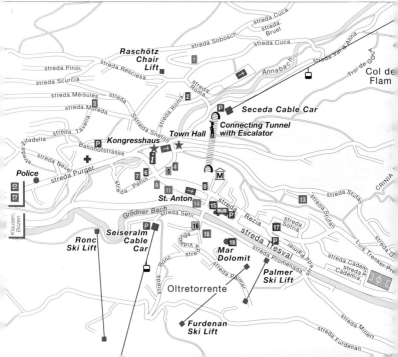

making, including some from the important Vinazer family, who were established here from 1622 until 1817. Next to the religious statues and madonnas you'll see marionettes, jumping jacks, pull-toys and other toys dating from between 1810 and 1940. There are also **minerals** from the Dolomites and other parts of the world, a very interesting **geological section** describing how the Dolomites were formed, and finally an entire room with memorabilia of **Luis Trenker** (see page 107) and archaeological finds. In the entrance to the upper floor there is a huge **fasting cloth** from the church of St. Jakob, with 20 scenes from Christ's Passion (17C). In earlier times this would have hung in the church choir during Lent. *Museum open Feb/Mar, Tue/Fri from 14.00-17.00 and Thu 10.00-12.00; Jun and Sep-mid Oct, Tue-Fri from 14.00-18.00 and Thu also from 10.00-12.00; Jul/Aug, Mon-Fri 10.00-12.00 and 14.00-18.00, Sun 14.00-18.00. Entry fee 3 €, children under 7 free.*

The village of **St. Jakob/S. Giacomo** (Sacun in Ladin; ✘) is a short way east of St. Ulrich. The spire of **St. Jakob's church** rising above the trees gives it away before you get up to it. This Gothic church (unfortunately always closed) and its circular cemetery (always open) stand behind high walls in a clearing in the woods half an hour above the village. If you come by car, park by the signposted turn-off and walk on to the church (there is no road).

Part of its baroque furnishings can be seen in the folk museum (see page 104), like some of the altar statues and the magnificent fasting cloth. On the outside south-facing wall (best light at noon) are very beautiful, recently restored late Gothic frescoes, including a gigantic St. Christopher carrying the Christ Child on his shoulder.

Walking tip: to Wolkenstein on the Luis Trenker Promenade and the old railway. How pleasant it is to be able to get to Wolkenstein and Plan via St. Christina on this lovely walkway rather than the road. The promenade has been laid out over a narrow-gauge railway built during the First World War. It's now a lovely stroll, slightly descending, between the three villages. At the outset, at Streda Stufan in St. Ulrich, it's called the '**Luis Trenker Promenade**'; shortly after you pass the tunnel to the Seceda lift on the left, and outside St. Ulrich it's called the '**Alter Bahnweg**' (Old Railway Line). From St. Ulrich to Wolkenstein

ating and drinking   **A** **ccommodation**

Concordia
Mauriz
Traube
Vedl Mulin
Dolomiti Madonna
Anna Stuben
Mar Dolomit

ight life

Mario's Bar
Mauriz
Winebar Cascade

3 Planlim
4 Adler
7 Am Stetteneck
10 Pichler
12 Rodes
13 Grones
18 Grödnerhof
20 Hartmann

C **afés**

1 Art-Café Funtanela
8 Demetz
11 Corso
14 Haiti

150 m

St. Ulrich/Urtijëi
(Ortisei)

20

Streda Josef Skasa
OLD RAILWAY LINE

, Christina,
Volkenstein

The Ladins

The Ladins of the Dolomites live around the massive Sella Group in the Ladin valleys — the Grödner Tal, Gadertal, Fassatal, Buchenstein and Ampezzo. They make up the majority of the population in these areas. The Ladin-speaking area became part of the Roman Empire in 15 BC. The Romans introduced Latin, which evolved into Dolomites-Ladin in this area — part of the Rhaeto-romance language, also spoken in Surselva and Engadina in eastern Switzerland (Romansh) and the Comelico-Ladin spoken in the upper Cadore (for example in Auronzo) and Friulian. All speakers of Rhaeto-romance languages can understand each other. Until now there has been no Dolomites-Ladin official grammar or written rules, but this is being developed on the Swiss model.

Even Italians have problems understanding Ladin, despite having learned (over three generations) to cope with German in South Tyrol. This has political repercussions: while most German speakers in the province of Bozen-South Tyrol have a great deal of autonomy, Ladin is spread over three provinces, but is still without political representation. A Ladin province is certainly not on the cards at present.

The German-speaking South Tyroleans, the Italian-speakers in the province of Trentino and the Ladins have a long common history, having lived together since the Bavarian land acquisition in the early Middle Ages in one region — Tyrol. For 500 years the Habsburgs ruled over all three peoples. Together they developed a culture, they wore the same clothing, ate the same food, built the same style of house and practised the same life-style. Thus south of the Sella Group, where the neighbours were Italian, not German, the Ladins thought of themselves — and still think of themselves — as Tyroleans. Even in Cortina d'Ampezzo, otherwise so strongly Italian in character, Ladins are members of the typical Tyrolean 'Schützen' (see page 21). And in the Fassatal, Buchenstein and Ampezzo the Ladins feel more empathy with the German Tyroleans than with their Italian neighbours. After the First World War the Ladins, who all previously belonged to the Austrian Tyrol, were divided up between the provinces of Bolzano/South Tyrol, Trentino and Belluno. But this has not changed their feeling of being one people.

takes about 1h30min; you can either walk back in about the same time or take one of the regular SAD buses.

The **Raschötz chair lift** runs up from Streda Resciesa in St. Ulrich (1280 m) via an intermediate station to the alm pastures of the **Ausserraschötz** at 2093 m. From up here the view to Schlern, the Seiser Alm and the Langkofel Group is phenomenal. An easy walk, with only 80 m of ascent, runs from the top station to the **Raschötz Hut**; everybody can manage this. The more hardy can then go on to the **Ausserraschötz summit** (2281 m) and look out over the imposing rock flanks in the Villnösstal on the other side of the mountain. The chair lift operates from early June to mid-

Oct, from 08.30-17.30; one way 9 €, up and back 12 €.

A **cabin lift** runs up to **Seceda**. The valley station indicates how important this lift is: from the pedestrian area (Plaza S. Antone) there is a series of covered escalators up to the Luis Trenker Promenade, from where another escalator (in a tunnel) runs straight to the cable car! In winter the top of the mountain is well served by all kinds of lifts, but at the start and end of the skiing season one can only go as far as the intermediate station. In summer Seceda is a real walkers' paradise. Those just out for a stroll stay on the slopes of the **Aschgleralm** and visit the Troier and Daniel snack bars. But if your knees can take it, you can walk 1200 m down to St. Ulrich or Wolkenstein. In summer the Seceda lift is normally open from mid-Jun to mid-Oct, 08.30-17.30; one way 16 €, up and back 24 €.

From St. Ulrich it's also easy to reach the **Seiser Alm:** take the cable car from **Oltretorrente** on Streda Setil. In high season this runs from 08.30-18.00; in Jun and from the end of Sep to mid-Oct from 08.30-12.30 and from 13.30-18.00. One-way 9 €, up and back down 12 €. This lift rises to the **Col da Mesdi** on the Seiser Alm (2005 m; see page 45).

The views from here to Langkofel are so fantastic that you might be tempted not to go any further. But there are plenty of walking trails through the flower-filled meadows of this alm — and snack bars and inns all within a stone's throw of each other. The mountain restaurant Mont Sëuc with 'panorama windows' has both snacks and warm meals

Luis Trenker (1892–1990) *came from St. Ulrich — the very heart of the Dolomites. Although he studied as an architect, he built a career as mountain climber, author, actor and director — all based on a characteristic mix of adventure, mountaineering, nerves of steel, 'schmalz' and sex appeal. The silent film 'Kampf ums Matterhorn' (in English called 'The Challenge') catapulted him to fame in 1928. This film — and later films like 'Berge in Flammen' (Mountains in Flames) — idealised living close to nature, in contrast to 'spoiled' town life. This romantic approach appealed to the Fascist powers in Berlin and Rome as much as to the public. Since Trenker didn't protest against the dictatorships, after 1945 he was persona non grata in Germany. But because of the way he projected himself — the attractive, if eccentric, mountaineering enthusiast with a pipe — his films have become icons in the German-speaking mass culture. Many of his films are available in English — just surf the web!*

daily; on Wednesday evenings there are 'candle-light dinners' (when the lift runs till 23.30).

Cycling tip: *from the Seiser Alm down into Gröden by mountain bike.* Since mountain bikes are allowed on the Seiser Alm cable car to the Col da Mesdi, this makes a delightful day out (see Tabacco 1:25,000 map N° 5). A little road begins at the upper lift station: take this down to the **Schgaguler Schwaige** (inn) and a small pass, where a wider road joins from the right. Follow the road in a big bend to the left over

Walk 11: From Seceda to the Regensburger Hut and Wolkenstein

Time: 3h
Grade: straightforward mountain walk on mostly good tracks across alms; ascent of only 100 m; descent 1070 m
Access: Seceda cabin lift from St. Ulrich; return by bus from Wolkenstein
Refreshments: Troier Snack Bar (Tyrolean cooking), Regensburger Hut/Rifugio Firenze, Juac Hut
Map: Tabacco 1:25,000 N° 5

Up on Seceda your heart beats faster — if only from the sight of the massive scree-slopes ahead, falling from the mountain down to the west. Fantastic views await you up here — the Geisler peaks, Puez Group and across alms to Sella and Langkofel.

Start out at the **top lift station on Seceda**: at the fork, go left on the slightly descending route signed to the Panascharte — heading towards Sass Rigais and the Geisler peaks. At the **Panascharte** ('gap'; 2450 m) there is a

On Seceda, with Langkofel opposite

vertiginous view down to the north side of the Geisler peaks, but almost nothing to be seen of the Villnösstal.

From here go down the slope, ignoring two turn-offs to the left. Pass the **Troier Snack Bar** and go more or less straight ahead on **Route 1**, keeping straight on at a crossroads. Drop gently and then (beyond a fence) more steeply to the **Regensburger Hut** (2037 m, **1h15min**).

An access road begins here; follow this downhill for about 20 minutes, then turn left on **Route 3**, a track. From the shoulder near modern **Gasthof Juac** (1903 m) you can already see Wolkenstein below. Keep on Route 3, crossing an asphalt road. Go through the hamlet of **Daunei**, and from there take the road. On the big bend to the right, you can take a short-cut left across meadows down to the Puez road and **Wolkenstein** (1560 m, **3h**).

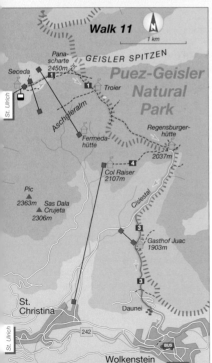

the high expanses of the alm —
first to the **Ritschschwaige** (keep
left at the fork just before this
inn), to the **Radauer Schwaige**
(where you go left again). Now a
forestry road is followed through
the **Val de Iender** almost all the
way down to the floor of the
Grödener Tal. At this point keep
left at a fork, and lightly-
trafficked roads will take you
back to **Oltretorrente** and
St. Ulrich.

St. Christina/S. Cristina (✖)

Of the three large places in
Gröden, St. Christina (S. Crestina
in Ladin) is the most unspoilt,
even though it's geared for
tourists and full of businesses.
It's an ideal starting point for
walks in the Puez Group, to the
Seiser Alm and to Langkofel. A
whole array of good hotels,
pleasant restaurants and other
facilities cater for leisurely, active
and very active holidays.
There are a few **parking places**
on the main road below the town
hall (Rathaus) and large **car
parks** by the Iman Sports Centre.
(*Tip:* Don't miss a visit to the
Nativity by the Iman Centre,
reputed to be the world's largest.
It's open all year round. All the
life-sized figures in this 72 sqm
stall are of hand-carved wood;
they stand, sit or kneel before
Mary with Child, Joseph, the
Three Kings and a shepherd — to
say nothing of the animals!
There are **bus stops** below the
Rathaus, at the entrance to the
village and at the exit (by the
Marciaconi supermarket).
The Gröden is narrower here
than at St. Ulrich, so St. Christina
is a long strung-out village, built
to avoid the steep slopes. Only on
the sunny terrace between

Plesdinaz and Ulëta are there
houses again — and the inhabitants enjoy fantastic views to the
Langkofel Group, Sella, the Seiser
Alm and Schlern. To the south
the cool steep shaded slopes
constrain settlement. No one
wants to live there, only skiers
find these slopes interesting,
since their pistes go right down
into the valley. Sights? Just the
parish church and the Fischburg;
all the rest is nature. Note:
Strictly speaking, the left side of
the stream, in the Cislestal,
belongs to Wolkenstein (for
example the Maciaconi supermarket), but in daily life it's
considered part of St. Christina
and so described here.
The original Romanesque **parish
church**, of which the tower still
remains, was rebuilt in Gothic
style in the 15th century (the
choir dates from this time).
Around 1730 the church was
enlarged and modernised in the
baroque style; from 1840-45
historicism also played a role.
The main altar, in gold, amber
and white still remains from the
baroque era (by Dominik
Vinazer, around 1690). The
reliquaries below the side altars
are also baroque, the bones of
several saints lie behind glass.
The cemetery in front of the door
is most inviting for a little circuit,
as most of the graves have
beautiful wrought-iron crosses.
Don't miss the massive stone
houses below the church, several
stories high, now the elementary
school. They are the only remains
of the time before tourism
invaded the village.
On the other, shady side of the
valley is the beautifully-kept
Fischburg. Two arcaded
courtyards, two living areas, a

walks and mountain treks. The easy walk to the **Rifugio Comici** is especially popular (1h30min return), because you can always get a meal there. And naturally you can start the famous circuit of Langkofel here (Walk 12). There are fantastic views to the Seiser Alm and Schlern on one side and the Sella Group on the other.

The **Col Raiser** (2107 m; ✕; see map on page 108) is quickly reached by lift, and the **Col Raiser Hut** a pleasant place to take a break. In high season the lift operates from 08.00-17.30; from Jun to mid-Jul and from mid-Sep to mid-Oct until 17.00; one-way 10 €, up and back down 13 €. But even less energetic visitors like to take a little stroll, and for that the short walk from Col Raiser to the **Regensburger Hut/Rifugio Firenze** in the **Cislestal** is ideal (only 60 m descent and return ascent; 30 min each way). This 'classic' mountain hut serves authentic Tyrolean dishes. Or one can do the very beautiful little walk through the flowering meadows of the **Aschgleralm** to the **Troier** Snack Bar with the old and new alm huts. If you have more energy, you can climb Seceda (Walk 11, in the reverse direction) or even Sass Rigais (if you have the right climbing equipment).

chapel, two four-cornered main towers and three minor towers combine to create a very eye-catching ensemble. The castle was initially built between 1622 and 1641 by a man from Wolken-stein, at a time when no one built this kind of residence. Unfortunately it cannot be visited, as it is privately owned.

From not far above St. Christina's parish church the old Calvary (**Via Crucis Col da Mëssa**) runs up to the strung-out hamlet of **Plesdinaz** on a sunny terrace. It's a trail lower down, but a road near the top. The 14 Stations of the Cross have been recently restored by Gröden artists (bronze on porphyry).

From **Monte Pana** south of St. Christina (reached by chair lift) there's another chair lift up to **Mont de Sëura** (2025 m). Both lifts operate mid-Jun to mid-Sep, from 08.30-12.15 and 13.15-17.00 or 18.00; one way 5/9.50 €, up and back 7.50/13.50 €. In winter skiers tackle a quite difficult run down from here to Monte Pana, but in summer this top station is the starting point for magnificent

Wolkenstein/Selva

Wolkenstein is the most active of the three large villages in Gröden; the 'shoulder season' is unknown here! What was just a hamlet a few decades ago is today an internationally known holiday centre.

Most of the accommodation is in quite expensive hotels and apartments, but there are a few economical private rooms; 'cheap' does not exist. People don't come here, however, because of the good hotels or food; they come for the action. Winter sports dominate, with skiing, ice-skating (large covered rink) and tobogganing. Three lift areas give access to the surrounding mountains — Langkofel, Sella and the Puez Group, all of them around or above 3000 m. Summer sports are also catered for: walking, mountain climbing, mountain biking and paragliding. Or you can just go out mushroom-hunting in the beautiful spruce woods on the north slopes of the Langkofel Group.

Parking on the main road is not allowed; there are covered **car parks** near the pharmacy and the Hotel Gran Baita. There are **bus connections** to Bolzano, Brixen and Plan de Gralba; in summer there are also buses over the Sellajoch to Corvara in the Hochabteital and Canazei in the Fassatal, with several bus stops along the main road.

The remains of **Wolkenstein Castle** are unspectacular, but the setting is most impressive. The castle was built below a rock overhang and in some places into the rock itself, so it's hard to tell where the rock ends and the ruins begin. The castle was destroyed during the German Peasants' Revolt of 1525.

Even the least energetic walker can get deep into the heart of the **Puez-Geisler Natural Park** on the easy trail in the **Langental/Vallunga** — the route to the **Pra**

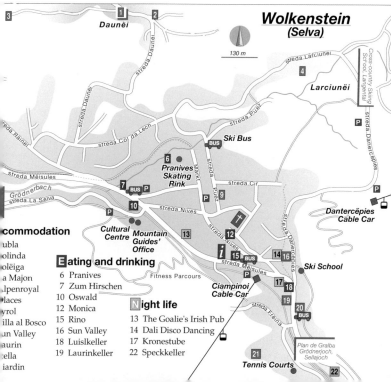

Wolkenstein (Selva)

Daunëi

130 m

streda Larciunei

Cross-country Skiing Sci-fondi Langental

Larciunëi

streda Puez

streda Daunëi

streda Col da Lech

streda Rainel

streda Mëisules

Grödnerbach
streda La Selva

Ski Bus

BUS

Pranives Skating Rink

Markt

streda Puez

streda Cir

streda Nives

streda Danercëpies

Dantercëpies Cable Car

commodation

ubla
olinda
olëiga
a Majon
lpenroyal
laces
yrol
illa al Bosco
un Valley
aurin
ella
iardin

Cultural Centre

Mountain Guides' Office

Eating and drinking

6 Pranives
7 Zum Hirschen
10 Oswald
12 Monica
15 Rino
16 Sun Valley
18 Luislkeller
19 Laurinkeller

Fitness Parcours

streda Nives

streda Danercëpies

Ski School

streda Mëisules

Ciampinoi Cable Car

Night life

13 The Goalie's Irish Pub
14 Dali Disco Dancing
17 Kronestube
22 Speckkeller

streda Fraina

Plan de Gralba
Grödnerjoch,
Sellajoch

Tennis Courts

Walk 12: Circuit round Langkofel/Sassolungo

Time: 6h30min-7h; or start at the Sellajochhaus (bus stop, car park) and shorten the walk by 1h by omitting the detour to Ciampinoi
Grade: strenuous mountain walk requiring endurance; ascent/descent of 550 m. *A couple of tricky sections demand care.*
Access: Ciampinoi lift from Wolkenstein
Refreshments: Plattkofel Hut, Rifugio Sandro Pertini, Rifugio Friedrich August, Sellajochhaus, Rifugio Emilio Comici
Map: Tabacco 1:25,000 N° 5
The walk begins at the **upper Ciampinoi lift station (2280 m).**

Take the trail down to the **Tiesasattel** (2127 m) and, just past it, head right along the clear route signposted to 'Rif. Comici'. Ignore two forks up to the left, beyond which the trail is numbered **Route 526a**. You cross the large corrie below the northern walls of Langkofel — first descending slightly, then climbing. There's a lot of scree and mountain rubble to be crossed on the fairly strenuous ascent to the **Ciaulonch saddle** (2113 m, **1h**), from where you have fantastic views — above all to Schlern and the Seiser Alm.

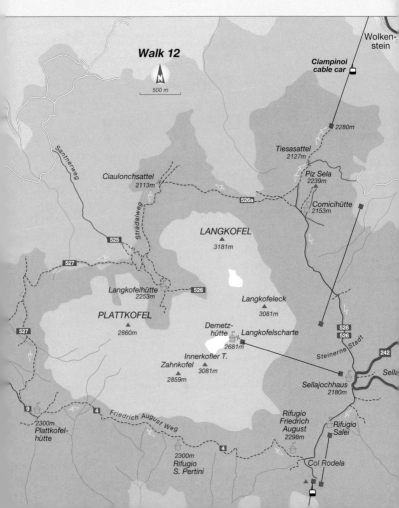

Taking a break on meadows below Langkofel, with a fine view to Sella

From here the **Stradalweg** takes you into the Langkofel corrie: *take care* on the first steep and somewhat exposed part of this trail; it is very short, and the way quickly improves. The trail forks in the **Langkofel corrie** (**1h30min**): ignore the route up left to the Langkofel Hut and a trail rising from below. After crossing the little road to the hut, **Route 527** takes you across the corrie and past three turn-offs to the right. Eventually you meet **Route 9** and follow it to the **Plattkofel Hut** (2300 m, **3h15min**). (The toilets here are exemplary!)

This is where the popular **Friedrich August Weg** (**Route 4**) begins, named for the Saxon king who loved to walk; it has tremendous views and a rich array of flora, including the many-frayed pink, *Dianthus superbus.* The trail contours past the **Pertini Hut**; then you come to the **Friedrich August Hut** (2298 m, **4h30min**) and shortly afterwards to **Col Rodela** with its lift. From here take the new footpath on the left, then the little road past the **Salei Hut**. At a small saddle, follow the track down towards the Sella-joch-haus (and do watch where you're walking, despite the view to Sella!).

Once at the **Sellajochhaus** (2180 m, **5h15min**) — a misnomer, since it's 1km below the pass — pick up **Route 526/528** (on the far side of the car park and signed to the Rif. Comici). This first runs through the so-called 'Stone City' (**Steinerne Stadt**), where you cross a fence and go straight over a crossroads. *Take care* in this wild area of fallen mountain rock.

At the **Comici Hut** (2153 m, **6h**) take some refreshment on board for the last leg back up to the **Tiesa saddle** (ignore the fork to the left before it) and final steep spur to the **upper Ciampinoi lift station** (**6h30min**).

da Rì at the end of the valley is really easy (allow about 1h). Beyond Pra da Rì the trails are narrower and more demanding. Experienced hill walkers can go on from Pra da Rì, heading over the top of the valley with its bubbling karst springs and up to the modern Puez Hut on a steep trail (Route 14). Those with climbing experience and equipment can take Route 14a to the Somafurcia Pass and continue on Dolomites High-Level Route 2 through the corrie above Lake Crespeina to the Forcella Danter les Pizes and down to the top station of the **Dantercëpies** cabin lift (operates from end Jun to end Sep, 08.30-12.30 and 13.30-17.00; one way 7 €, up and back 11 €.

Ciampinoi (Ciampinëi in Ladin) is reached from Wolkenstein by cabin lift (end Jun till Sep, from 08.30-12.30 and 13.30-17.30; one way 8 €, up and back 13 €). Not only is there a world-famous ski route from this peak down into the valley, but also walks in the area north of Langkofel and around the mountain. Even if you just stay at the lift station, your day is made: the panorama — south to Langkofel, east to Sella, north to the Puez Group and west to the Seiser Alm and Schlern — is breathtaking. But for the energetic, the walk *par excellence* is the circuit round Langkofel described on pages 112-113.!

The **Grödner Joch/Passo di Gardena** is the pass that links Gröden with the Ladin Hochabteital and Gadertal and is the shortest route to Bruneck. The **Sellajoch** links Gröden with the Fassatal in Trentino; this is also Ladin country between Canazei

(which you reach on the other side) and Moëna. The Grödner Joch is full of inns, whereas there is hardly a building on the Sellajoch (the **Sellajochhaus**, named for the pass, is in fact 1 km further north and downhill). It's only down here at the Sellajochhaus that you'll find **parking places** and a gondola lift (mid-Jun to about 9 Oct, from 08.15-16.30; one way 10 €, up and back 14 €) to the **Langkofelscharte** with the **Toni Demetz Hut** (2685 m), where a couple of walking routes begin. If you like, you can start Walk 12 at the Sellajochhaus and save about an hour's walking. Only climbers tackle the mighty walls of Sella from this pass (via the protected Pössnecker climbing route).

Sella Ronda

Whatever drivers and motorcyclists can do, a skier can do: that must have been the basic idea behind the Sella Ronda. There are so many lifts on the mountain, and the network of pistes is so tightly woven, that it's possible to ski round the Sella Group in just one day. But of course to do this is extremely strenuous and has the added disadvantage that the last lifts go down at 17.00 (or even 16.30). So what do you do when you're stuck in Corvara but your room is in Wolkenstein (of course it's no problem if you have a mobile and someone willing to play taxi). The organisers describe the 'ronda' as 'not difficult', but with 26 km of pistes (40 km total distance) and a height difference of 4500 m, it's unlikely you'll have much energy for après-ski.

9 GADERTAL/VAL BADIA

Hochabteital • Corvara • Kolfuschg • Sella Group • Puez Group • Stern • St. Kassian • middle Gadertal • Abtei • Wengen • St. Martin in Thurn • Campilltal and the Val di Molins • Enneberg • Fanes-Sennes-Prags Natural Park

Walks: 7, 13, 14, 15, 16; *walking tips:* Rifugio Scotoni; Heiligkreuz pilgrimage church; Val di Molins; *cycling tips:* from St. Martin towards Brixen; Fanes and Sennes by mountain bike

Web sites
www.altabadia.org
www.museumladin.it
www.sanvigilio.com
Opening hours: see individual attractions

The Gadertal/Val Badia stretches for more than 30 km from the Pustertal/Val Pusteria at Bruneck to the foot of the massive Sella Group. Although it is one of the most intensely touristic valleys in the Dolomites, it is one of the least affected by tourism.

If you're staying in the shadow of the mighty Sella massif in the upper valley (Hochabteital/Alta Badia) — for instance at Corvara, Kolfuschg, Stern or St. Kassian — you'll notice that despite the glorious nature all around, many *viles* (as the Ladins call their narrowly built hamlets) give the impression of being locked in a time-warp. The Hochabteital attracts masses of mountain climbers and walkers with its many hotels and *pensions,* as well as dozens of alm huts doing business. In contrast, the hamlets of Pedratsches, St. Leonhard and St. Martin in Thurn in the lower valley are hardly visited. The valley is greener here, wider and more plentiful than further up. The Enneberg/Marebbe area, the third landscape of the Gadertal, borders Bruneck and Kronplatz, and thus the German-speaking areas. St. Vigil, its main village, grew very quickly and is a bustling tourist centre, but the *viles* on the sunny terrace above it still live from agriculture. The old parish village called Enneberg Pfarre is today just an unimportant hamlet.

The Gadertal (including all its tributary valleys) is often called the Abteital in German. The Italian (and also the Ladin) name, Val Badia, means exactly the same thing: both translate to Valley of the Abbey. In the Middle Ages and in early modern times the whole valley (except for the area of St. Martin in Thurn and Kolfuschg) belonged to the Sonnenburg Nunnery in the Pustertal (see page 73).

Hochabteital/Alta Badia

When you descend the hairpins from the Grödner Joch, the basin of Kolfuschg and Corvara between the Puez Group with mighty Sass Sóngher and the precipitous rock walls of the Sella Group looks like a green paradise. But it's a paradise in which there has been a lot of building in recent years; you have to look hard to find the old farmhouses clustered around the church at Kolfuschg. The quality of the accommodation is high, and so are the prices — Kolfuschg and Corvara advertise on quality, not on price. It's the same story in Stern, a bit further down the valley, and in St. Kassian in its own friendly valley. Obviously there are many restaurants to cater for all the hotels and *pensions*.

There are also walking trails wherever you look: walks through meadows at the foot of Sella, walks on the alms of Piz la Ila and Pralongia in the east, walks in the Fanes Group to the lovely Fanesalm and from there perhaps even further on Dolomites High-Level Route 1. Then there are high-mountain routes in the Sella and Puez massifs, climbing routes like the difficult protected climb (the 'Pisciadu'), and in winter all kinds of lifts and ski trails — including the Ski World Cup's famous Gran Risa black piste, on which the great Alberto Tomba celebrated his retirement.

Corvara is dominated by Sass Sòngher

The tourist board for the whole area (see 'Web sites' above) offers a **TouristCard** giving some reductions, for instance to sports centres and lifts. When visiting the valley you can **park** by the lift stations (for instance at Corvara and Kolfuschg). **SAD buses** link the valley villages with each other and with Bruneck, but connections to the west and south are poor. Instead there is the **'Sella Ronda' bus** service (summer only) which rounds the Sella Group in both directions several times a day. The **Alta Badia Mountain Pass** gives free travel on all the above buses and lifts; passes are available for 3-4 days (30 €, concessions 26 €) and 5-7 days (38 €, concessions 32 €); there are also 12-14 day passes and season cards.

Corvara (✕)

You'll get the best overall impression of Corvara in the upper part of the village, where the **Streda Col Alt** describes a curve to gain height. You look through the whole new town and up to the slopes of Pescosta, where there are more houses every year. Above this the mighty walls of Sass Sòngher rear up; its tent-like peak forms the southeastern viewing point of the Puez Group. The magnificent setting is Corvara's greatest asset — apart from the golf coursea bit above the village, on the road to the Campolongo Pass. Otherwise Corvara is fairly uninteresting,

View to the Sella Group (Walk 13)

with pseudo-Tyrolean architecture (often with false-looking decoration and a surplus of balcoies) and too much asphalt on unbuilt areas. Hotels are good, but expensive.

The new church is a typical 1950s building, but it's worth having a look at Corvara's **old church**, now just a chapel. Its altar triptych dating from 1520 has a painting ascribed to the Donau School (perhaps a pupil of Albrecht Altdorfer), depicting the decapitation of St. Catherine.

A particularly lovely **walking route** runs from the valley station of the Boé lift to the Pisciadú waterfalls and the Val de Mesdi. From there you can follow flower-rich meadows to Kolfuschg (Route 650) with wonderful views to Sass Songher.

Lifts run from Corvara to **Col Alto** (one way 5.30 €, up and back 7.60 €), **Boè** (one way 7 €, up and back 9 €), **Vallon** (one way 4 €, up and back 6 €), and **Pralongià** (one way 3.70 €, up and back 5.40 €, closed Thu).

Kolfuschg/Colfosco (✖)

While Corvara looks north, Kolfuschg has a sunny south-facing aspect and a view to the imposing, almost vertical north wall of the Sella Group, rising to 1000 m. The old part of the village (at 1650 m!) is almost completely hidden in the mass of new buildings. It's hard to believe that Kolfuschg, so easily reached today, was once totally isolated. Until the late 19th century there was no road through the Gadertal and the village wasn't even a parish in its own right; it belonged to Lajen in the Eisacktal (as did all of Gröden). But there was no road there either, until one was built over the Grödner Joch (only fully completed around 1970) — just a mule track. Once Kolfuschg was joined to the Gadertal road, it came under the administration of Buchenstein on the far side of the Campolongo Pass, where there had already been a road down to Arabba in existence since 1901. It's worth seeing the late Gothic

Walk 13: Piz Boé, the highest peak in the Sella Group

See also the photograph on page 5

Time: 7h30min-9h. It's best to allow two days for this walk; really strong walkers can do it in one day, but then it is *very* strenuous.

Grade: strenuous hike, with an ascent of 1200 m and descent of 1150 m. You must be sure-footed and have a head for heights.

Access: bus from Gröden or the Hochabteital to the Grödner Joch (2121 m); return on the Boé cable car to Corvara

Refreshments/overnight stay: Pisciadú Hut/Rifugio F. Cavazza, 2585 m, run by the CAI Bologna; Rifugio Boé, 2871 m, SAT, 55 beds; Capanna Piz Fassa, 3152 m, private, 4 beds; Rifugio Franz Kostner al Vallon, 2500 m, CAI Bozen (www.rifugio kostner.it)

Map: Tabacco 1:25,000 N° 7

Start the walk at the **Grödner Joch:** at the pass pick up **Route 2** signposted to Sella. This runs over the grassy **Col de Frea** at the foot of the pillar-like wall of the Sella Massif (see photograph on page 117).

A traverse across mountain rubble leads to **Val Selùs**, where the way leads steeply downhill. There's a good but narrow route down the loose scree, with wire ropes on the upper sections protecting the steep steps (inexperienced walkers are likely to cause hold-ups here). On the far side of a low pass you reach the **Pisciadú Hut** in a karst basin (2585 m, **2h**); somewhat lower down is a lake with the same name.

Walk past the lake on **Route 666** (also Dolomites High-Level Route 2) below the rock walls of **Cima Pisciadú** and into **Val Tita**.

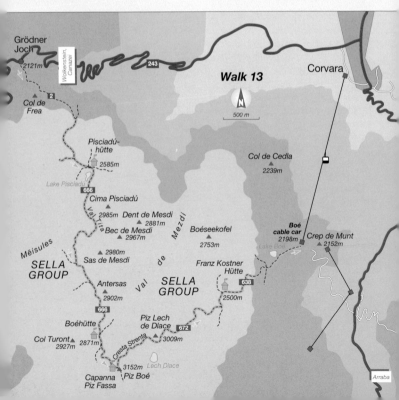

From its upper reaches an old snow gully leads to the high alm plateau of **Mëisules**, with a fine view to the south. From here the route crosses the stony plateau, making for **Antersas**. Again protective wires are in place where you pass to the right of this peak. Just afterwards you reach the **Boé Hut** (2871 m). Behind this hut there is another steep ascent, scree, a rock ledge with wire ropes; finally a fairly easy clamber over boulders and you're on **Piz Boé** with the modern hut, **Capanna Piz Fassa** (3152 m; **5h15min**).

The ongoing route runs a short way back over the ridge, until you can head right on **Route 672** via the **Cresta Strenta**, a somewhat exposed path again protected with wires. This takes you to **Piz Lech de Dlace** (3009 m), below which you can see the glimmering ice lake, Lech Dlace.

From here the way continues over easy slopes down to a large terrace before entering a narrow rock valley (more protective wires).

Turn left at the bottom end of this valley and you'll come to the **Franz Kostner Hut** on a low hill (2500 m, **6h45min**). Signposts at the hut point the way to the end of the walk — **Crep de Munt**. En route you pass pretty **Lake Boé** before coming to the **upper station of the Boé cable car** (2198 m, **7h30min-9h**).

Walk 13: view from the secured trail down into Val de Mezdi

church of **St. Vigil**, with arched windows and a small baroque onion dome. One or two old Ladin houses *(ciasa)* with stone walls on the ground floor and some wooden cladding on the upper floors (for insulation) can still be seen in the old village, and in the surrounding hay meadows one can see a few old *majun* (the simple hay barns).

Sella Group

Whether you round Sella by car, motorcycle, bicycle, on foot or on skis, it will be a memorable experience. This mighty massif, culminating in Piz Boé at 3152 m, lies just in the centre of the Ladin lands, where all the Ladin valleys to Ampezzo begin.

Massive walls encircle a wild high plateau; they can only be mastered by experts using the protected climbing routes. Karst dominates the region, so there's

119

no flowing water, mostly very dry vegetation, and bright chalk, its layers still easily seen. This is not a place for walkers; those who approach Sella must be climbers and have the right equipment. From the north the Boé lift from Corvara is the easiest approach for most people; from the south they come on the lift from the Pordoi Pass on Sass Pordoi.

Puez Group

Sass Sòngher (2665 m) above Corvara is just one of many viewpoints on the gigantic plateau of the Puez Group. This massif is shared by the Grödner Tal, Hochabteital and Villnösstal: access from the Hochabteital is via the Grödner Joch, Kolfuschg (Plan Frara funicular, one way 10 €, up and back 14 €) or Stern. In spite of the proximity of so

many tourist centres, the wide area of the plateau is quite lonely — people are just more attracted to Sella opposite.

Read more about this massif under Villnösstal (page 40), Grödner Tal (page 108), and the Puez-Geisler Natural park (page 42).

Stern/La Villa (✕)

Nothing much has changed here in the old village above the road; only a few houses stand between the church and the Renaissance **Ansitz Ciastel Colz** (now a hotel and restaurant). The view to the Fanes Group (see Walk 14 over-leaf) is fantastic: from right to left you see the Cunturines peaks (3064 m), Lavarela (3034 m) and the north-facing rock wall of Kreuzkofel.

What attracts tourists, however, is the lift to **Piz la Ila**; it can carry

View to the flanks of the Sella massif from the Puez Group — the Gadertal begins at its feet.

Lagazuoi in the most southerly reaches of the Fanes Group. The highest point is the Passo di Valparola (2168 m), from where the Falzàrego Pass is only 2 km distant. There are **parking places** (and a **bus stop**) by the community building, on the main through road, and by the Piz Sorega lift.

Accommodation in St. Kassian matches up well against that in the much larger villages, and it doesn't lack for walking routes either: the Fanes, Puez and Sella groups are around the corner, and there is a lift straight up to the gorgeous meadows of Pralongia (Piz Sorega lift: one way 5.80 €, up and back 8.30 €). Moreover, it's only an hour by car to Cortina.

2200 people an hour! (Open daily Jul to mid-Sep and winter, one way 6.90 €, up and back 9.90 €.) That's especially important in winter, when for example the Ski World Cup Race on the famous 'Gran Risa' black slope down from Piz la Ila down to Stern takes place in December. Alberto Tomba won it eight times.

In summer, however, the area between the mountain station on Piz la Ila and the **Pralongia ridge** is a family-friendly walking area: meadows and pastures wherever the eye can see, a lot of water to paddle in, no dangerous places. And huts with good food and play areas for children.

St. Kassian/S. Cassiano (✕)

St. Kassian's valley runs from Stern via the main village of St. Kassian and the hamlet of **Armentarola** up to the walls of

Walking tip: Rifugio Scotoni. This easy walk along the trail from Stern to Lagazuoi starts from the car park at Capanna Alpina (reached by an access road south of St. Kassian). The Rifugio Scotoni is open summer and winter, with good home cooking in a pleasant atmosphere. Allow 45min each way; see the map for Walk 14 on page 122.

The middle Gadertal/Val Badia

The middle valley between Stern/La Villa and St. Martin in Thurn is, after Buchenstein, the most unspoilt of the Ladin valleys. You don't notice this so much from the valley road as you do in the little villages above and in the many *viles*, the Ladin hamlets.

The villages of Pedratsches and

Walk 14: From Stern to the Fanes Group and St. Kassian

Time: 9h30min-12h; a two-day walk for really fit hikers; an overnight in the very comfortable Fanes Hut is highly recommended.

Grade: strenuous hike, with an ascent of 1300 m and descent of 1050 m. You must be sure footed and have a head for heights, especially for the hour-long stretch before the Lavarela Hut.

Access: bus or car to Stern; return from the Bar Saré to Stern by bus or taxi

Refreshments/overnight stay: Rifugio Lavarella; Rifugio Fanes; Capanna Alpina

Map: Tabacco 1:25,000 N° 7

The contrast between the steep ascent through unyielding rock walls and the following stretch — striding out across a rolling plateau — could not be starker. This walk is full of high points.

From **Stern** (1420 m) take the road towards **St. Kassian** and, past the bridge over the Gader stream (1385 m) and the following S curve, turn left on **Route 12/13**. Then go right immediately on **Route 12**. It's a steady climb through meadows and pastures — at first there are even a few houses. Finally you rise through forest. You cross forestry road 15 (1743 m) in a clearing and, 10 minutes later, come to a **damp area** with springs on the right.

As the forest makes way for buckled trees and then loose rubble, the route forks (2000 m). The left fork goes to Heiligkreuz; keep right for Fanes. As you rise up the right-hand wall of the **Val de Medésc**, please ignore all the short cuts, which are causing bad erosion. Then cross more

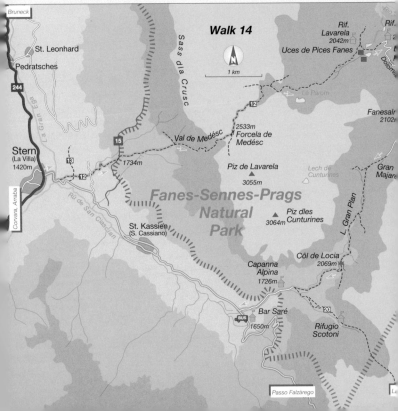

very loose rubble before arriving, rather tired, at the **Forcella de Medésc** (2533 m, **3h45min**).

The ongoing route across the plateau is mostly slightly downhill. You pass a lake (**Lé Parom**; in high summer dry as a bone), and then a view opens out to the Fanesalm, 300 m below you. There follows another rather tiring descent through woods, where you pass to the left of the strong karst springs of the Vigil stream. Descend to the **Rifugio Lavarela**, which you can see below to the right; you walk between the two ponds on the alm and beyond them rise easily to the large, very pleasant **Fanes Hut** (2060 m, **6h**).

The next day, take the alm road to the south; this is marked with the coloured triangle of **Dolomites High-Level Route 1**. Climb to the **Limo Pass** and lake (**Lé de Limo**), then go on to the large **Fanesalm** (2102 m, **7h**) with snack bar. Cross the floor of this alm to an area of fallen rock, where both the valley and your route fork: to the right is a route back to Lavarela (involving an easy scramble), to the left is St. Kassian and the **Falzàrego Pass**.

Take the almost-level route to the left. At the next fork go right, cross the **Col de Locia** (2069 m, **8h15min**) and descend to the St. Kassian road — perhaps first taking a break at the **Capanna Alpina**. Once on the road, you will find a bus stop to the left, by the **Bar Saré** (1650 m, **9h30min**).

The parish church of St. Leonhard, with the Puez Group in the background

St. Leonhard (together sometimes confusingly referred to as Abtei/Badia), Wengen, and St. Martin in Thurn are the centres of a widespread settlement which reaches up to the rock walls of Heiligkreuz-kofel and Peitlerkofel. Here the old customs and skills, seldom seen elsewhere, have been preserved; the crafts are still carried on by some families. Most of the ham still comes out of a smoker. Pilgrimages, like the one to Säben Monastery in Klausen, have been undertaken on foot for centuries. St. Leonhard still puts on its 'Leonhard-Ritt' (religious procession featuring riders on horseback, horse-drawn carriages, etc), in honour of its patron saint. In the Val de Molins you can see how corn was ground until quite recently. And in the farmhouse kitchens they cook it as they have done for centuries. This is a region for the

123

nostalgic visitor, who can explore it on foot, mountain bike, or on horseback (raising horses is an important mainstay of the valley's economy).

Abtei/Badia

The Gadertal widens a bit at Abtei — enough to make room for two separate settlements, **Pedratsches/Pedraces** (on the road; ✕) and **St. Leonhard/ S. Leonardo** (on the eastern slopes). St. Leonard lies below the mighty rock walls of Heiligkreuzkofel, at the foot of which stands an old pilgrimage church and hospice. *Viles* lie scattered in the meadows and pastures. Some still seem to be living in the 19th century, so little have they changed since the coming of tourism.

The large **parish church in St. Leonhard** above Pedratsches is very obvious; it's dedicated to St. Leonard, the patron saint of cattle. The church is one of the most holy places for the farmers of southern Germany and Austria. There's rich rococo decoration by Franz Singer and Matthäus Günther, which is a must! There is also a beautiful view to the church, with the Puez Group in the background, from the small play area with artfully laid-out pond further uphill.

Walking tip: Heiligkreuz pilgrimage church. Standing at 2045 m, the **Heiligkreuz Wallfahrtskirche** was built in 1484 under the direction of Bishop Konrad of Brixen. It was later extended in the baroque style and a tower added. The original **hospice** (✕), where pilgrims once spent the night, is run as a hut today. The host is both verger and cook; do

try his rustic food! To get there, take the **chair lift from Pedratsches** (5.20 € up, 7.80 € up and back). This goes up to 1841 m, then it's a steep climb of 200 m to the church. Allow 1h30min return; Tabacco 1:25,000 map N° 7.

Old votive panel in the Heiligkreuz pilgrimage church

Wengen/La Valle (✕)

The village of Wengen found itself a nice sunny slope in a tributary valley (all the Ladin *viles* get the sun, not a single one is on the shady slopes south of the village).

Wengen is at the centre of a group of hamlets in the Rü de Ciampló Valley; it has a church (of which only the tower is old), inn, town hall and post office. But what is really meant by its Ladin name, 'La Val', are the *viles*, the hamlets scattered round the slopes: going up from **Pederoa** (✕) in the Gadertal you come to **Campló** and **Lunz**; higher up is **Runch** (✕), with a stone Gothic building (once the courthouse), **Ciablun**, **Miribun**, **Tolpëi**, none with more than 10 houses of which many are old. Walking through this cultural landscape on the old farm tracks and speaking to the people is a journey into the past. Walk 15 is a beautiful little circuit.

St. Martin in Thurn/
S. Martino in Badia

Two valleys come into the Gadertal from the west below Wengen: the Campilltal and the valley of Untermoi/Antermoia. Between them the prettily situated village of St. Martin in Thurn (Ladin: San Martin de Tor) is spread across a green hill.

This is where the Archbishops of Brixen had their administrative seat for the Gadertal. Magnificent Schloss Thurn, which today houses the Ladin Museum, testifies to their wealth. In the village and the valleys life goes on at a quiet pace. If you would like to know more about life in the scattered Ladin settlements, this is your last chance.

The Ladin Museum in Schloss Thurn (Ciastel de Tor) opened in 2001 and is well worth a visit. In the heart of the landscape between Peitlerkofel and the Sennes, the historic castle with its romantic main building, large keep and the many later additions is an ideal setting. Where once the Archbishops of Brixen ruled from their seat in the Gadertal, today we can have a good look at the history and culture of the Ladins of the Dolomites. You can visit four floors of the castle and the massive keep. The most interesting exhibits are those devoted to **specialist handcrafts** (including a complete dollmaker's workshop), **geological displays** (minerals and fossils from the Dolomites), the **farmhouse room** which has been replicated in detail, and finally the presentation of the **Ladin language** through multi-media and several PCs. The Ladin **Micura de Rü**

Walk 15: Wengen and the 'viles'

Time: 2h-2h30min
Grade: easy, with an ascent/descent of 150 m
Access: bus or car to Wengen
Map: Tabacco 1:25,000 N° 7
Start out at **Wengen**: take the road towards **Cians** but, in the last curve to the right, turn left on **Route 4**. This runs through woods to the totally isolated hamlet of **Ciampëi**, where you will see one house made entirely of wood.

From the upper end of the hamlet the route heads uphill to the right through meadows. Just below Biëi you come to **Runch**, with its Gothic building made completely of stone, once the courthouse.

Keeping on in the same direction, continue on the narrow road to **Ciablun** and **Tolpëi**, where you turn sharp right on a drive that ends at the stream. Cross the little bridge over the stream and continue ahead on the track (no waymarks). You will soon come to **Route 6** and a little chapel with beautiful views. From here walk down to **Wengen** (**2h-2h30min**), which you can see diagonally below.

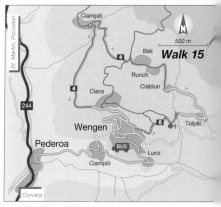

The 'viles' of the Gadertal

Visitors to German-speaking Tyrol around the Pustertal are already familiar with the isolated, grouped farm buildings (you seldom see even two farms near each other) — a result of the population explosion in the 17th century, when many farms were divided up. As in the German Tyrol, the farms here consist of two buildings — the living quarters and the work-places. But only in Ladin areas will you find hamlets with seven, eight or even 10 of these buildings so close together. The ones in the Gadertal are especially well preserved and today present the characteristic settlement of the area. Why the Ladins built their settlements like this and the German Tyroleans in a completely different way nobody knows. In all other respects the two groups are so similar culturally, that except for the different language you can hardly tell them apart.

But the 'viles' are distinctive: wells and baking ovens in the centre, the houses narrow, with narrow passageways between them and benches for sitting on and gossip-ing at the end of the working day. The lower parts of the houses are built of stone, with wood above (often with lovely carvings), and steeply pitched roofs. A balcony surrounds the wooden part, where the harvest could be dried in the fresh air. Many of the plastered stone walls have frescoes depicting saints (usually Mary with Child). Window frames and walls are often decorated with geometrical 'graffiti', as was usual in farming areas during the Renaissance.

The working buildings lie on the slopes or are built into the slopes, so that at the back a ramp runs up to the first floor, where hay was kept, while the stables are on the ground floor. Usually there is a little chapel nearby, and in many of these hamlets there are still huge 'scaffolds', used for drying broad beans in the autumn.

Cultural Centre is attached to the museum. *Museum open from Palm Sun to end Oct, Tue-Sat 10.00-18.00, Sun 14.00-18.00; also from Dec to the Sat before Palm Sun, Wed-Fri 14.00-18.00. Entry 5.50 €, families 11 €. Cultural Centre with displays and library open Mon-Fri 10.00-12.00 and 15.00-17.00.*

Campill/Longiarü and the Val di Molins (✕)

The quiet Campilltal is ideal for a peaceful holiday. One of the most interesting places is the stretch called Val di Molins (Valley of the Mills), an open-air museum. The farmers built water mills alongside the Sères stream, where corn was ground in the old days. Corn is no longer ground here, the farms have changed to raising cattle, and the fields have disappeared. But the mills still stand and thanks to EU money have been beautifully preserved. The two narrowly built *viles* of Sères and Misci are amongst the most unspoilt and attractive in the Gadertal. Some-times in summer corn is ground in one or other of the mills; ask for information in St. Martin, where you can also get a leaflet about the valley. In August there is a 'Festival of the Mills' in Sères and Misci, with tasty local farm products.

Lunz is typical of the Gadertal 'viles'.

Walking tip: circuit in the Val di Molins. An idyllic **circular walk** runs along the stream and past the eight mills. It begins in **Sères** (1568 m) at the end of the road through the valley and climbs to about 1730 m, taking in all the mills. On the return route you walk through **Misci**. Leaflet from the tourist office.

Cycling tip: from St. Martin towards Brixen. From St. Martin there's a little road down to Plose and Brixen. Although you can do it in a car, it's an excellent route for racing or mountain bikes. It first runs through little **Untermoi/Antermoia**, where refreshments are available at the Ütia de Börz hut. There are two different 'baths' here at Untermoi — the Sarighela Hay Bath (see page 47) and the Valdander Baths. The latter is one of the very few South Tyrolean farm baths that survived the 20th century. It lies in a narrow, cool, wooded valley on the opposite side of the Untermoi valley and dates from 1820. The waters are rich in calcium, iron pyrites and fluorine. The water is soft, tastes slightly salty and somewhat bitter, and helps with 'women's problems' and chronic rheumatism and arthritis.

The road then rises to the **Würzjoch** (2006 m), the pass between the Gadertal and the Eisacktal. From this pass there is a magnificent view to the northern flanks of Peitlerkofel — and a good restaurant. Continue via the top end of the **Lüsner Tal** and the **Halsl** (1987 m) to a fork: from here you can go left to Villnöss and Afers or right to Brixen.

Enneberg/Marebbe

The sunny valley of Enneberg (Mareo in Ladin), another tributary valley of the Gadertal, has become a popular holiday area. In summer you can walk in the Fanes and Sennes groups, in winter you can ski on Kronplatz (reached from the south of Enneberg).

Typical Ladin *viles* cluster around the main village of **St. Vigil** (✖) and especially around tiny **La Pli**,

Poor souls in Purgatory, as depicted in the pilgrimage church at La Pli de Mareo

while below in the valley are row upon row of hotels and apartments. But in the background, just at the edge of the village, the Fanes-Sennes-Prags Natural Park begins — pure and solitary Dolomites nature with a couple of unforgettable alms, like the large Fanesalm below Lavarela. The tourist office offers free booklets with walks and cycle tours.

The rococo **parish church at St. Vigil/S. Vigilio** has not changed since it was built in around 1728; it's an historical gem and a feast for the eyes. As in St. Leonhard, the painter Matthäus Günther and stucco artist Franz Singer have been at work here. The architect was Giuseppe de Costa, a local. The **statue of Caterina Lanz** in the church square is a memorial to the Ladin heroine who fought in the French Wars (see page 159).

At the end of St. Vigil, on the road towards Pederü, is the **Naturparkhaus Fanes-Sennes-Prags**, an information centre shaped like a wood-panelled rotunda. The displays are very child-friendly. *Centre open May-end Oct and Christmas to end Mar, Tue-Sat from 09.30-12.30 and 16.00-19.00 (Thu 21.00/22.30); entry free.*

Tiny **Enneberg Pfarre/Pieve di Marebbe**, north of St. Vigil, is more commonly called by its Ladin name, **La Pli de Mareo**. It is the site of a pilgrimage church dedicated to Our Lady of Good Advice. This was the parish church for the whole Gadertal until about 1100; Abtei didn't get its own church until 1449. The original Gothic structure was rebuilt and decorated in the baroque style; the façade and the beautiful high altar date from this time (1638); the chancel is late baroque (1760). Four large votive paintings are of special interest, showing pilgrimage processions which the people of Welsberg in the Pustertal make every hundred years, in thanks for being saved from the Plague in 1636 (the paintings date from 1637, 1738, 1838 and 1936).

Another interesting building in La Pli is the **Gran Ciasa** (✗) behind the church — an old mansion, now an inn with Ladin cooking.

From La Pli you can take a lightly-trafficked little road (signposted to **Bruneck**), to **Maria Saalen** and **St. Lorenzen**. (Since none of the following roads or hamlets are on any touring maps and they are so lightly-trafficked that you can walk as well as drive them; you may like to get Tabacco map N° 31.) In the next valley you will come to an **old watermill** which, although not in use, does still work. You can also take roads up to the most beautiful *viles:* continue on the road to **Pliscia**, go back to the Ciaseles turn-off, and from there to **Ellemunt**. Return as far as **Brach**, then go to **Corterei** and **Frontü** and then back to **La Pli**.

Fanes-Sennes-Prags Natural Park

The **Rautal/Valle di Tamores** (Ladin: Val dai Tamersc) leads from St. Vigil deep into this natural park which comprises 25,680 hectares. You can drive there or take a bus along the public road as far as **Pederü** at 1548 m, with a hut and good alpine cooking. (It's a toll road; those with guest cards are entitled to a reduction.) From Pederü there are little roads into both the Fanes and Sennes groups, but they are closed to motor traffic. See the 'Cycling tip' overleaf.

View to the Fanes Group

Fanes and Sennes are both huge karst plateaus with widespread alms. The few water courses disappear very quickly. Tiny lakes lie in clay hollows, surrounded by steep chalk peaks giving the impression of gigantic steps. The Rautal is the only largish valley running into the park; almost all other approaches require steep climbs. There are several pleasant alms offering bed and board.

A little road leads from Pederü into the **Fanes Group**, to the Kleine Fanesalm with the Lavarela and Fanes huts; half an hour's walk uphill you pass a little lake fed from a stream and a strong spring. Then the road runs higher, to the Grosse Fanesalm, where there is also a hut with refreshments (but no overnight accommodation). From here the road rounds the east side of the range and runs down into the Ampezzo, to the Toblach/Cortina road. The whole stretch (about 12 km) is quite easily done on foot or by mountain bike. There are also magnificent walking routes from the Lavarela and Fanes huts across the plateau to the surrounding peaks — Heiligkreuzkofel, Lavarela, Cunturinesspitze — as well as the Dolomites High-Level Route 1 to the Lagazuoi War Museum and the Falzàrego Pass or down to St. Kassian (see Walk 14).

To get into the heart of the **Sennes Group** you first have to climb a steep hairpin road dating from World War I (it's almost too steep for mountain bikes, with a lot of loose gravel — although the cycling tour described on page 131 *does* come down this road, *carefully*). Once you get to the hut on Fodara Vedla at 1980 m, however, you'll be glad you've made the effort. It's a lovely green, hilly alm, with old

Walk 16: Across the Sennes to the Seekofel Hut

Time: 6h30min

Grade: easy alm walking, but the ascent/descent to/from the Sennes plateau is steep and strenuous; ascent/descent of 800 m

Access: car or bus from St. Vigil to Pederü (car park/bus terminus)

Refreshments: Gasthaus Pederü; Ütia Fodara Vedla, 1966 m; Ütia de Sénes, 2126 m

Map: Tabacco 1:25,000 N° 31

You can get into the Sennes in half a day from Pederü, but this full day's walk takes in three pleasant huts.

Start out at Pederü: take the little road that turns left into the **Valón de Rü** (not far past the Gasthaus Pederü). This old military road rises in hairpins, and the loose gravel slows you down. Finally the climb levels out and soon you

reach the pastures and meadows of **Fodara Vedla** on the far side of the (usually dry) stream. The **Ütia de Fodara Vedla** (1966 m, **1h30min**) is a perfect alm hut, with a sunny terrace. Somewhat higher up is the alm village itself, a pretty grouping of beautiful old wooden houses.

Take the little road further north uphill. **Route 7** sometimes runs along this road, and you can use some of its short-cuts to avoid the bends (red/white/red waymarks, plus the '1' of the Dolomites High-Level Route). In a basin with a little lake (**Lé de Sénes**) you come to another hut, the **Ütia de Sénes** (2116 m, **2h30min**).

Continue along the road from this alm, but after 10 minutes turn right on **Route 6** (also Dolomites

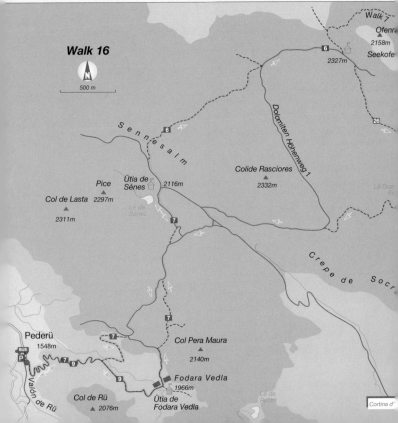

Old alm village by Ütia Fodara Vedla

buildings and overnight accommodation. From the hut there are
easy walks across the plateau to
the Sennes and Seekofel huts
(Walk 16), to Kreuzkofel, down to
Lake Prags and Prags (see Walk
7) or over to Hohe Gaisl (tough)
and down to the Toblach/Cortina
road in Ampezzo.

Cycling tip: Fanes and Sennes by mountainbike
Time/length: 4h with ease; 34 km
Grade: ascents and descents of
1250 m
Map: Tabacco 1:25,000 N° 31
You don't have to be a crack
mountain-biker to enjoy this
circuit, provided that you break it
down into two days, with an
overnight stop at either the Fanes
or Lavarela huts.
From **Pederü** take the little
private road up to the **Kleine
Fanesalm** with the two above-
mentioned huts and from there
up to the **Grosse Fanesalm** (steep
in places, but otherwise not a
problem).
From the alm carry on down the
good road through **Val di Fanes**
to the **Cortina/Toblach road**,
which you reach on a hairpin
bend with a fantastic panorama.
From here head uphill through
the upper **Val Boite**, to the **Ütia
de Sénes**, then take the road to
the **Rifugio Fodara Vedla** and
back down to **Pederü**. *Take care
on the final steep and winding
descent over loose rubble.*

High-Level Route 1) towards
the Seekofel Hut. You cross a
stony plateau and reach the
little road again, just before the
hut. Take a break at the
Seekofel Hut (2327 m,
3h30min) and enjoy the good
food!
To end the walk you *could*
simply retrace your steps, but it
is more interesting to make a
detour via **Route 26**: continue
along the road, then go right at
the first fork.
Follow this to a placid lake,
Gran de Foses (2142 m,
4h15min), then take the first
fork to the right. This takes you
back to your outgoing route. On
the descent you can avoid the
detour via Fodara Vedla by
following **Route 7** to the right
when it meets the road. But you
can *not* avoid the skiddy
descent on the military road
back down to **Pederü**
(**6h30min**).

10 FASSATAL/VAL DI FASSA

Fassatal • Vigo di Fassa • Pozza di Fassa, Pera and Meida • Soraga • Moèna • Valle di San Pellegrino and the Monzoni Group • Canazei • Ciampàc • Pordoijoch • Marmolada and the Fedaia Pass • Campitello

Walks: 12, 17, 18, 19; *Walking tip:* Val Contrin; *Walking and cycling tip:* from Penìa to Pozza and Moèna
Web sites
www.fassa.com

www.tierre-pro.com (for the Rampilonga bike race)
www.polotin.com/museo
www.istladin.net
Opening hours: see individual attractions

The Avisio stream rises at the foot of Marmolada and runs into the Etsch north of Trient. Its upper reaches — running between colossal Sella, Langkofel, Rosengarten, and Latemar on the right-hand side of the valley and the less well-known but equally spectacular mountains between Marmolada and the Monzoni Group on the left — is the Fassatal, one of the five Ladin valleys.

The Fassatal (Ladin: Fascia) is well equipped for both summer and winter sports and has even more accommodation than the Gadertal (especially apartments) — so places like Vigo di Fassa, Pozza di Fassa, Moèna, Campitello and Canazei (Ladin: Cianacei) are good alternatives to the valleys north of Sella and Langkofel. Italians are the most frequent tourists here. Like all Ladin valleys in South Tyrol, the Fassa is Italian, although the valley belongs historically to the Tyrolean cultural area.

The Fassatal can be reached from South Tyrol via the Great Dolomite Road from the Karer Pass or via Predazzo and Cavalese (Fleimstal), from Gröden via the Sellajoch, and from Belluno via the Pordoijoch or the Passo di Fedaia and Passo San Pellegrino. In summer all these connecting routes are covered by the **Trentino Transporti** buses (some stretches also by the South Tyrolean service, SAD). In winter buses only cover the Penìa/Canazei/Predazzo/Trento route and the stretch via Vigo and the Karer Pass to Bolzano, but there is also a free ski bus Tiers/Lake Karer/Karer Pass/Vigo/Pera and another ski bus between Canazei

and Pera. There are also winter transfer buses from the Verona, Bergamo and Venice airports (the 'Fly/Ski Shuttle' run by Trentinoviaggi). The nearest **railway stations** are at Bolzano and Trento (Bolzano is much quicker).

A **Panorama Pass** costing 42 € (4-7 days) or 55 € (6-13 days) can be bought at lift stations; it gives access to all the lifts in the Fassatal, neighbouring valleys and the Fleimstal. The valley tourist offices usually have a folder available called 'Val di Fassa — mappa delle idee', with walking and skiing overview maps. In July and August there are organised walks to various alms (the 'Andar per Malghe'), with tastings of traditional foods. High summer also sees various music programs ('I suoni delle Dolomiti') — from classical and chamber to jazz and pop. In mid-September the Rampilonga — the 42 km-long mountain bike race over all the Trentino passes (1800 m) —takes place here (from Moèna to Alpe Lusia).

Vigo di Fassa (✕)

In contrast to other, larger places in the Fassatal, Vigo (Ladin: Vich) is not in the valley itself but up on a sunny slope. It is surrounded by extensive meadows which until three generations ago were cultivated fields. The backdrop is a steep wooded slope and the rock walls of Rosengarten. From Vigo one looks out over the upper Fassatal to Langkofel and Sella; the peaks of the nearby Monzoni Group on the far side of the valley glow red in the evening.

Good **places to park** are on the second curve of the Via Nuova below the village, on the Piazza Europa, or by the Ciampedié lift.

The **SAD Bozen/Predazzo bus** stops in the village centre, the **Canazei/Cavalese bus** only stops on the first curve of the Via Nuova below the village. Although Vigo is a beautiful place to stay, with fine food and accommodation, it isn't packed out — even in high season. It's a good place for getting around anywhere between Bolzano and the Sella and Cavalese, although less well placed for Trento. Thousands of years ago this sunny slope attracted settlers, and from the Middle Ages until modern times the church of San Giovanni, somewhat lower down, was the *pieve* (parish church) for the whole valley. Vigo is proud to be a Ladin village. Ladin is spoken by almost every-one, and both the Ladin Cultural Institute and one of the five Ladin museums are located here. The cabin car up to Ciampedié below the walls of Rosengarten makes Vigo a good starting point for mountain walks, climbing and hair-raising ski slopes. Tandem paragliding is also popular

Vigo di Fassa, with Rodella (centre) and Langkofel in the background

— with a guaranteed view of the Dolomites!

Despite tourism there are many **old stone Ladin houses** to be seen in Vigo. Some of them have beautiful old frescoes on the outside walls — like the houses at the beginning of Via Pontac and Via Vael. In the part of the village known as Costa and in Larcioné (both below the road to the Karer Pass) there are more beautiful old houses — take a look at N° 2 in Larcioné: it has

---

Wall paintings

It seems wherever you look in the Fassatal you see wall paintings. That was as true in olden times as it is now. The oldest preserved frescoes here date from the 14th century, but every year more are painted. Whether it was a St. Christopher or a Mary with Child, a saint or an evangelist, the themes almost always had a religious content, whereas today landscapes are also in evidence. It would appear that the painters of the Brixen School were especially industrious in Campitello and Vigo in the 15th century. Some baroque painters include Giovanni Forcellini from the Agordino (17C), to whom the St. Christopher in Campitello and frescoes in Moèna and Soraga were ascribed, and Valentino Rovisi (1715-1783), a student of the great Tiepolo, who painted the St. Christopher at the church in Gries (Campitello) and frescoes in Moèna and Vigo.

---

two outside baking ovens, one on top of the other.

San Giovanni, once the parish church for the whole Fassatal, lies somewhat below Vigo; it's a beautiful late-Gothic building with three naves. The pillars, made from stone from the Monzoni Group, are without capitals and so reach right up into the Gothic net vault, making the room look higher than it actually is. The baptismal font in Gothic-Renaissance style (1538) is a reminder that up until 1554 all valley baptisms took place here — as well as all weddings and burials. Frescoes in the choir depict scenes from the life of St. John the Baptist (the patron saint); these date from the time the church we see today was built (dedicated in 1489).

The **Museo Mineralogico Monzoni** is a small private museum in a old log cabin-style barn (*tobià*) with beautiful minerals — above all from the volcanic Monzoni range. It is at 8, Via Pilat (downhill, off Via Nuova). *Open 10 Jul-10 Sep and Christmas Eve/New Year's Day from 16.00-19.00 and 20.00-13.00. Free entry.*

There is another Gothic church high above Vigo, the pilgrimage church of **Santa Giuliana**. The nave was dedicated in 1519, and the church has a deeply sloping roof. The tower is older than the nave and chancel, as shown by the Romanesque windows. Its southern wall also boasts a huge fresco with a St. Christopher and Christ Child, while inside are three frescoes portraying the martyrdom of St. Juliana (the patron saint). The choir frescoes are especially beautiful, being examples from masters of the Brixen School (15C). The chapel of **San Maurizio** next door, first documented in 1297, is probably the oldest stone building in the whole valley. *Open daily from 16.00-18.00.*

The **Museo Ladin de Fascia** is a modern museum in an old stone building. On display are a complete *stua* and *musha* (see 'Ladin houses' on page 143), beautiful panelling, carnival masks (very popular throughout the valley in olden days and still worn today, with long noses and a dangling carrot!), life-size figures with carnival dress and local costumes, farming implements and memorabilia, folk art, carvings, etc. There are also videos with historic films about life on the farm (those taken in Penìa and dating from 1982 look as if they come from the 19th century). Unfortunately, documentation is only in Italian and Ladin. *Museum open Tue-Sat, 15.00-19.00; from 20 Jun to 10 Sep and 20 Dec to 6 Jan daily from 10.00-12.00 and 15.00-19.00. Entry fee 4 €.*

The cabin lift from Vigo to **Ciampedié** holds 100 people and operates daily from 08.30-13.00 and from 14.00-18.00; one way 7 €, up and back 12 €; you can used this same ticket on the Paolina chair lift to/from Lake Karer (for instance for Walk 17). From the top station (1997 m) you have a fantastic view to Rosengarten, Langkofel and Monzoni. In winter skiers whizz down the red Thöni Run to Vigo; two chair lifts are just nearby; the black Tomba Run goes to Pian Pecei (1900 m). But in summer the mountain station is the starting point for walks in the Rosengarten area, above all to **Roda de Vael** with its two huts and on to the Karer Pass (see Walk 17) and the Vajolet Hut, from where there are many ascent routes up Rosengarten, the Vajolet Towers and Kesselkogel (see Walk 18).

Pozza di Fassa (Poza), Pera and Meida

These three adjacent villages in the Fassatal are all recent except for some old barns in log cabin style that can be seen in **Meida** along the banks of the San Nicolò which runs up the eponymous side-valley. The **Val di S. Nicolò** makes an excellent excursion; the road ends somewhat above the **Alm Ciampié**. The **Buffaure Group** in the north and the **Monzoni** in the south are pretty much unknown territory for tourists. The Buffaure don't look as though they belong to the Dolomites. No wild peaks, no high plateaus, dark basaltic stone instead of bright chalk, and lots of water — these mountains are of volcanic origin. There are few waymarked walking trails; everyone makes for Rosengarten on the other side of the valley. Isolated, pristine **Val Jumela** is unforgettable. At the top lift station there is a botanical garden; the hut, Baita Cuz at

Walk 17: From Ciampediè to Paolina

Time: 2h45min-3h
Grade: all on good trails (suitable even for children); ascent 350 m; descent 250 m
Access: bus or car to the Ciampediè lift in Vigo (see previous page), return with the Paolina lift and then the bus running from Lake Karer to Welschnofen and the Fassatal. The Paolina lift runs from end May to about 25 Oct, midday break 12.15-13.30.
Refreshments: Paolina Hut, open daily; Rifugio Roda de Vaèl/Rotwand Hut), CAI Trento, 2283 m; Baita M. Pederiva, private, 2283 m, no overnight accommodation; Rif. Nigritella, private, 1986 m; Rif. Ciampediè, SAT, Rosengarten, 1997 m, and at the top station of the Ciampediè lift.
Map: Tabacco 1:25,000 N° 6
This straightforward walk gives fine views to the Rosengarten area and Latemar, but also to the Monzoni Group on the far side of the Fassatal, with Lagoraides in the background.
Take the cabin lift from Vigo up to the **Ciampediè** mountain station (1997 m), then **start the walk**: from the station follow the motorable track to the left, past the **Ciampediè** and **Nigritella huts**. Not far past the latter hut, turn off right on **Route 545**, which takes you through a lovely wood and without any significant height gain to the floor of an alm, **Malga Vaèl**. (A short, signposted detour is possible here, to buy some milk or cheese.) You cross the **Vaèl** stream, which is usually dry (1985 m, **45min**), then climb to the two huts below the walls of Rosengarten, the **Roda de Vaèl Hut** and the little **Baita Pederiva** (2275 m, **1h45min**). These are good places to take a break, especially at Baita Pederiva just at the pass (the Rifugio Roda de Vaèl is a bit higher up). As at all mountain huts, there is polenta with goulash, cheese or mushrooms, various cakes, seasonal fruit with whipped cream, and other regional delicacies.

From here the route continues along the south side of Rosengarten, directly under the southern ridge of Rotwand. It's very easy underfoot, so you can enjoy the magnificent views. At one point you pass a memorial with a huge eagle, dedicated to Theodor Cristomannos (see page 59, 'On the Great Dolomite Road'). After another short flat stretch, you descend to the **Paolina Hut** (2125 m, **2h45min**), from where you can take the chair lift down to **Lake Karer**.

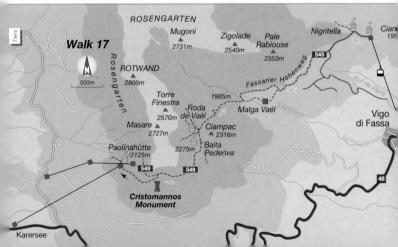

By the Aviso in Moèna, with the Monzoni Group in the background

2200 m, is manned and has a delightful view to the Rosengarten area. Cabin lift Pozza/Buffaure and chair lift Buffaure/Col Valvacin together 9.50 € one way; up and back 13 €; open 08.30-12.30 and 14.00-18.00.

In **Pera** there is a restored mill run by the Museum of Ladin Culture called the **Molin de Pèzol**. ***Mill open Mon-Sat from 10.00-12.00 and 15.00-19.00; entry free.*** From Pera you can get to the huts in the Rosengarten area via the **Valle del Vaiolet**, and from the village of **Mazzin** (where Walk 18 begins) just a bit further up there is access to Val de Dona, the Antermoia Hut and — via the Tierser Alpl Hut — to Schlern and the Seiser Alm.

In **Pozza** some old frescoes are preserved on the outside walls of a handful of houses, but because of through traffic they are becoming more and more damaged.

Soraga

This little village (Ladin: Sorega), with its beautiful old *tobià* (wooden barns) lies somewhat above the road; the isolated church somewhat below. There are some venerable old Ladin houses to be seen in the village centre, in the higher part of the village called **Soraga Alta** and in **Palua**. Several of the houses in Soraga Alta have beautiful outdoor frescoes, for instance **Ciasa Zepelin** (Madonna with Child and two saints).

Moèna (✕)

Moèna, at the junction of the Fassatal and the San Pellegrino Valley makrs the beginning of the Ladin-speaking area. The village is only built up along the main through road; on the edges you can still see the old hamlets that grew together to form the village. Back in the Middle Ages, Moèna was taken from the princes of Brixen and given to Trento, so its history is rather different from the rest of the valley. But it has kept its old language — Ladin (and a very special dialect thereof, with many Italian words).

Walk 18: From Mazzin to the Vajolet Hut via the Antermoia Hut

See also photograph page 62
Time: 6h15min-8h
Grade: very strenuous mountain hike on sometimes less than good trails; ascent 1400 m; descent 1200 m. You need a fine day; take local advice, there is a danger of hailstorms in this area.

Access: bus or car to Mazzin
Refreshments: Rifugio Antermoia, SAT Trento, 2476 m; Rif. Passo Principe/Grasleitenpass Hut, private; Rif. Vaiolet/Vajolet Hut, CAI Trento, 2243 m; Rif. Gardeccia, private, 1963 m, at the end of the motor road in the Vajolettal
Map: Tabacco 1:25,000 N° 6
Start out at the **bus stop** in **Mazzin** (1370 m): take the forestry road into the narrow **Val de Udai**, which at first runs to the right of the stream but soon crosses it on a bridge. Follow this forestry road until it ends, then continue up the valley on a good but little-used track. At one point you will come close to a strong spring coming out of a rock wall, the **Spina da Lago** (1772 m). From here on the way gets steeper, but the views improve. Finally you come to the flat floor

View from the Passo di Antermoia to the Vajolettürme (Towers)

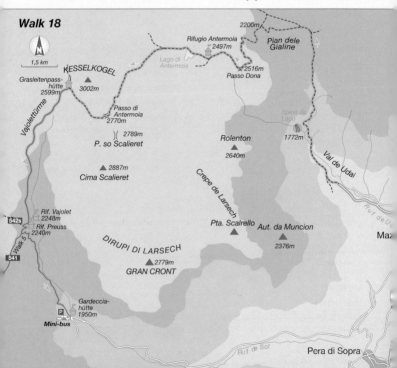

of the alm **Pian dele Gialine** (2200 m, **2h45min**), where you turn left on a crossing track, still ascending. A well-used route comes in from the right (from the Val Duron); it is well used because it is shorter, but it's not as beautiful! You cross some rubble and rock ribs and come to a little hut on **Passo Dona** (2516 m) — just a shed. But just around the bend is the much longed-for **Antermoia Hut** (2497 m, **3h45min**), where the view to Kesselkogel opens out.

After taking a break at the hut you pass **Lago di Antermoia,** a mountain lake embedded in rubble. It covers 2.4 ha and is 5 m deep. This is a karst lake with no surface inlet or outlet; only seasonally is there any noticeable water. No fish live in the cold clear water under Kesselkogel.

From the lake take the trail to the **Passo d'Antermoia** at the left of Kesselkogel. This ascent is quite strenuous, since it is both steep and covered with loose gravel. Once at the pass (2770 m, **4h45min**) you're in for a surprise: Rosengarten and the Vajolet Towers are before you — magnificent!

A short way down from the pass you come to the little **Grasleitenpass Hut**, built into a rock overhang. Then you follow a wide track down into the Vajolettal, passing just below the Vajolettürme (Towers).

Next come the **Vajolet** and **Preuss huts** and the **Gardeccia Hut** at the end of the walk, where you'll find mini-buses waiting (1950 m, **6h15min**).

In the lanes round Piaz de Ramon on the left side of the Avisio and Piaz de Sotegrava on the right side are a couple of dozen old houses with frescoes, among them some log cabin-style *tabià* — like Tabià Janac on Via San Pelegrino and Tabià Deville dating from 1567 in Via F. Filzi (both near Piaz de Ramon).

As well as the neo-Gothic **parish church** on a hill west of the village, it's worth visiting the nearby little **Wolfgangskirche** (S. Volfango). Inside is a cycle of frescoes dating from the 15th century showing several motifs, for instance a beautiful St. Martin, the Annunciation, and scenes from Christ's Passion. The key to the church is with the parish priest. On Tuesdays there are free guided tours of Moèna's churches at 16.00.

On Strada de Cernado (the main road to Canazei) there's an old **Bottega del pinter** (cooper's workshop) worth visiting, since the house is run by the Ladin Culture Museum in Vigo. Cask repairing was carried out here until 1937. *Coopers open Jul-mid Sep, Mon-Sat from 10.00-12.00 and 15.00-19.00; free entry.*

Valle di San Pellegrino and the Monzoni Group

The valley of the Rio San Pellegrino forks off from the Fassatal in Moèna; a road runs over the Pellegrino Pass to **Falcade** and into the Agordino of Belluno. The attractive and hardly developed Monzoni mountains rise on the left-hand side of the valley with their dark basaltic stone; to the right are the even lonelier ranges around **Cima Bocche** and **Cima di Laste.** There are no huts up at these heights, only bivouacs. In

Canazei

100 m

A Accommodation

1 Stella Alpina
4 International
6 Schlosshotel Dolomiti
7 Astoria
9 Genzianella
10 Al Viel
11 Pareda
12 Peter
13 Camping Marmolada
14 El Ciasel
15 Alpe
16 Edy
18 La Cacciatora

E Eating and drinking

2 Laurin
3 Le Gourmet
5 La Stalla
8 De Tofi
12 Peter
16 Edy
17 Vecchio Vernel

both summer and winter only the surroundings of **Alpe Lusia** are visited, as there are lifts and roads from the south and north.

Above the **Passo San Pellegrino** (Ladin: Pas de Sèn Pelegrin), at a height of 1918 m, is the little church of **Sant'Antonio de Padova**, built in 1934. It marks the site of a pilgrims' hospice from the Middle Ages (14C) and its church, both of which were destroyed in the mountain war in 1915. Today mass is celebrated here on Sundays and holidays (even in winter), and both local people and tourists attend. A little road goes to the idyllic **Lago di Pozze** (✗), flanked by meadows and woods (the colour of the larches in autumn is magnificent). There is just one building at the lake, the Gasthaus Miralago, with a good restaurant and rooms.

Walking Route 604 begins at the

places by the Eghes Wellness Centre, opposite the Pecol lift station, and in Alba in front of the Ciampac valley lift station. **Buses** connect with Cavalese 10-12 times a day, and an express bus runs 6 times a day to Trento. **Trentino Transporti** has an office here. The **'Fassa Express'** (a minibus dressed up to look like a train) links Penìa, Alba, Canazei and Campitello.

Langkofel and Sella rise in the north, Marmolada in the east. The Sellajoch and Pordoijoch attract motorists who enjoy pass roads and racing round Sella by car, motorcycle or bicycle. But maybe they shouldn't move on so fast, since both Canazei and nearby Campitello are as suitable as places in the Gröden or Hochabtei valleys for a holiday at the foot of the Sella Group. Lifts give access to the Sella Ronda in both summer and winter.

The traditional 'Skyrace' takes place here at the end of July, when runners go from Canazei to Piz Boè (9 km) and return by a different route (11 km) — an exhausting race, with a height difference of 1700 m. The famous Sella Ronda (see page 114) takes place in February.

Canazei consists of several different areas that have gradually grown together. In the centre, the settlement around the **Piaz de sènt Floriàn** with the church of **St. Florian** and old stone houses still forms a recognisable nucleus. (From here, after the bridge, there is a road to Sellajoch via Ruf de Antermont.) A little lower down, the council has treated itself to a modern world-class building by top architect Ettore Sottsass, the **Neue Rathaus** (with tourist information office).

pass: this leads in about 2h to Passo Selle with its little hut (2528 m); yellow Rhaetian poppies grow by the remains of Austrian emplacements from the War in the Dolomites.

Canazei

Canazei (Ladin: Cianacei), the lively centre of the Fassatal, stands at 1500 m; it's quieter in the shoulder season, when the lifts are closed. There are **parking**

Protected farmhouse in Gries, with the onion dome of the parish church behind it

The western part of the village, still quite agricultural-looking in places, is called **Gries**. At the parish church of **Madonna della Neve** (Mary of the Snow) the eye is drawn to a huge 18th-century wall fresco. It's a St. Christopher by the Tiepolo School painter Valentino Rovisi. **Majón de Roces,** a beautifully kept 17th-century Ladin house (part of the museum), stands somewhat above the Strèda Dolomites; it opens for exhibitions.

Penìa (✖) is the highest year-round settlement in Trentino; the dwellings cluster around the Gothic parish church of **San Sebastiano** with its large outdoor fresco of St. Christopher. Despite the new buildings, it's not a wealthy place, as can be seen from the route to the two farms of Vèra (1680 m) and Lorenz, the highest farm: the old village roofs are mostly patched or covered with 1950s corrugated iron. How antiquated the farming methods here were a generation ago can

be seen from videos — like the ones showing hay-making in 1982. Potatoes are still farmed on the steep slope above the village, and the soil, prone to landslides because the slope is so steep, has to be carried back up to the tops of the fields.

In the lower village, on Strèda de Treve (the main road), the **Museo Colombo Dantone** is worth seeing — a private museum of Ladin farming traditions in the 19th and 20th centuries. Another important part of the display shows military objects from the First World War on the Dolomites Front. *Museum open end Jun-early Sep, Mon-Fri from 17.00-19.00, entry is free, but donations are welcome.*

Penìa has a carnival with old masks and costumes (from 20 January).

Walking and cycling tip: from Penìa to Pozza and Moèna

A beautiful track for both walkers and cyclists begins above the

Ladin houses of the Fassatal

In contrast to many other places in High Tyrol, houses in the Fassatal are often plastered stone buildings, decorated on the outside with frescoes. Only the roof will be of wood. In a second building (almost always made of wood in 'log cabin' style and called the 'tobià') are the working areas with stable and barn. As in Gröden and many parts of German Tyrol, this building stands on a hill and is partially built into the hill, so that the cattle can be easily taken in and out from below and hay can be brought to the upper floor via a wooden ramp. Up until two generations ago, there were scaffolds here (as in the Gadertal) for drying broad beans in autumn, but none remain.

In the house is the 'stua' (living room), panelled in wood carved with various motifs, with wooden furniture. A passageway leads to the little kitchen. There is also the 'musha', a room with a traditionally painted chimney, adjacent bench and wooden table for drying clothing. This room is usually in the southeastern part of the house and next to the elders' bedroom (which is also panelled). All rooms, including the kitchen and other bedrooms lead on to a central hallway called the 'pòrtech'. In the old days there was no running water in the house; it had to be drawn from the well. Well-kept old wells can be seen in many of the valley hamlets.

Penìa, above Canazei

bridge over the Avisio in Penìa (the **Strèda dò Veisc**, on the left). The whole distance (see Tabacco 1:25,000 map N° 6) is about 20 km, so allow 4-5h on foot or 1h by bike. But you can break off any time, since at all villages by the river there are buses in both directions. When you get to the next bridge, you cross to the far bank. The route then stays on that side of the river, passing the Ischia sports area of Campitello and usually keeping close to the river. You bypass Mazzin. In Pozza there's a short ascent and then the almost-flat, always asphalted and well marked track continues to Someda and Moèna. In winter the track is an easy cross-country ski route down to Moèna and Predazzo — part of the Marcialonga.

Ciampàc

The Ciampàc walking and skiing area lies south of Canazei's Alba district, on the way to the Fedaia Pass. The Ciampàc lift from Alba (the motorable track is *not* recommended) operates from about 08.30-17.30 (with mid-day break). It runs up to 2160 m, from where a connecting chair lift goes up to Sela Brunech at 2440 m; one way 8.50 €, up and back 12.50 €.

The skiing area, with a magnificent black piste, lies between 2100 and 2440 m on the snowy northern side of the mountain chain west of Marmolada, culminating in the Colac peak at 2715 m.

In summer the green alm around the cable car station is a good **walking area for families**, with several huts offering refreshments (for instance, Tobià del Ghiagher, 2200 m, near the top station, a traditional hut with rustic food and a little botanical walk, open summer and winter).

But the main goal of the da out is in any case to see the view: the mighty flanks of Sella rise just opposite. From the **Sela Brunech** there's a straightforward route down to the **Ciampàc alm area** or into the **Val Jumela** towards Meida/Pozza (mostly on motorable lanes), from where you can get back by bus. The walks over the ridges to the west and east are only suitable for experienced mountain climbers (the Roseal ridge can only be attempted with climbing equipment).

Walking tip: Val Contrin. Just to the south of Alba is the Ruf (River) **Contrin** with its two alms, the **Malga Robinson** in the middle of the valley and the **Malga Contrin** with a hut. To get there (see Tabacco 1:25,000 map N° 6) take **Route 602**, a steep motorable track that begins at the Alba lift station. The climb takes 1h30min, the descent 1h15min. Once up there at 2000 m, you'll be sitting just below the wild, western flanks of Marmolada, rising another 1300 m above you.

Knowing this makes the food all the tastier! The Rifugio Contrin, at 2027 m, really appeals to lovers of alpine food, with home-made butter, cheese and yoghurt.

Pordoijoch/Passo Pordoi

However they get there — on foot, by bus or car, by bicycle or on the Pecol cable car (from Strèda Roma), one of the first things every visitor to Canazei does is go to the pass below the south wall of Sass Pordoi. You can get there by bus in summer; **buses** run from the **car park** opposite the Pecol lift. Or you can take the Pecol cabin lift, then the connecting Belvedere chair lift: 08.45-12.15 and 14.00-17.45; one way 9 €, up and back 13 €. The Sass Pordoi cabin lift operates from 09.00-17.00; one way 7 €, up and back 12.50 €. For the Pecol cabin lift (1), the Col de Rossi cabin lift (2) and Sass Pordoi cabin lift (3) there's a combination ticket available: going up it is valid for all three; coming down it is valid for (1) and (3) only: 20 €. The Sass Pordoi lift operates in summer from mid- May until about 20 Oct.

From the Belvedere there are fantastic views to Marmolada. But if you follow the easy **Bindelweg** (Walk 19) to Lake Fedaia (from where you can take a bus back to Canazei), you'll see a lot more! The Bindelweg is one of the most beautiful walks in the Dolomites, saturated with flowers and full of gorgeous views. But of course this means that it is also saturated with walkers. It's a must on account of the dramatic views to the Marmolada, even if masses of people get on your nerves.

Walk 19: The Bindelweg

Time: 2h45min for either route
Grade: easy walk on good trails.
Fedaia route: descent of 400 m
(you must be sure-footed and
have a head for heights); Porta
Vescovo route: ascent of 200 m
Access: bus from Canazei,
Arabba or Gröden to the
Pordoijoch; return from Lake
Fedaia by bus to Canazei
(connections to the Grödner Tal)
or bus from the Arabba lift
Refreshments: Rifugio Viel da
Pan, 2432 m
Map: Tabacco 1:25,000 N° 6

From the hut the path is
somewhat narrower and less well
used (most people having turned
back from the hut). Lake Fedaia
(a reservoir) draws ever closer,
until you are almost above it.
At a fork (2349 m, **2h**) you have a
choice: go left uphill to **Porta
Vescovo** (2478 m, **2h45min**), from
where you can take the Arabba
cabin lift, or go right on a
somewhat exposed, but well
protected and not difficult path
down to the dam of **Lake Fedaia**
(2044m, **2h45min**).

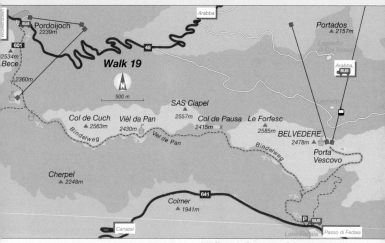

Start the walk at the **Pordoijoch**:
take **Route 601** (also Dolomites
High-Level Route 2) south uphill
to a pass (2360 m, **30min**) from
where you will have your first
fine views of the mountains to
the south. Marmolada is still
somewhat hidden, but as you
progress it will gradually reveal
its full width. The route traverses
the southern flanks of the **Padon
ridge** and crosses alpine
meadows with interesting flora.
The food is good in the **Vièl da
Pan Hut** (2430 m, **1h15min**), so
linger a while on the terrace,
enjoying the fine views.

*Walker at the start of the Bindelweg,
with Sella rising above the Pordoijoch*

Take the lift up to **Sass Pordoi** at 2950 m, and you will be completely surrounded by high, wild mountains. The views are so astounding that you may not be tempted to go any further. But **Piz Boé**, the highest peak of the Sella massif (3152 m), beckons strong walkers. It's fairly easy to get there (about 2h, with a little scrambling at the end) and, once there, you have the Capanna Piz Fassa with a snack bar. Trails link up with the road to the Grödner Joch and right across Sella to Kolfuschg, Corvara and the Grödner Joch; there are also protected climbing paths to both the Grödner Joch and Sellajoch. Take *plenty of water*; there is not a drop on this high plateau!

Marmolada and the Fedaia Pass

Perhaps you'll agree that Marmolada looks like a gigantic coral reef in a tropical Mesozoic sea. Today the highest point is measured as **Punta Penia at** 3335 m. The somewhat less steep north side of the range is covered with glaciers; the south side is a single massive wall 800 m high. The glaciers, while impressive, are just small remains; general glacial shrinkage is very noticeable on Marmolada. Melting ice has created little lakes on the edge of this glacier, which is a very popular **summer ski area**. You can get there from **Malga Ciapela** (1467 m; ✕) in the Belluno region east of the range. The cabin lift up to it first lands at **Serauta** (2950 m), just at the edge of the glacier; another lift goes from there to a point below the eastern peak of Marmolada (3250 m). There are no 'normal' routes up, they are all the

preserve of well-equipped, experienced climbers. The only exception is the ascent to the Pian de Fiacconi Hut at 2626 m, below the glacier: two routes lead up to this, as well as a small gondola lift.

In summer there are **buses** from Canazei (and 7 a day direct from Trento) to the Passo Fedaia, where there is a **World War I Museum** (a small but interesting private collection located in the Rifugio Alla Seggiovia). *Museum open Tue-Sun from10.00-12.00 and from 15.00-18.00; entry 3 €.*

From the dam of the Fedaia Reservoir there is a gondola lift to the **Pian de Fiacconi Hut**; mid-Jun to Sep, from 08.30-17.30; one way 4.50 €, up and back 8 €. A cable car runs from **Malga Ciapela** to **Serauta** and then from Serauta to **Marmolada**; end Jun to beginning of Sep and in the winter season, both stretches up and back 20 €.

The whole Marmolada area was a war zone during the War in the Dolomites (1915-1917); terrible fighting took place here, above 3000 m. Before the offensive in autumn 1917 the Austrian emplacements lay in view of the Italians. To avoid them, they built ice tunnels through the glacier.

En route to the cable car at Malga Ciapela you first pass a once-large expanse of water, **Lake Fedaia**. There are in fact two Fedaia lakes, the natural one at 2028 m, and the man-made reservoir at 2053 m; both lie before the **Fedaia Pass** in Trentino. The reservoir is in fact a plus in the landscape; it's the only one you can see from the Bindelweg itself, as the little

'Lech de Fedaa' is only visible once you are descending to the pass.

At the pass it's worth taking a break and visiting the private war museum mentioned above, before continuing on to Malga Ciapela or back to Canazei.

Campitello (✖)

Quieter than Canazei, the neighbouring village of Campitello (Ladin: Ciampedel) is more traditional and agricultural, even though it is totally dependent on tourism. If you walk from the stream along Via SS. Filippo e Giacomo and then Salita alla Chiesa up to the church, you'll get a good impression of what remains of the agricultural character of the place. It's above all evident in **Pian**, the sunny part of the village on a slope 100 m higher up. The stream that runs through Campitello, the Ruf Duron, has its source up on Rosengarten. The church of **SS. Filippo e Giacomo** stands on a hill; it has an unusual tower which looks more like a castle tower. As so often in this area, there is a large fresco of St. Christopher outside, as well as other wall paintings.

From Campitello a cable car runs up to **Rodella** (23 Jun to 13 Oct, from 08.45-12.30 and 14.00-18.00; one way 9 €, up and back 13.50 €. Rodella is the panoramic mountain of the Fassatal *par excellence*. From the peak with its hut you see Rosengarten, Schlern, the Seiser Alm, Langkofel, the Puez and Geisler groups, Sella's massive base, Antelao, Pelmo, Marmolada, and the Monzoni Group — and above that you can even make out Cimone della Pala and the Cima d'Asta, Lagorai … and, to the left of Latemar, the Brenta Dolomites.

You can walk to the foot of **Langkofel** in half an hour, then pick up the route round the mountain at the **Friedrich August Hut** (see Walk 12). Or you can do the beautiful walk over to the Comici Hut on the north side of Langkofel, crossing the **Steinerne Stad**t (Stone City), a magnificent landscape of fallen mountain rock. Or you can just wander around the flower-filled alm meadows at will.

The mountain hut **Rifugio Col Rodella** (✖) lies on the summit, about a 20-minute walk from the upper station; good cooking.

You are likely to see **hang-gliders** here; both the top lift station and the hut are good starting points; the large landing place in Campitello is directly below you.

11 FLEIMSTAL/VAL DI FIEMME

Cavalese • Predazzo • Val Travignolo and the Rolle Pass

Walk: 20
Access: via good roads to Auer in the Etschtal or slower via the winding road in the Fleimstal.
Buses: good connections to Trento (via Auer) and the Fassatal, as well as San Martino, Primiero and twice a day to/from Bozen. 'Fly/Ski Shuttle' bus from the northern airports (see page 132). Italy station (Trentino Transporti). The nearest **railway station** is Auer.
Web sites
www.visitfiemme.it
www.magnificacomunitadi-fiemme.it
www.parcopan.org
Opening hours: see individual attractions

In contrast to the Fassatal, the Italian-speaking Fleimstal is less developed for tourism. The bordering mountains have no huts, and only trekkers use the bivouac shelters. So the landscape is more pristine and lonely — but hardly less imposing than that further north.

From Auer or Neumarkt in the Etschtal a narrow, rather exposed road with fantastic views leads via Montan to the pass of Kaltenbrunn. Then the road drops along a sunny slope into the Fleimstal. The view is fantastic: you look along the valley and over to Monte Agnello and the wild, jagged Lagorai range, and then to beautifully sited Cavalese. You come to Tèsero with its large parish church with a Gothic tower, baroque decoration and a huge fresco of St. Christopher. Only when you reach Ziano does the road meet the valley floor and fork: to the left is Predazzo and the Fassatal, to the right is a road along Val Travignolo up to the Rolle Pass, San Martino di Castrozza and on to the Pala Group.

Cavalese (✕)

Cavalese lies on a sunny terrace above the Fleimstal and has been the major centre for the whole valley since the Middle Ages. As you approach Cavalese from Auer, the village, with its Gothic parish church in front of the jagged profile of the Lagorai Group on the south side of the valley, looks like the lid of a chocolate box. Cavalese is a good place for both winter and summer sports: there's a cable car straight up to the Alpe Cermis on Lagorai, and in Pampeago (7.5 km northeast) a connection to the Fleimstal/Obereggen ski area.

There was a terrible accident on the Alpe Cermis cable car in 1976, when the cable snapped and the gondola fell, killing 42 people.

Village events include the 'Processo alle Streghe' during the first week of January, a folk festival in commemoration of the Witches' Trials, and the 'Desmontegada de le càore', usually in the third week of September, when the goats and sheep come down from the mountains and are driven in herds through the streets.

The **Palazzo della Magnifica Comunità di Fiemme** in the

The Lagorai Group (seen here from the Rolle Pass) borders the Fleimstal in the south; it's one of the most isolated ranges in the Dolomites.

middle of town, was once the summer seat of the Archbishop of Trento and the seat of government in the Fleimstal; it still bears their coats of arms. The building dates from the Renaissance, when the Archbishops Bernard von Cles and Cristoforo Madruzzo ruled, but the whole building, including the façade, has been much rebuilt. The façade bears the image of St. Vigil, as is usual in Trento and the whole Trentino area. In 1850 the palace was the seat of self-government in the valley, the so-called 'Magnifica Comunità di Fiemme'. The building may only be seen on a guided tour. The 'Comunità' still exists, principally to administer woodlands; profits are used for supporting animal husbandry and agriculture in the Fleimstal. The palace museum was closed at press date.

The parish church of **Santa Maria Assunta** was dedicated in 1136 and rebuilt in late Gothic style with a tall clock tower. Nearby stands a temple-like classical building, the **Heiligtum der Sieben Schmerzen Mariä**, in which there is an old statue of St. Mary, a Gothic Pietà.

Four kilometres east of Cavalese, in **Tèsero** (✕), the Gothic church of **San Leonardo** with its Romanesque clock tower stands on the highest point in the village. Inside are frescoes and an altar painting by Francesco Unterperger (1542). In the village itself, with its beautiful baroque town hall, Gothic parish church, façades decorated with frescoes and the Renaissance chapel of San Rocco, there are several woodcarving workshops. A good time to visit is during Advent, for the 'Tèsero and its Cribs' festival, when both small and life-sized Nativity scenes are displayed in the village squares.

The peaks of **Lagorai**, one of the most isolated ranges in the Dolomites, rise up south of Cavalese. The many little lakes high up in

149

the corries (and completely atypical of the Dolomites), are visited by very few walkers, since most of the range is uninhabited. Only the **Alpe Cermis** area south of Cavalese sees some visitors. You can get there from Cavalese by changing lifts twice: from cabin to gondola to chair lift; Jul to mid-Sep and in winter, from 08.30-12.00 and 14.00-17.30; one way 10.50 €, up and back 12.50 €.

In summer there are some lovely walking trails, among them a 45-minute walk to three lakes teeming with char, the **Laghi di Bombasèl**. In winter it's popular on account of its slopes. But apart from a manned hut just by the cable car, there are no other huts. To the south the Lagorai range borders the massive **Cima d'Asta Group**, which is completely unlike other mountains of the Dolomites as it consists of a crystalline primitive rock.

Predazzo (✄)

In contrast to Cavalese, Predazzo lies along the valley floor. The **bus station** is in the southeastern part of the village. There are some fine old buildings tucked away off the main through road. The general impression is one of a completely Italian mountain village. The surroundings are worth seeing: Latemar, the whole Fassatal and **Val Travignolo**, which begins here and runs via the Rolle Pass into the Primiero Valley. Predazzo comes to life in winter: it is one of the most important cross-country skiing centres and has a marvellously well-equipped ski-jump centre. Among the events staged here are the 'Dieci giorni equestri della Valle di Fiemme' lasting 10 days in the first half of July, with 'Middle Ages' jousting tournaments, cultural programmes, folklore and concerts, and the 'Giro dei 12 Masi' on the first Saturday in August, an evening event in the old town with folk music, traditional costumes, and tastings.

The late gothic cemetery chapel of **San Nicolò** (somewhat west of the modern parish church) still has frescoes in the choir dating from the days of its founding.

The **Geological Museum** is also worth a visit: In the Mesozoic Era there were large volcanic eruptions in the southern part of Latemar, and the museum holds a collection of rare and interesting minerals and crystals (the **Dos Capèl geological nature trail** between the mountain station of the Predazzo cable car and Alpe di Pampeago give a good introduction). *Museum open in summer Mon-Sat from 10.00-12.00 and 17.00-19.00; in winter Sun-Fri from 15.00-18.00 (sometimes closed for restoration work).*

A cabin lift runs from the ski centre north of Predazzo on the Fassatal road to an intermediate station, from where one takes a chair lift to the south slopes of **Latemar**. Lifts operate from the end of Jun to end Sep and in the winter season from 08.30-13.15 and 14.15-18.00. Cabin lift one way 5 €, up and back 7 €; cabin and chair lift one way 8 €, up and back 11 €. From the top station there's an easy walk to the **Torre di Pisa Hut** on the south side of Latemar (from where you could continue down to Obereggen).

Time: 2h
Grade: easy woodland walk on well-built trails; ascent/descent 50 m
Access: bus or car to Malga Rolle, on the road to the Rolle Pass (request bus stop)
Refreshments: restaurant at Malga Rolle; Rifugio Colbricon, 1927 m, private
Map: Tabacco 1:25,000 N° 22

Begin the walk at **Malga Rolle** (1890 m): take the lane that begins here and runs to the lift stations below the Rolle Pass. Before you get to the lifts, turn right on **Route 14**.
This recently rebuilt and well-graded trail rises gently through woods to the **Colbricon Lakes**. The two lakes lie in a landslip area, and there is a beautiful view across them to the mountains in the north. There's a friendly little hut here (with just three beds!) and good food (1927 m, **1h**).
Retrace your steps to **Malga Rolle** (**2h**) or, if you don't have to return to a car, you can take **Route 14** down to **San Martino di Castrozza**, although this does cross some ski pistes and, lower down, follows an asphalted road.

Val Travignolo and the Rolle Pass

The road to the Rolle Pass, San Martino di Castrozza and the Primiero Valley runs through Val Travignolo. While the Lagorai mountains in the south are little visited, the **Lusia Group** in the north has various lift installations starting from the small meadows of Bellamonte. You pass **Bella-monte**, beautifully situated on a plateau and, after the next curve in the road, you come into the thick **Paneveggio Forest**, the largest in Trentino. Then there is a long stretch beside a reservoir, the **Lago di Paneveggio** (1458 m). A clearing introduces a visitors' centre for the **Paneveggio-Pale di San Martino Natural Park**, the main purpose of which is to protect this forest. *Centre open from second week in June until Sep, 09.30-12.30 and 14.30-17.30/18.00; in winter Tue/Thu from 10.00-17.00; entry fee about 2 €.*
The landscape changes completely at the **Passo Rolle**, where the unbelievably steep walls of **Pale di San Martino** fill the picture. The next peak is **Cimone della Pala**, a huge rock tooth reaching 3184 m. A detour (on foot) to the **Baita Segantini** is recommended: take either the little road (closed to cars in summer) or the unmarked track which avoids some of the bigger bends in the road. In winter you can get there by chair lift. From the first-floor terrace of this hut (open 20 Jun to 20 Sep and Christmas till Easter; good rustic cooking) there is an unforgettable view to Cimone della Pala.

12 PRIMIERO VALLEY

San Martino di Castrozza • Paneveggio-Pale di San Martino Natural Park • Pale di San Martino • Fiera de Primiero • Val Canali

Walk: 21	www.parcopan.org
Web sites	**Opening hours:** see individual
www.sanmartino.com	attractions

South of the Lagorai range, the Primiero runs south as a narrow valley dominated in the north by the rock needles of the Pale di San Martino. At the furthest northern point is the tourist centre of San Martino di Castrozza lying at almost 1500 m; pretty Fiera di Primiero, only 14 km away, lies at only about 700 m. The difference in climate between these two villages is as great as the height difference would indicate.

Four places lie in the flat Primiero basin: Fiera di Primiero, Tonadico, Siror and Transaqua, of which the last three are villages. The many hay huts in the extensive meadows, often built closely together, are still used. In summer the cows and smaller cattle are up on the alms. Their return to the valley, called the *Desmontegada*, is the time of a big festival, celebrated with polenta from giant serving dishes, bratwurst and smoked alm cheese. Although tourists also come to the festivities, this is still essentially for the farmers who are happy that their animals are back down in the valley after the long summer.

San Martino di Castrozza (✕)

The setting of San Martino is fantastic — on a slope totally dominated in the north and east by vertical walls and the needles of Pale di San Martino 1500 m higher up. In the west are the less severe eastern flanks of Lagorai, and in the south San Martino overlooks the Primiero.

Before the place was 'discovered' by English tourists to the Alps, there was only a little hospice here; for hundreds of years it gave shelter to walkers crossing the Rolle Pass. Today San Martino has a large touristic infrastructure catering for almost all tastes, quite frenzied in high season but all closed otherwise.

Buses stop at the church; there are two a day to Trento and 10 to Feltre, as well as buses to Predazzo and Bolzano.

The **Via Passo Rolle**, the main street, runs past the **parish church** with its Romanesque campanile. The most important hotels and restaurants, shops and public services are concentrated here. The church tower is the last remains of a **Middle Ages hospice** that the monks deserted in 1418. At that time the crossing of the Rolle Pass was an undertaking that had to be catered for on both economic and strategic grounds: the Habsburg interests in the Primiero were vital (in the south the Primiero borders Venice, thus foreign territory). The Counts of Welsperg, the Habsburg's governors in the Primiero, thus took over the well-kept building and turned it into a fortress and toll point.

In the 19th century English tourists started coming — the vanguard of the masses who now flood in during August and at Christmas. Four young men from San Martino worked for them as mountain guides, and an Irish mountaineer, John Ball, built an hotel to cater for them (the Cima di Ball is named after him). Called the 'Alpino', it was ready in 1883 and had 15 beds. In 1893, greatly enlarged, it opened as the 'Hôtel des Dolomites'. The one-time hospice became the 'Hotel Rosetta' in 1888, a predecessor of today's 'Hotel des Alpes' (opened in 1908, but not built on the same site). When in 1915 the Austrians pulled back to the Rolle Pass for strategic reasons, they burned the place down. Only the church is original; everything else you see today was built after 1919.

Paneveggio-Pale di San Martino Natural Park

The Paneveggio Forest, one of the largest forests in the region, and the Pale di San Martino, one of the most spectacular mountain groups in the Dolomites, come together here in one natural park. You can learn more about the park's climate, geology, archaeology, flora and fauna at the **park information centre** on Via Laghetto in the western part of San Martino: open end Jun to beginning of Sep, daily from 09.00-12.30 and 16.00-19.00; entry about 2 €.

A lovely **nature trail** begins at this park information centre; one of the highlights is the protected damp area called **Prà delle Nasse**

(signposted). Unfortunately the signposting and information panels in general are not very edifying. Damp areas are very rare in the karst Dolomites, so it is not surprising that the trail only touches on the edge of the protected area.

There are other visitors' centres for the park in Val Canali and Paneveggio, as well as a nature trail and the Prà de Madègo Ecological Museum in Caoria.

Pale di San Martino

The easiest way to climb the massif is to take the cabin lift from San Martino up to the **Col Verde** (usually daily in high season from 08.00-17.00; with connecting Rosetta gondola lift). There are lovely views even from the col, and then it gets really wild: the little gondola lift which runs from here up to **Cima di Rosetta** crosses a gorge, taking everyone's breath away. Up here you first have the impression that you can't walk a metre in any direction, but then you find yourself on a rolling plateau and the little walk over to the **Pedrotti Hut** is so easy you could take your auntie … *unless* it's snowing or freezing — which can even happen in August, since you're at 2600 m!

The plateau is like a moon landscape as far as the eye can see, and you will only see any of the tiny plants that survive here if you look really hard. The plateau's highest reaches were once full of glaciers, but these have almost all melted since 1870. What many people come here for is the fantastic climbing — peaks like Sass Maor, Schleier Edge, Cima di Ball, Pala di San Martino, and Cima Canali. As

Time: 6h
Grade: magnificent high-level hike for experienced mountain walkers. You must be sure-footed, with plenty of stamina, and have a head for heights. Ascent 300 m; descent 1400 m. Only suitable in fine settled weather
Access: Col Verde cabin lift from San Martino, then gondola lift to Rosetta (times on page 153)
Refreshments: Rifugio Pedrotti alla Rosetta, 2581 m, SAT; Rifugio Pradidali, 2278 m, CAI
Map: Tabacco 1:25,000 N° 22
This is one of the most fascinating walks you can take in the Dolomites without being a mountain climber. You will come very close to the famous Sass Maor climb. And you'll have a little frisson of excitement, too, as you traverse a long exposed ledge secured with wire cables.
Start out at the top of the **Rosetta**

lift (2609 m): walk along to the left, to the **Pedrotti Hut** (2581 m, **15min**), which lies on the high karst plateau of the Pale Massif. Almost nothing grows here; rubble and rock cover the rolling landscape. Take **Route 707/709**; then, after forking right, **Route 709**. This leads south uphill, crosses snow fields (where until quite recently there were glaciers) and comes to the saddle known as **Passo Pradidali Basso** (2658 m). From here you have your first view to the high corrie of **Pradidali**, into which you now descend. The path seeks out the best line between rubble and fallen rock and crosses to the other side of the valley just before a little lake. From here you can see the **Pradidali Hut** (2278 m, **3h**) below the imposing peak of Sass Maor.
From the hut continue uphill on

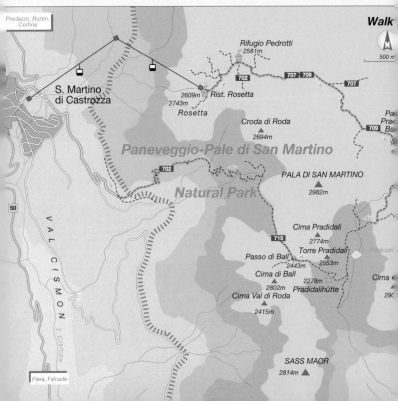

with so many peaks in the Dolomites, the first climbers to master them were the Viennese and English tourists, as the name 'Ball' reminds us. Walk 21 is a magnificent hike round the Pala di San Martino.

Fiera di Primiero and surroundings

Mining and agriculture were the traditional occupations in the Primiero. With the breakdown of the mining industry after 1500 because of competition from the Spanish Habsburg holdings in America came centuries of poverty. Only tourism, which took hold in Fiera at the end of the 19th century, but really only got into its stride in about 1970, brought a new source of income. The number of hotels continues to rise, albeit more hesitantly and not so overwhelmingly as in San Martino.

Fiera di Primiero and the three villages of **Tonadico**, **Siror** and **Transaqua** (✖) form a single world, cut off from the rest of Trentino. Ties with nearby Venetian Feltre are stronger than with those of Trento, to which the Primiero belongs adminis- tratively. The outside world can only be reached via passes or through the narrow **Cismon Gorge** in the south. There are up to 10 **buses** a day to Feltre and San Martino.

Fiera's parish church with its high tower is Gothic, built on the site of earlier churches. The interior, with its complicated net vaulting, has a choir decorated with late Gothic frescoes. Behind the church is the little church of **St. Martin**, with frescoes inside and out, and somewhat higher, an old house with a magnificent

Alm hut at the southern foot of Pala di San Martino in the Val Canali

Route 715 (also Dolomites High-Level Route 2) to the **Passo di Ball** (2443 m), named for the Irish mountain climber. On the far side, descend into the wild corrie below **Pala di San Martino** (on the right). Some passages at the foot of the **Cima Immink** are protected with fixed cables (even so, this is *not* a place for those who suffer from vertigo!).

Just after this passage Route 702 turns left, away from the Dolomites High-Level Route 2: follow **Route 702** and descend in seemingly endless hairpin bends down to the woodland belt, where you meet a forestry road (1650 m). Turn right, back to **San Martino di Castrozza** (1500 m, **6h**).

fresco portraying the Madonna of Charity. On the road below is the **Palazzo delle Miniere**, built in Renaissance style by the Habsburgs during the heyday of copper, silver and iron mining in the Primiero. In the interior, the history and culture of the area is well documented. *Palazzo documentation centre open Jul-Sep and Christmas; entry fee about 2 €.*

Transaqua is the scene of the annual **Hay-cutting Festival** at the end of August. To commemorate how hay used to be brought down from the mountains on wooden sledges, several laden sledges are dragged through the village to the church, with attendant competitions like wood-sawing, etc — a programme lasting three days.

Another, important festival is celebrated in the whole area: the **'Gran Festa del Desmontegar'**. This takes place at the end of September and celebrates the animals' return from the mountain pastures with colorfully decorated animals, wagons and people dressed in local costume. Folk music groups start at **Siror** and pass through Fiera and Transaqua on their way to **Tonadico**, an old village with beautiful farmhouses and a hilltop Gothic church, where there is a folk festival and stockbreeding exhibition. All the restaurants in the area display and sell traditional dishes.

Val Canali

This valley reaches from Tonadico to halfway up the Pale di San Martino massif. Lower down

are the ruins of **Castel Pietra** — a castle built on a rock in the middle of a wood to protect the Passo Cereda/Agordino road. In 1377 it came into the hands of Tyrol and in 1401 became the seat of the Counts of Welsperg. Only in the 19th century did the castle fall, although it was burned many times; today it belongs to a branch of the Thun family. *Only open to visitors by permission of the owners (at Castel Braghèr); and only for sure-footed walkers with a head for heights!*

The province of Trentino has established the main office of the Paneveggio-Pale di San Martino Natural Park in the old counts' **Villa Thun-Welsperg** nearby. The **visitors' centre** has all information about this natural park *(open daily Jun-Sep from 09.00-12.30 and 15.00-18.00; entry 2 €).*

Opposite: Agordino — Arabba, with a view west towards the Passo Pordoi and the Padon ridge at the left.

Arabba • Buchenstein • Andraz • Porta Vescovo • Passo di Campolongo • Col di Lana • Passo di Falzàrego • Àgordo • Dolomiti Bellunesi National Park • Valbiois • Àlleghe • Monte Pelmo • Zoldano Valley

Walks: 19, 22, 23; *Walking tips:* stroll through the *viles;* Col di Lana

Web sites
www.infodolomiti.it
www.arabba.it
www.austro-hungarian-army.co.

uk/battles/coldilan.htm (the battle for the Col di Lana)
www.grandeguerra._dolomiti. org
www.dolomitipark.it
Opening hours: see individual attractions

The Cordevole rises in Buchenstein, and its long valley, together with all its tributaries, is called Agordino (after the main conurbation of Àgordo). Before the river emerges in the lowlands between Belluno and Feltre and runs into the Piave River, it flows through a beautiful mountain landscape.

Coming from Sella, the Cordevole first runs past the Ladin farmland area of Buchenstein, then, at Caprile, it flows through Italian-speaking Agordino. Averau, Nuvolau, Croda da Lago, Pelmo, Civetta, Moiazza and Schiara rise to the left, Marmolada and the Pale di San Martino to the right. In Buchenstein and in the side-

valleys there are still old farming villages with *tabià* (log cabin-style barns) — for instance in Rocca Piètore, in the Zoldano Valley and in the hamlets above Canale di Àgordo.

This Dolomite landscape *par excellence* has one surprising feature: except for a few key centres (Àlleghe, Selva di Cadore, Rocca Piètore, Falcade) one meets hardly any tourists, and then only during high season.

A whole array of passes links Trentino with the Agordino area: Pordoijoch, Fedaiapass, Passo San Pellegrino, Passo di Valles (on a turn-off from the road to the Rolle Pass) and the Passo di Cereda between Fiera di Primiero and Àgordo, the largest and most important town in Agordino. There is also an easily-driven road without any passes (but not without bends!): the road between Fiera, Feltre and Belluno, along which you can drive to Àgordo through the valley straits called the Canale d'Àgordo.

Arabba

The Great Dolomite Road descends between the Pordoi Pass and the Passo di Campolongo into the Cordevole Valley and runs past the highest village in Buchenstein, Arabba (called Reba, its Ladin name, by the inhabitants). It's the only large place in Buchenstein, but still only a village. There is a large **car park** by the valley station of the Porta Vescovo lift. In the school period there are up to five **buses** a day to Àgordo and Belluno, but only three otherwise (and none on Sundays). In summer up to five buses a day to the Pordoijoch and Canazei, Wolkenstein and Corvara.

The **parish church** of **Saints Peter and Paul**, dedicated in 1664, is one of the few buildings to have survived the inferno of the First World War — the village itself was reduced to rubble and ashes by firing from the Italian emplacements higher up. Today Arabba is a tourist centre (the only really touristic place in Buchenstein) and a good base from which to explore the central Dolomites.

Walking tip: stroll through the 'viles'. To get to know some Ladin hamlets *(viles)*, you can stroll from Arabba along the road to the Campolongo Pass as far as **Varda** and from there take beautiful **Route 22** through meadows and woods: you will walk above **Mazarei** and come to **Cherz**. In the lower part of this hamlet there is a very attractive old holy statue (like a crucifix, but God the Father holds the crucifix on his knees). From there you *could* follow a path to the fort on the main road (with hotel), but since this is not easy to find, it's better to take the little road to **Renaz** and return from there by bus. Total time about 1h-1h30min (Tabacco 1:25,000 map N° 7).

Pieve di Livinallongo/ Buchenstein village (✕)

On the village square in Buchen-stein (Ladin: Fodóm) in front of the church is a memorial (1912) dedicated to **Caterina Lanz**, the 'Heroine of Spinges'. In 1797 in Spinges village (near Mühlbach in the Pustertal) this young woman used a pitchfork to fight the invading French, before spending the rest of her life cooking for the parish priest in Andraz. After her death, as nationalism bloomed in the second half of the 19th century, this fighting Ladin became the symbol for Austrian justice. Caterina Lanz is still considered a heroine today, who defended the Ladins and Tyroleans against their enemies.

The village **Ladin Museum** displays the Ladin culture of Buchenstein with many everyday objects and photographs. *Museum open Jul/Sep Tue or Wed and Thu from 16.00-19.00, Aug Mon-Fri from 16.00-19.00; entry fee 3 €, concessions 2 €. www.ladins.it.*

Andraz

It's hard to believe that this little roadside hamlet, just a handful of houses, was once the seat from which Brixen's bishops adminis-tered Buchenstein. But in fact **Andraz Castle** ('Andraz' in German translates to 'Buchen-stein', thus giving the village and area its name) is not located here, but further up the valley towards the Falzàrego Pass at Ciastèl ('Castle'). You reach the well-restored ruins via a little road that turns left off the pass road (sign: 'Castello'). Or you can take local walking **Route 26** that goes off the first hairpin bend past La Baita (an inn). There could hardly be a more beautiful setting for a castle: it stands on a gigantic isolated rock in the middle of a meadow; the old walls appear to grow out of the rock itself.

Porta Vescovo

Looking south from Arabba, the dark **Padon ridge** hides the Mar-molada glacier, which can only be seen from points above Arabba. A cabin lift runs from Arabba (Jul-Sep and winter, 08.30-12.30 and 14.00-17.30; one way 7 €, up and back 9 €) up to a pass on this ridge called **Porta Vescovo** ('Bishop's Gate'). Once you're up there, the whole Marmolada panorama opens up, the view is one of the most attractive on the whole Padon ridge — and best seen from the famous **Bindelweg** (Walk 19). In winter the Porta Vescovo is the starting point for magnificent ski runs which unfortunately have so disfigured the slopes that in summer this is not a worthwhile walking area.

Passo di Campolongo

The alm landscape around this pass into the Hochabteital is a most pleasant **walking area** with a whole array of manned alms and huts. In winter the terrain changes into a real *ski circus,* undemanding, and suitable for families and inexperienced skiers. Walking Route 636, one of the most attractive routes up to the base of Sella, begins just at the pass.

Col di Lana

This small grassy mountain in the centre of Buchenstein appears to be nothing special. But on the peak (2425 m) is the huge cavity left by a 5000 kg mine that the Italians exploded on April 17th, 1916 to take the peak from the Austrians. Col di Lana was a strategic point of the first order, overlooking four passes: Falzàrego, Valparola, Campo-longo, and Pordoi — as well as the approach from Agordino, one of the most important Italian lines of aggression. (The story of the battle is movingly told, in English, on the recommended web site.) A cross and chapel on the peak are a reminder that this will be the last war between neighbours on this **Col di Sangue** ('Blood Mountain', as the Italians call it).

Walking tip: Col di Lana. Take **Route 23/21** from the **Rifugio Valparola** (2168 m, only manned in high summer) at the **Valparola Pass**. The walk is straightforward (see Tabacco 1:25,000 map N° 7), but the ridge between Monte Sieg and Col di Lana is only recommended for sure-footed walkers who have a head for heights. Return the same way, allowing 2h30min-3h there and back (ascent/descent of 260 m).

Passo di Falzàrego

Between Arabba and Cortina the Great Dolomite Road must cross a high pass — the Falzàrego at 2105 m. Here you'll find a large **parking area**, bars, shops, and a restaurant. On the left a steep block of rock towers over the pass, the **Sasso di Stria** (Witches' Stone).

From the Falzàrego a road runs over the Valparola Pass into the Gadertal to St. Kassian; if you take this you will pass a most

attractive Austrian fort, today called **Forte Tre Sass**. You can visit it, as it is part of the **Open-air Museum** (www.lagazuoi 5torridolomiti. org) that takes in areas around the Falzàrego Pass, Monte (Piccolo) Lagazuoi in the north (with the Rifugio Lagazuoi at 2752 m) and the Cinque Torri (in Ampezzo). On Lagazuoi (reached via a lift straight from the pass, Jun-Oct and Dec-Easter, 08.30-17.00, one way 9 €, up and back 11 €), the Austrians and Italians were so close together that they had to dig themselves into tunnels, in order not to be constantly shot at. Most of these tunnels have been opened to the public — although without lighting, so take a torch! Not only do the tunnels remain; there are also trenches and many ruined buildings. In some of the latter the conditions of 1917 have been reconstructed, right down to the potatoes and ration bowls which were warmed in field ovens.

Museo all'aperto del Monte Lagazuoi (Open-air Museum)

This museum has no boundaries; the entire area is an open-air museum and entry is free. The trails are generally well protected and well marked, with panels explaining individual sites. But be sure to wear suitable shoes for mountain walking, take a torch (and head protection!) for the tunnels. More information is available from the tourist offices in Arabba and Cortina, as well as the web site shown on page 157.

The museum's biggest under-taking is the **Kaiserjägersteig**, a path that climbs from Lagazuoi

Walk 22: From the Falzàrego Pass round Averau and Nuvolau

Time: 3h30min
Grade: moderate mountain walk on usually good trails; ascent and descent of 400 m. Orientation skills required at one point on the climb to the Averau Pass
Access: bus or car to/from the Falzàrego Pass
Refreshments: Rifugio Averau, 2416 m, with good rustic cooking; Rifugio Scoiattoli, 2255 m
Map: Tabacco 1:25,000 N° 3

Start out at the **Falzàrego Pass** (2105 m), where a sign indicates the way (**Route 441** to Nuvolau). You cross hilly, fairly damp terrain, rising to a rougher landscape. Arriving at a high valley, which appears to run to a pass, you will suddenly be led to a crevice taking you out of the valley and back onto the slope. But the *next* high valley leads to the pass, the **Forcella Averau**. Here you switch to the other side of the ridge and thus round the steep massif of Averau.

After an easy climb in loose rubble you come to another pass, the **Forcella Nuvolau**, with the **Averau Hut** (2413 m, **1h45min**). This hut is known for its good cooking and has a beautiful terrace with a view to Marmolada.

Your walk (**Route 439**) continues on the northern, Ampezzo side of the ridge, with the strange rock formation of the Cinque Torri ahead. Crossing mountain meadows you descend to the **Scoiattoli Hut** (2225 m, **2h15min**) above the **Cinque Torri**. The 'Five Towers' are a paradise for climbers and form part of the **Lagazuoi/Cinque Torri Open-air Museum**.

Retrace your steps from the hut a short way, then go right on **Route 440** (also Dolomites High-Level Route 1). This descends towards the road to Lagazuoi, but just before you get there (just before the steam), take the ascending route to the left. This takes you to the **Col Galina Hut** and back to the **Falzàrego Pass** (3h30min).

Left: on and in Monte Lagazuoi the Open-air Museum is a reminder of the War in the Dolomites. The Cinque Torri, seen from above on this walk, also form part of the museum.

The main square in Àgordo, with Moiazza in the background

to the Austrians' highest emplacements and then crosses a dicky suspension bridge to the Front emplacements and continues down to the **Sperre Tre Sassi** (now a museum) at the Campolongo Pass (2h, *climbing skills required!*). On one Sunday in August the museum comes to life, when volunteers dress in Austrian and Italian uniforms. *Museum open mid-May to mid-Oct daily from 10.00-12.30 and 13.30-17.30; entry 4 €. www. cortinamuseoguerra.it.*
The area south of the Falzàrego Pass is an ideal starting point for **walks** on Averau and Nuvolau as well as the Cinque Torri, all wild Dolomite peaks which rise out of green alm meadows. Most of the walking routes here are also suitable for cycling.

Àgordo (✖)

What a picture! The two attractive side-towers of the parish church with the peak of Moiazza behind them. If you have a good wide-angle lens, you can even capture the second 'sight' of Àgordo in the picture — the Palazzo Crotta, with its statues on the wall. A Venetian villa with Dolomite peaks in the background — quite unusual!
Àgordo is also home to the world-famous Luxottica, Italy's largest manufacturer of sunglasses for the European luxury market: Armani, Chanel, Ferragamo, Moschino, Ungaro and Yves St. Laurent. It's the town's main livelihood.
Àgordo has its own bus station and good **bus connections** to Belluno(12 a day) and Àlleghe/Caprile (3 a day); there's also one bus a day to Corvara and one serving Cortina and the Drei Zinnen.
The **parish church** with its wide front and side-towers was built between 1836 to 1852, but in the interior you will find paintings from the previous building, among them the works of the early baroque Venetian painter Palma il Giovane.
The **Palazzo Crotta-De Manzoni** is the most northerly Venetian villa and the only one in the mountains. It was built in the 18th century and enlarged in the 19th century; inside it is divided into individual private apartments and cannot be visited. But you *can* take a peek into the courtyard with its side arcades.
The **main square** lies between the church and the villa; there are beautiful arcades below which some cafés and shops have opened. The old part of town lies beyond this — two, three narrow streets, a couple of old houses with outdoor frescoes — and that's it. If you're interested in sunglasses design and manufacture, visit the private

Optical Museum. *For opening hours call at the tourist office in Àgordo or contact the Luxottica factory direct; free entry.*

Dolomiti-Bellunesi National Park

The most southerly reaches of the Dolomites lie in Belluno and are protected in a national park, one of the few national parks in Italy to encompass a mountain region. With the exception of the Schiara Group southeast of Àgordo, the park lies in the pre-Alps, so can't hold a candle to the nearby mountain giants.There are virtually no walking routes or huts; it's a place to see rare plants and animals which otherwise have died out or are very rare in the southern Alps.

Valbiois

The Valbiois (www.falcade.it) begins at **Cencenighe Agordino** as a narrow gorge before opening up by **Tis** and then at **Canale d'Àgordo** (✕). **Vallada**, north of Canale, is a monument to the agricultural past; its church (San Simón) has a cycle of frescoes from the Titian school. **Falcade**, in a sunny position high in the Valbiois, is a totally touristic sports centre. In summer this valley is a good base for cyclists who can't tackle the Dolomite passes. There are five **buses** a day to Àgordo year-round, one to Bozen (via Vigo di Fassa), three to the Passo di San Pellegrino (summer only), and up to three a day to the Fedaia Pass (via Caprile).

Àlleghe (✕) and Civetta

The setting could not be more beautiful: a mountain lake on the doorstep and mountains behind the village. From the far side of the lake you can see the pointed spire of the parish church of San Biagio; behind it, mighty Civetta rises above a green apron.

There is a large **car park** in front of the ice skating rink; covered car park between the ice skating stadium and Via Monte Pape. Good **bus connections** to Àgordo, but for Arabba only two buses a day (and those only in the school term); some buses to the Falzàrego Pass in the summer.

Winter sports are writ large in Àlleghe; it's the centre for skiing on Civetta, and the ice-skating stadium is just five minutes from the centre of town. Mountain climbers and free climbers visit in summer, since not only is Civetta on the doorstep, but other colossal mountains of the central Dolomites are nearby — Marmolada, Sella, Pelmo. Since the number of beds is limited,

Àlleghe with its lake and Civetta

you must reserve in high season.

The **parish church of San Biagio** hides its Gothic origins rather feebly under its baroque outer dress. The adjacent **chapel** with its Loreto Madonna is an important goal for pilgrims and the oldest building in the valley. Two little roads, Via Europa and Via Monte Pape, run from the church forecourt down to **Lago di Àlleghe** with its beautiful **lakeside promenade**. To photograph the famous view of Civetta, you have to drive south along the edge, round to the far side of the lake, to the small village of **Masarè** and then over the Cismon bridge on a little road that ends at a snack bar. From here the view sweeps over the lake and Àlleghe to Civetta. If you walk (or cycle) further, you can continue on an easy, well-marked track (mostly in woodland and by the banks of the river) to **Caprile** (🍴). The lake is not old; it came about in 1771 as the result of a massive landslide — you can see where this happened quite clearly, on the western mountain slopes above Masarè.

A cabin car runs from Corso Venezia at the southern entrance to Àlleghe up to the **Piani Pezzé** (where there is the Fontana inn and pizzeria by the ski run, with rustic food) and from there you can take a chair lift to the **Col dei Baldi** (1852 m). These two lifts operate from end Jun to mid-Sep and in winter, 08.30-17.30; one way to Piani Pezzé about 4.50 €, up and back about 6 €; both lifts one way 7 €, up and back 9 €; you can take a bike. A one-day pass for all five Civetta lifts (with bike) is 10 €. (The Malga Boi

Walk 23: below the wild western walls of Civetta, a welcome signpost tells walkers that the Tissi Hut is not very far away.

Vescovà, an alm with hut below the Col dei Baldi, can be reached by a tarred road from the Forcella Staulanza; rustic cooking, wine; 🍴).

Taking the lift to the Col dei Baldi and then doing Walk 23 makes a full day's outing. On the other hand, those up to following Route 565 with its unprotected climbs through the Val d'Antersass are *really* ready for refreshments when they get to the Tissi or Coldai huts.

Civetta (3220 m) is a long strung-out reef, and its peaks are really the preserve of climbers. The most famous climbing route on Civetta is the extremely bold **Via ferrata degli Alleghesi**. You come to this if you take Route 557

Walk 23: Under the walls of Civetta

Time: 7h30min (an overnight stay at the Tissi Hut is recommended) **Grade:** long, strenuous, but technically straightforward mountain walk; ascent 500 m; descent 1800 m
Access: lift from Àlleghe to the Col dei Baldi (see opposite); return by bus from Listolade
Refreshments: Rifugio Coldai, Zoldo Alto, 2191 m; Rifugio Tissi, 2262 m; Rifugio Vazzoler, Taibon Agordino, 1714 m; Gasthof Monte Civetta in Listolade
Map: Kompass 1:25,000 N° 620
The walk starts at the **Col dei Baldi** (1922 m). With Civetta in front of you and the huge bulk of Monte Pelmo to the left on the far

side of the upper Zoldano Valley, head south to the **Forcella di Àlleghe** (1892 m). Your onward ascent path (broken in places due to people taking short-cuts) winds up from the alm at this pass to the **Coldai Hut** (2135 m, **1h15min**) between Cima di Coldai (right) and the northern ridge of Civetta (left).

You cross a low pass and come to the basin of **Lago Coldai**, a typical karst lake with no surface inlet or outlet. Further on, take the path to the left (**Route 560**, also Dolomites High-Level Route 1), to cross another low pass. You then traverse below the wild west wall of the main Civetta ridge, avoiding the scree slopes at the foot of the wall by going right and slightly downhill. From the **Forcella Col Reàn** (2107 m) it's half an hour up to the **Tissi Hut** (2262 m, **3h15min**), on a slope up to the right.

From here go back down to the Dolomite High-Level Route and follow it along the western flanks of Civetta all the way to the ruined alm **Casón de Col Reàn**. Keep to the same route, gently descending into the woodland belt. There are spectacular views along the southern foot of Civetta, with the vertical **Torre Venezia** just above you on the left. The way continues along a forestry road and passes near the **Vazzoler Hut** (1714 m, **5h15min**) in the woods, with its alpine garden.

Still on the forestry road, hairpin down into **Val Corpassa** and the manned **Capanna Trieste** (1135 m, **6h15min**), from where you are on asphalt all the way to **Listolade** (663 m, **7h30min**).

south from the Coldai Hut, which then joins Route 559 to traverse the eastern flank of the ridge. If you can handle the first 40 m of this without problems (vertical, sometimes overhanging drops, metal pins and grips), you won't have any problems further on. If it gives you the jitters, just turn back — there is another route perfectly suitable for hill walkers: Walk 23. What looks so difficult when seen from Àlleghe is in reality a quite normal — but totally spectacular — mountain walk.

North of Àlleghe, heavily built up **Caprile** (✖) lies at the turn-off to the Falzàrego Pass; its church is somewhat higher up. It is a good base for outings in upper Agordino, Buchenstein and Ampezzo — and an alternative to expensive and crowded Cortina!

Monte Pelmo

From Caprile you can drive via Selva di Cadore to the **Forcella Staulanza** (1773 m); alternatively you can get into the Zoldano Valley from Àgordo via the **Passo Duran** (1601 m), but this route is quite poorly built.

Driving via the Forcella Staulanza Civetta is on your right; on the left **Monte Pelmo** offers a textbook picture of a Dolomite mountain: steep rock walls all around, just a couple of flecks of snow in the gorges, and a flat area on top. The **Città di Fiume Hut** on its northern flank is good starting point for the famous circuit of Monte Pelmo on Routes 472 and 480; both of

these are perfectly within the capabilities of 'normal' mountain walkers (a few short protected stretches). The peaks, including the karst plateau between the main peak and the eastern shoulder are, by contrast, out of bounds — the preserve of climbers.

Zoldano Valley

Whether up in **Zoldo Alto** or in the main village of **Forno di Zoldo**, the attractive chain of villages and hamlets that stretch along the Zoldano Valley have one thing in common: in summer hardly anyone lives here, but it's very busy in winter. The cars almost all have German licence plates. Why? The local people specialise in ice cream. In Germany eight out of ten ice cream parlours are run by Italians. Almost all of them come from the Zoldano and drive home at the beginning of winter.

Right: Cortina d'Ampezzo — where the chic meet the sports enthusiasts

14 AMPEZZO

Cortina d'Ampezzo • Passo Giau • Great Dolomite Road to Passo Falzàrego • Tofana Group • Höhlensteintal and Monte Piana • Cristallo • Sorapis and Antelão

Walk: 24; *Walking tip:* Monte Piana from the Bosi Hut
Web sites
www.infodolomiti.it
www.cortina.dolomiti.org

www.regole.it
www.vajont.net
Opening hours: see individual attractions

Ampezzo lies in the highest valley of the river Boite between Dolomite giants. At its centre is Cortina d'Ampezzo at 1200 m — a popular winter and summer sports centre for a century. The peaks around Cortina rise up to 2200 m above the town: Tofana di Mezzo 3244 m, Cristallo 3216 m, Sorapis 3205 m. The *enrosadüra,* the pink Alpine glow of sunset, is most evident on the west wall of Sorapis.

Ladin Ampezzo and the adjacent Italian Cadore were separated until 1919, when Ampezzo belonged to Austrian Tyrol. Today both are part of the province of Belluno. But maybe not for long: Cortina may take advantage of the new law allowing a change of province and become part of South Tyrol. In principal Ampezzo has always had special rights: it's had autonomy since the Middle Ages, when it was ruled

by Venice. These rights were given them in 1511 under Kaiser Maximilian, when Ampezzo joined Austria of its own free will. Called the 'Regoles', they were last written down in 1971 as part of an agreement between Ampezzo and Italy. The people of Ampezzo are proud of their autonomy, and if they move over to the province of South Tyrol it will be their own decision, as it was in 1511. Ladin is spoken by very few people here today, and you hardly ever see the old local dress — only amongst churchgoers and at festivals, when 'Schützen' (see page 21) come together. As an old Tyrolean region *of course* Ampezzo has 'Schützen'!

Cortina d'Ampezzo

All that is left of the tiny Cortina of 100 years ago is the parish church, the Ciasa de ra Regoles (seat of the autonomous government) and the church cemetery. Cortina is a modern tourist area *par excellence*, and the Tyrolean atmosphere of most other places in the Dolomites only surfaces in a few examples here.

There are two large **car parks** near the old railway station; the Corso Italia and adjacent lanes are all pedestrian zones. The **bus station** is in the old railway station. **Dolomitibus** operates to San Vito and Belluno; in summer also daily to the Falzàrego Pass (6-8 buses), Corvara (3 buses) and the Trecroci Pass/Auronzo Hut (5 buses). **SAD** (the South Tyrolean bus company) has six services to Innichen and four to the Auronzo Hut. In winter there is a free ski bus between Borca, San Vito, Cortina, Misurina and the Falzàrego Pass. The nearest **railway** stations are Calalzo di Cadore and Toblach.

Prices are high, *very* high. You are paying for the privilege of being in Cortina. The season is short; on September 15th most of the shops close down and don't reopen until the middle of December. If you want to see a farmhouse, you will have to go up to one of the places above Cortina, where the sunny slopes spread out below Tofana.

Cortina is the place where Italian chic and money come together, with women in expensive designer dirndels, and some of the men in even more expensive lederhosen. Whoever can afford it takes a villa while staying in Cortina, but you can also stay in a hotel, and the only two five-star hotels in the Dolomites are located here.

Whether you come to enjoy yourself or you only come to be seen, there's a lot on offer — from the turbulent nightlife in high season (but *only* in high season) to the slickest sports. Restaurants are 'in' one minute and 'out' the next, so that one winter you'll meet here, and the next winter who knows where. If you 'do' the *corso*, strolling along the Corso Italia early in the evening, you'll soon learn where to be seen and where not to be seen under any circumstances!

Among the various events held are the Cortina-Toblach mountain bike race (42 km) on a Sunday in the second half of July, the Coppa d'Oro delle Dolomiti,

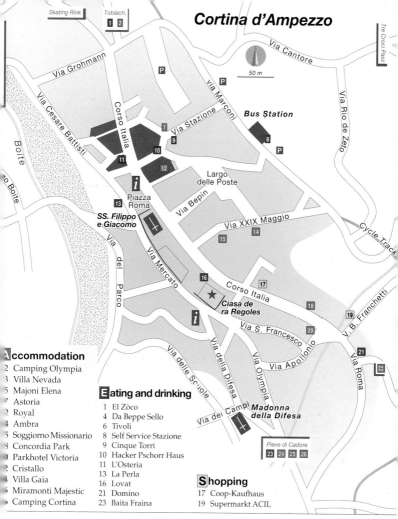

Cortina d'Ampezzo

a classic car rally in September, and the Festa delle Bande, when bands from Ampezzo get together in local costume (two days in August).

The **Corso Italia**, the middle stretch of which is a pedestrian zone, runs a long way through the town, taking in the **Via dell' Alemagna**, which was built by the Austrians in 1830 to link Venice (which at that time belonged to Austria) and Toblach in the Pustertal. This was, of course, a very old route, since the Fugger family sent their fabrics from Augsburg to Venice along the 'Alemagna'. Some older buildings break through the front of the modern hotels and shops, including above all the **parish church SS. Filippo e Giacomo** with its 71 m high, Venetian-style campanile (1851-1858). The church itself is baroque, with a very beautiful Lady altar (the first side-altar on the left) decorated with woodcarvings by Andrea Brustolon (1703); the ceiling paintings are the work of

---

Cortina 1956: the year of Toni Sailer

The first time the Olympic Games were shown on television was in 1956, when the Winter Games took place in the then little-known Cortina d'Ampezzo. Italy had done all it could to get the games — built a new ice-skating stadium and toboggan run, and run a huge international publicity campaign. It was the first time a Russian team had attended the Olympics. Despite a shortage of snow — but a lot of ice — the outstanding performance belonged to an Austrian skier named Toni Sailer. By winning the downhill, slalom and giant slalom, he became the first skier to sweep all three Alpine events. Triumph for Toni Sailer — and for Cortina, which gained world-wide fame.

At the time of those Olympics Cortina already had a 60-year-old skiing tradition. In 1894 August Kolitsch from the Sudetenland, a teacher at the local art school, first brought a pair of skis to the Ampezzo — and used them, to the great astonishment of all. The Cortina Ski Club, founded in 1903, is the oldest in what is today Italy. The first skiing competitions took place here in 1907. Since 1924 there has also been an Ice Hockey Club, which plays on Lake Misurina and may soon be able to practice in the stadium. Cortina may be a wonderful destination for summer, but it really comes into its own in winter

Franz Anton Zeiller. In the church square are the shell-shaped **Tribüne** for live performances and a memorial to Cortina's famous mountain guide, Angelo Dibona (1879-1956).

The large **Ciasa de ra Regoles** next to the church was the seat of the autonomous government of Ampezzo from 1511 to 1915, when Cortina came *de facto* under Italian rule (in the peace treaty of 1919). The building houses the **Museo delle Regole**, which comprises three sections. The **Rinaldo Zardini Paleontology Museum** is devoted to the geology of the Dolomites — the rocks, fossils and minerals. Good dioramas show the development of the Dolomites over the last 200 million years. The **Mario Rimoldi Pinacoteca** is dedicated to contemporary Italian and classical modern art. In the **Ethnographical Museum** there is information about the handicrafts and dress of the Ampezzo Ladins. *Ciasa de ra Regoles open Jun-Sep and Christmas to Easter from 16.00-19.30; in high summer also 10.30-12.30; entry about 3 €.*

Passo Giau

Passo Giau (2233 m) is an alternative connection to Buchenstein and the Agordino; it has far more curves than the Falzàrego Pass road, so it's very popular with bikers. Two buses a day cross the pass (Cortina/Selva di Cadore route). Approaching the pass you have the jagged profile of **Croda da Lago** on your left, with **Becco di Mezzodi** in front of it — both isolated reefs in a green alm landscape. Becco means 'beak' — the beak-shaped peak rises just south of Cortina.

Below Croda da Lago there's a pretty little lake with a hut (Rifugio Croda da Lago), which can be reached on foot from the road to Passo Giau in 2h (Route 437/434 from Ponte di Rucùrto at 1700 m). From the hut it's 1h to the start of the climb to Becco di Mezzodi, a 45min ascent (Grade II).

Tofana di Mezzo

At **Passo Giau** (photograph page 15) there are very fine views to the rock bastion of **Ra Gusela**, the southern spires of **Nuvolau** (which is also obvious from Cortina itself). A not especially difficult *via ferrata*, called Ra Gusela, runs to Nuvolau; it ends by the attractively-sited Nuvolau Hut on the peak.

Great Dolomite Road to Passo Falzàrego

If you drive from Cortina on the Great Dolomite Road to the Falzàrego Pass (2105 m), the **Tofana** massif dominates the panorama. (The Dolomitibus to Falzàrego and SAD bus to Wolkenstein also cover this route.) The famous **Cinque Torri** can be reached from this road, either on foot or by chair lift (from 09.00-17.30/18.00; one way 9.50 €, up and back 13 €). These massive rock lumps, looking like gigantic toys, are one of the most-loved photographic images of the Dolomites. There are two very pleasant huts nearby, where you could spend the night, the Rifugio Scoiattoli and the Rifugio Cinque Torri.

With its countless, easy-to-difficult (2min- to 1h-long) climbs, the Cinque Torri make an attractive **climbing area**. The highest peak is Torre Grande at 2366 m (normal climbs on its three needles of Grades I, II and III; note that sometimes a route may be closed due to rockfall). Or, if you like scrambling over boulders, you can do so to your heart's content in the **climbing garden** — even if you're a beginner. This is a good place to learn climbing techniques in straightforward surroundings.

In 1915-1917 the Cinque Torri were at the Front; the Italians dug in here. As at Lagazuoi, trenches, artillery posts and shelters have been restored, rebuilt and made accessible thanks to the **Open-air Museum**. *For details see page 160 and Walk 22 on page 161.* Only when you leave the pass to return to Cortina does the panorama over Ampezzo gradually open up — with Cristallo, Sorapis and Antelao on the horizon, as well as Pomagagnon towering over Cortina itself.

Tofana Group

Tofana di Mezzo (3244 m) and **Tofana di Rozes** (3225 m) dominate the horizon northwest of Cortina; the third Tofana, **Tofana di Dentro** (3238 m) is hardly noticeable. The Tofanas are **climbing mountains** and, except for Tofana di Rozes, classed as moderate to difficult. If

Falzàrego Pass, all the while with views to Averau, Nuvolau and the Cinque Torri.

Höhlensteintal and Monte Piana

The southern approaches to the Fanes and Sennes groups begin in the Höhlensteintal north of Cortina (see Toblach, page 88). From **Lake Dürren** in the valley an old, eroded military road runs up to isolated Monte Piana, where the plateau was the front line in 1915-1917. During the war in the Dolomites the north peak, **Monte Piano (2321 m)**, was in Austrian hands, the south peak, **Monte Piana (2325 m)** in Italian. There are many remains of emplacements, tunnels and shelters; a circuit round the old fighting area can be done in about 2h30min.

Walking tip: Monte Piana from the Bosi Hut. For something tamer than the climbing trail mentioned above, take your car or mountain bike up to the **Bosi Hut** and begin the walk there: anyone can do the first part of the yellow- and black- waymarked route; it's easy, with only 100 m of ascent (Tabacco 1:25,000 map N° 10).

Cristallo/Cadin peaks

One of the best drives (or cycle tours) from Cortina is the circuit round Cristallo. Take the Great Dolomite Road to the **Passo di Tre Croci (1809 m)** and down to idyllic **Lake Misurina (1735 m)**. The view from its northern bank across the lake to Sorapis is one of the most famous mountain motifs in the world. From the

you take the Freccia di Cielo ('Heaven's Arrow') cable car to the Tofana di Mezzo peak, you will see that there's no room to fool around: except for the terrace of the hut at the top, there is not a single square metre of flat land.

Walkers take the road from **Gilardon** (on the Falzàrego road) to the **Baita Piè Tofana** at the end of the road (1557 m, rustic restaurant with terrace), then take the chair lift (in two sections): Piè Tofana to Duca d'Aosta (with hut), one way 5.60 €, up and back 7.70 €; Duca d'Aosta to Pomedes, one way 4.60 €, up and back 6.60 €). In winter the lightning-fast Canalone Run dives down into the valley (red, with a black alternative); this was the run used in the 1956 Olympics. From the Pomedes Hut at the mountain station (2300 m) they take Route 421 down to the Dibona Hut (more good food) and from there Route 412 to the

See also photographs on pages 98 and overleaf

Time: 3h

Grade: straightforward mountain walk with magnificent views; ascent/descent 350 m

Access: bus or car (toll road) from Misurina to the end of the toll road at the Auronzo Hut

Refreshments: Langalm (2245 m); Drei Zinnen Hut/ Rifugio Locatelli, 2405 m, open end Jun–end Sep

View to Rautkofel from the Col de Mezdi

NB, mountainbikers: The only part of this route open to bikers is the track to the Lavaredo Hut.

Map: Tabacco 1:25,000 N° 10

The walk begins at the end of the toll road that runs from Lake Misurina up to the Drei Zinnen. At this point 98% of visitors make for the Auronzo Hut (2320 m) and head east on Route 101. Do *not* join them. Instead, take **Route 105**, heading west. There are magnificent views to the Cadin peaks, Monte Cristallo and Hohe Gaisl. The route rises very gently below the southern walls of the Drei Zinnen to the **Forcella del Col de Mezdi** (2324 m), where you have a new view: the alm landscape on the floor of the Rienztal (the river has its source up here) and the fearful ridges of Rautkofel and Bullköpfe.

A scree slope is crossed on a good path and you reach the alms. Beyond three pretty little lakes you come to the new hut on **Langalm** (2245 m), where there's fresh milk to be had. At this point the panorama of the Drei Zinnen has unfolded (the most famous view of it is the one taken from the north). To carry on to the Patternkofel and Drei Zinnen Hut, you now cross the alm — 100 m down, then 200 m back up (keep right at two forks, then head left on the track). On this quite steep ascent your attention will be drawn to some relics of the War in the Dolomites (rusted barbed wire).

At the top, head right to the **Drei Zinnen Hut** (2405 m) and the famous view to the Drei Zinnen, with the peaks of the Sexten Dolomites rearing up on the far side of the pass.

To return, take **Route 101** to the **Paternsattel** (2454 m) east of the Drei Zinnen and walk past the Lavaredo and Auronzo huts to the **car park/bus stop** (**3h**).

173

begins at this hut. Named for the great Angelo Dibona, this runs over into Valgrande between Cristallo and Pomagagnon and then to Ospitale in the Höhlensteintal (medium difficulty; walking time without stops 6h).

Sorapis and Antelao

When Cortina's first cable car to Faloria opened in 1939, it was a sensation — the latest in technology. Today's cable car to the Faloria Hut (2123 m, open Jun-Sep and in winter), on a ridge in the **Sorapis** massif, is just one of many. But what's nice about it is that it starts in Cortina itself (in the part of town called Pecol). Once you get up to the top, however, it's tricky: only properly equipped expert mountaineers can tackle the crossing.

That's even more true for **Antelao**, somewhat further south (by San Vito di Cadore). You get a good look at Antelao's profile from the west side of the Ampezzo: it is a completely symmetrical mountain. There is not even one hut on Antelao, only two bivouacs to protect you from the loneliness of the heights.

lake you can continue along the road to the **Auronzo Hut** (toll) and explore around the Drei Zinnen (Walk 24) or the wild landscape of the **Cadin peaks**. The national road runs further downhill into the Höhlensteintal and meets the Toblach/Cortina road in **Schluderbach** (from where those with bikes could take the cycle track back to Cortina or Toblach).

West of the Passo Tre Croci the Rio Gere chair lift runs up to the Rifugio Son Forca, from where another chair lift goes to the **Forcella Staunies** with the Lorenzi Hut, under the neighbouring peak of **Cristallino**. (Tickets include both lifts; one way 14.30 €, up and back 20 €.) The climb to Cristallino, which begins at the hut, requires expertise. But more famous is the **Via Ferrata Dibona** (often photographed with its suspension bridge) which also

14 CADORE

San Vito di Cadore • Cibiana • Museu delle Dolomiti • Pieve di Cadore
and surroundings • Auronzo di Cadore and surroundings •
Marmarole Group

Walks: none	www.vajont.net
Web sites	**Opening hours:** see individual
www.infodolomiti.it	attractions

You'll see Cadore if you look south from Monte Cristallo at Cortina, from the Kreuzberg Pass at Sexten or from the main Karnische ridge on the Austrian border. The three valleys that run from the old main town of Pieve ('Parish') — the Boite, Ansiei and Piave — are collectively called Cadore.

Cadore was in Venetian hands from 1420. For centuries, since early modern times, the area was the main supplier of timber for this seafaring republic; the wood was floated down the Piave River to its mouth. But there are still forests in Cadore; the republic and later the Habsburgs made sure there was reafforestation.

While in Cortina you're tripping over people all the time, in Cadore it is supremely peaceful. Maybe too peaceful: in the lonely Marmarole Group there are days, even in high season, when you will meet no one at all. Cadore has only two large settlements lying within the Dolomites — San Vito di Cadore in Valboite, just near Cortina d'Ampezzo, and Auronzo di Cadore, the main town of the Ansiei Valley. Both make good bases if you want somewhere quieter than Cortina.

Lake Misurina and the Sorapis Group

San Vito di Cadore (✖)

You can swim at tiny **Lake San Vito** (1000 m), though it's *cold!* After Cortina, San Vito is the most important tourist centre in the Valboite. It is prettily situated at the foot of **Antelao**. The **parish church** is worth a visit; the painting on its high altar is by Francesco Vecellio, one of the brothers of Titian, who came from Pieve di Cadore. San Vito is a good base for climbing Antelao and Sorapis — and Monte Pelmo on the other side of the valley. The same is true for nearby **Borca di Cadore** 2 km away, but accommodation there is limited.

Cibiana (✖)

This little place lies on the pass road from Valboite to Zoldano (7 **buses** a day from the railway station at Calalzo di Cadore). It was one of the Italian villages decorated in the last century with **outside frescoes**. The villagers (all 500 souls) gave artists a free hand in 1980, with only one stipulation: the paintings should as far as possible have some connection with Cibiana — the buildings and the occupants. So on one house you will see two women with wooden clogs and backpacks ('Zocui e Zestoi'). Another is 'La Botega': the door on the fresco is the door to the house. One wall depicts two street musicians; 'L'Emigrante' shows one of the emigrants who left to find work decades ago.

Museo delle Dolomiti

From the **Forcella Cibiana** (pass) you can take an old military road up to an Italian fortress on **Monte Rite** at 2181 m. The extremely well-preserved stronghold has been made into an Alpine Museum by the Venice Region under the direction of **Reinhold Messner**. Using glass and metal, they've transformed the old artillery positions with shafts of light. It opened in 2002 — the 'International Year of the Mountain'. On display among other things is Messner's large collection of Alpine paintings dating over the past 150 years — including mountain 'portraits' by **E. T. Compton** (1849-1921), who pioneered a very romantic interpretation of realism. Another part of the collection is devoted to geology and **Deodat de Dolomieu** (see page 5). The museum (variously called Museum Reinhold Messner, Museo della Montagna or 'Museum in the Clouds') is 2h on foot from the pass, but in summer there is a mini-bus service ('Servizio Navetta') at 10.00: one way 5 €, up and back 8 €. There is also the Dolomitibus service up to 6 times a day from the Valboite to Cibiana and the Forcella Cibiana. *Museum open daily from Jun to Sep 10.00-17.00 (18.00 in Jul/Aug).*

Pieve di Cadore and surroundings

Pieve lies on a slightly hilly terrace at the exit of the Valboite; it's the main parish of Cadore. Pieve (and Calalzo) are linked by **train** and frequent **buses** with Belluno (14 buses a day to Cortina, 15 towards Auronzo). The railway station is at Calalzo di Cadore, 2km away.

The house where Tiziano Vecellio, better known as **Titian**, was born in 1490 is today a small **museum**, although it has none of his paintings. *Open summer only Tue-Sun from 09.30-12.30 and 15.30-18.30 (also Mon in Aug); entry 2 €.*

Pieve's main square is named after Titian, and a memorial to him stands there. But the most important building in the Piazza Tiziano by far is the **Palazzo della Magnifica Comunità Cadorina**. Today it is only the town hall, but earlier it was the seat of government for all of Cadore. It has a **local museum**, displaying among other things some paintings by the Vecellios, like the beautiful 'Dedication of Cadore to the Madonna' by Cesare Vecellio. In the **parish church of Santa Maria Nascente** there is a large 'Last Supper', clearly inspired by Leonardo, and also the work of Cesare Vecellio, a relation of Titian. If you make the effort to go up to the village of **Pozzale** on the slopes of Monte Tránego above Pieve, you'll find that its church has the only Titian that remains in the area where the artist was born — a Madonna with Child (on the left).

Pieve has virtually merged with neighbouring **Calalzo di Cadore**; the railway from Belluno up into Cadore ends here. In **Tai di Cadore**, on the other side of Pieve, the **San Candido Church** holds more works by Cesare Vecellios, for example a beautiful St. Apollonia. This village also has a worthwhile **optical museum** (Museo dell'Occhiale) with spectacles, lenses, magnifying glasses and optical instruments from the 16th century to today. *Museum open Jul-Sep daily (incl. holidays) 08.30-12.30 and 16.30-19.30; Oct-Jun 08.00-12.30; entry 3 €.*
Longarone lies at the junction of the Zoldano and Piave valleys. The village was in the 'line of fire' when the **Lago di Vajont dam** burst on 9th October 1963,

killing 2018 people. Longarone was rebuilt on the other side of the valley, although they say the dam is now safe. The Longarone council has a service called 'Informatori del Vajont', which allows you to visit the famous dam with a guide. For information about the dam, see the Vajont web site on page 167.

Auronzo di Cadore and surroundings

Auronzo can be reached by up to 15 **buses** a day to Calalzo/Pieve di Cadore (from where there are **train** connections); there are also buses to the Kreuzbergsattel in summer and up to three buses a day to Misurina.

Like the other large lakes in Cadore, **Lake Auronzo** is a reservoir. That does not stop it from being very attractive when the sun is shining and one or two sailboats are plying the waters. This lake is also the largest single expanse of water in the Dolomites where swimming and angling are allowed. It also has a very pretty beach for sunbathing. But if you came to climb a mountain, you have a large choice nearby — from Marmarole to Cadin with its protected but not very difficult **Bonacossa Weg**, Cristallo and the Drei Zinnen.

Marmarole Group

No group of mountains in the Dolomites is more isolated than the Marmarole, which culminates in the **Cimone della Foppa** at 2932 m. The only huts are at the south foot; on the mountain itself there are only two bivouacs. The crossing of the group from east to west (from Aronzo), is a strenuous undertaking of three to four days demanding climbing skills.

● Index

Bold type indicates a photograph; *italic type* indicates a map or plan; both may be in addition to a text reference on the same page. Suggested restaurants follow entries for some places, preceded by the symbol ✖ (restaurants at mountain huts near upper lift stations are usually mentioned in the main text). Obviously all hotels and many inns have restaurants, but these are not shown unless they are exceptional. Note that closing dates do not usually apply in high season (mid-Jul to mid-/end Aug, Christmas/New Year, and Feb in the winter sports centres). A cover charge *(pane e coperto)* is not always levied in the Dolomites but, if it is, it can be as much as 4 € — so check the menu! In recent years, fewer establishments include service charges either; check the menu and allow 10-15%. Price guide: €-€€€ very economical to fairly pricey; *op:* open; *cl:* closed; T: Tyrolean cooking; I: Italian cooking (see page 16).